"*Why Care about Israel?* is a user-friendly book that will help you navigate the rivers of a subject close to God's heart—Israel and the Jewish people. Common sense, a helpful biblical perspective and loads of experience in the trenches all combine in Sandy Teplinsky's life to give this book unique insight. Drawing on her active involvement in the American Messianic Jewish movement, as well as in the former Soviet Union and Israel, Sandy's viewpoints are clear and constructive. This book will draw you closer to God's heart for His ancient people and will be a joy to read at the same time!"

—AVNER BOSKEY, FINAL FRONTIER MINISTRIES,
BEERSHEVA, ISRAEL; AUTHOR, *A PERSPECTIVE ON ISLAM* AND
ISRAEL, THE KEY TO WORLD REVIVAL

"Inspirationally written, biblically accurate, well researched and understandable to the common believer—all these describe *Why Care about Israel?* I applaud Sandra Teplinsky for a job well done. This book sounds a clear trumpet call that is desperately needed for this very hour!"

—JAMES W. GOLL, CO-FOUNDER, MINISTRY TO THE
NATIONS; AUTHOR, *EXODUS CRY* AND
THE COMING PROPHETIC REVOLUTION

"God's prophetic promises concerning Israel are coming to pass today before our very eyes. Romans 11 tells us that Israel's restoration 'will bring life from the dead.' Sandra has finally provided us with a book that cuts through all the confusion about Israel and the Middle East and gives us a clear, balanced understanding of God's purposes for His people. Every believer who wants to be part of God's plan for these last days needs to read this book."

—JONATHAN BERNIS, MESSIANIC JEWISH RABBI;
PRESIDENT, JEWISH VOICE MINISTRIES INTERNATIONAL

"*Why Care about Israel?* powerfully draws all believers to the place we should be, on our knees for Israel and the Jewish people. Sandy Teplinsky has done each of us a special favor by opening our eyes to see and understand God's clear and compelling call to restore His people and why it's critical that we care!"

— DICK EASTMAN, INTERNATIONAL PRESIDENT,
EVERY HOME FOR CHRIST

"The message of Sandra Teplinsky's excellently articulated book *Why Care about Israel?* is a message the Church needs in this hour to come into its fullness. The Middle East crisis is bound up with this message. Get the book. Read it and pass it along, praying that it will invade the hearts of today's church leaders around the world."

— DON FINTO, PASTOR EMERITUS, BELMONT CHURCH,
NASHVILLE; AUTHOR, *MY PEOPLE SHALL BE YOUR PEOPLE*;
DIRECTOR, THE CALEB COMPANY

"Sandy Teplinsky writes a brilliant and anointed book that is theologically sound yet prophetically timely. I consider this must reading for every believer and pastor who loves Yeshua."

— CHE AHN, SENIOR PASTOR, HARVEST ROCK CHURCH,
PASADENA; AUTHOR, *INTO THE FIRE*

WHY CARE
about
ISRAEL?

How the Jewish Nation Is Key to

Unleashing God's Blessings in the 21st Century

Sandra Teplinsky

Chosen
Grand Rapids, Michigan

Published by Chosen Books
A division of Baker Book House Company
P.O. Box 6287, Grand Rapids, MI 49516-6287
www.bakerbooks.com

Printed in the United States of America

Library of Congress Cataloging-in-Publication Data
Teplinsky, Sandra.
    Why care about Israel? : how the Jewish nation is key to unleashing God's blessings in the 21st century / Sandra Teplinsky.
        p.   cm.
    Includes bibliographical references and index.
    ISBN 0-8007-9343-9 (pbk.)
    1. Israel (Christian theology) 2. Palestine in Christianity. I. Title.
BT93.T435 2004
231.7′6—dc22   2003024712

Photos on the part opener pages appear courtesy of the following:
Part 1: © Jack Hazut, J.H.M. Photography
Part 2: Greg and Jason Katz
Part 3: © Israel Talby, Israel Images
Part 4: © Jewish Voice Ministries International
Part 5: © Israel Talby, Israel Images
Part 6: Israeli Defense Forces
Part 7: © Rafi Magnes, Israel Images

This book is dedicated to every "Righteous Gentile" of the present and future, who, like those of the past, follows Jesus Christ (Yeshua HaMashiach) in His love for Israel, sacrificially.

Contents

Part 6 *Unraveling the Arab/Palestinian-Israeli Conflict*

Part 7 *Living Sacrifices*

Foreword

This is one of the most important books I have read on Israel and the Church in several years. Sandy Teplinsky asks all the right questions and gives all the right answers with passion and precision and prophetic insight. At times the book will move you to tears. At other times it will move you to anger and indignation. At all times it will confront you with the heart and voice of God. Readers who neglect this book do so to their own loss.

"But those are strong words," you say. I agree wholeheartedly. They are strong words because the book carries a strong message—namely, that God cares deeply about Israel and the Jewish people and that you, as one of His children, should also care deeply about them, regardless of your church background or affiliation, regardless of your particular burden or calling, regardless of your view of the Middle East conflict.

I especially urge readers who do *not* agree with some of Sandy's views to weigh carefully and prayerfully the evidence she presents. But I warn you: Exposure to biblical truth can be dangerous to one's theology. (Serious study of the Word has caused me to change my own theology more than once!) Don't continue reading unless you are willing to test your beliefs against the plain sense of the Scriptures. And don't continue reading unless you are willing to have your heart broken afresh by the Lord. (As one who has carried a strong burden for the salvation of the Jewish people for more than three decades, I can tell you that my own heart was broken afresh as I read.)

What, then, makes this book in particular so valuable?

First, Sandy Teplinsky is, above all, a lover of Jesus, and she has a special place in her heart for Israel and the Jewish people *because Jesus Himself does.* And so she does not write this book primarily because she is Jewish herself (as is her husband, Kerry); she writes it primarily because she loves the Lord. Second, she is a lover of the Word, and as she opens up the Scriptures, the Word will come alive to you as well. Third, as a former attorney, she has an eye for detail and writes with keen logic, so you will not find all kinds of specious arguments here, nor will you be frustrated by rabbit trails that lead nowhere. She has her goals set before her, and she writes clearly and cogently. Fourth, her own heart is broken, and that brokenness is contagious. You will not encounter dead theory and dry theology here. In fact, you will find many practical ways to respond to what is written. Fifth, her writing is personal and vulnerable, allowing you to join her on a lifelong journey, to come along on the quest to understand and respond to the eternal purposes of God. Sixth, the book is complete, dealing fairly with the key issues that need to be addressed, from the error of replacement theology to the horror of anti-Semitism in the Church; from the modern history of Israel to the real spirit of Islam. Seventh, the book is current as well as compassionate. That is to say, she addresses head-on the contemporary situation between Israel and the Palestinians, not pulling any punches (indeed, the carefully documented evidence she presents is deeply disturbing), but she does so with a heart of love for the Arab world, too, desiring to see both Jew and Gentile enjoying Jesus the Messiah together, as one people joined to the same God, children of the same Father.

As I read these pages for myself, I wondered, *Will she cover this issue? Will she address this point? Is she aware of this argument?* Over and over the answer has been yes, and she has done her homework. Readers unfamiliar with some of the material she covers can consult the endnotes for more documentation; others who only get bogged down with details can simply enjoy the powerful flow of the book, knowing they are in good hands as they read.

I close with a personal note. Almost twenty years ago, while doing some late night study, I had an unusual encounter with the Lord. I was reading some portions of the Siddur, the traditional Jewish prayer book, considering some of the petitions that my own people have brought (and continue to bring) to God through the centuries. Suddenly I felt a terrible agony of soul for my brothers according to the flesh, more intense than I could remember. Everything within me was crying out, *No one is so near and yet so far!* and it tore my heart open. Since then, when Christian friends have asked me what the greatest need is in Jewish ministry today, my answer has been the same: "More tears." A fresh baptism of tears for Israel, based on the truths of God's Word, is one of the most pressing needs in the Church today.

It is my fervent prayer that you will experience that baptism of tears for the lost sheep of the house of Israel, just as Sandy herself did years ago (described in deeply moving terms later in this book). Much is depending on it.

DR. MICHAEL L. BROWN, FIRE SCHOOL OF MINISTRY,
CHARLOTTE AND NEW YORK

Acknowledgments

Thank you to my constant companion, my treasured husband, Kerry Scott, whose love, encouraging support, research, editing and technical expertise made this truly a collaborative project. To Kasey and Tasha, who sacrificed a year of their mom's time and attention, thank you, my darling daughters and young women of God.

Messianic scholars Avner Boskey of Final Frontier Ministries in Israel and Bill Bjoraker of Operation Ezekiel Ministries in California, thank you tremendously for your academic input and perspectives. You contributed enormously to the accuracy of this book, theologically and factually. For reviewing the manuscript and also offering important input, much gratitude to Jim and Cheryl Hayman, Janna Christenson and Taysir Abu Saada. My deep appreciation to Esther Gerstein, Greg and Jason Katz and Jewish Voice Ministries International, who graciously provided photographs.

To the intercessors who prayed this book through to the finish, I remain eternally grateful. May your reward in God's Kingdom be beyond great. Though too many to mention, I especially thank those who committed to praying daily for a year: Janna Christenson, Marilyn Evenstad, Cindi Fink, Rhonda Guin, Marlene Hertz and Susan Shandroff.

To Chosen's extraordinary editor-in-chief, Jane Campbell, thank you for believing in this project and nurturing it along with outstanding expertise. Editor Ann Weinheimer, your talents and godly patience are reflected in every page. You were a pleasure to work with.

Lastly, thank you to my pastor-teachers whose life messages are indirectly heard throughout this book. You have poured yourselves out for the Lord and I have benefited from your labors. I shall always remain grateful to the late John Wimber, Ché Ahn and Larry Feldman, as well as my parents. Thank you for investing in my life as you served the King.

And to the King, all glory, honor and praise, as well as my humble gratitude, for the grace for *Why Care about Israel?*

PART 1

The Blessing of Israel

"I will bless those who bless you, and whoever curses you I will
curse; and all peoples on earth will be blessed through you."

GENESIS 12:3

CHAPTER ONE

God, Israel and You

In the scorching breeze of Chaldean antiquity, God prophesies to His friend Abraham.

"I will bless those who bless you."

Angels, I imagine, dance. Man's redemption rolls into motion; over the sands and cities of the ancient Near East, the Gospel glimmers.

Then, one night, Abraham's runaway grandson lays his head down on a pillow of stone, and blanketed by blinking stars, he, too, meets the Blesser. In a celestial dream in the desert, Jacob (renamed Israel) inherits the covenant blessing.

Four thousand years later, the world is changed but the Word is not. The heavens collide and God catapults the children of Israel back to global center stage. Instantly, the Jewish nation becomes an international battle zone—and stumbling stone. Why?

Because it's all about Him.

The Creator King picked an otherwise sorry little strain of humanity called Israel for the sake of His own glory—not just for Bible times, but for all of history, down to this hour and beyond. Israel in the twenty-first century is all about *Him.*

Do you want to know your God and His ways intimately? Do you want Him to find in you a friend with whom He freely shares His heart and mind in this increasingly complex world, with its changing set of realities? Then understand what He is saying to you through Israel. Because what He is saying through her, He is not quite saying—or doing—any other way. Appropriate that understanding, and you will not be the same. I think—at least I pray—you will be more like *Him*.

Why Israel, Why Now?

After decades of relatively quiet Messianic ministry to both Christians and Jews, I find that everywhere I go people are riveted with interest in Israel—and her God. Ministry leaders, prayer warriors, secular businessmen, college students and even my unchurched hairstylist have all awakened to a startling reality: Israel affects them. They want to know how to respond to the Jewish nation in war and peace. They ask questions that you, too, may have mulled in your mind, such as:

- What is the tiny nation of Israel about? Why does it exist?
- As a Christian, how should I understand the Arab/Palestinian-Israeli conflict and respond in love toward all involved?
- Is there a biblical solution to the conflict?
- How is the Holy Spirit working in the lives of Jews—and Muslims?
- What does Israel have to do with my personal relationship with God?

God wants you equipped to live for Him. In this clash of world kingdoms, He wants you seeing and hearing beyond the natural realm and into the realm of His Spirit. He wants you understanding that what He is doing in your life relates very much to what He is doing with His ancient covenant Jewish people. The beloved King is using Israel to grow in His Church a deeper prophetic knowledge of His ways and character. He wants to mature the Bride of Christ in love, steadfast strength, purity and purpose. His very nature in us will prove essential in the rousing days and years ahead as never before. Now is the time to know and grasp hold of Him as *the God of Israel*. For that purpose, this book has been written.

According to the Bible, we should not be surprised that Israel has become an unavoidable issue:

- Israel is God's irrevocable covenant people through whom He uniquely reveals Himself to the nations—and you and me.
- Blessings and cursings flow from Israel for us to sow and reap.
- Christianity does not supersede physical Israel or her covenant promises.
- The Jewish nation serves as a prophetic microcosm of humanity and God's dealings with all nations.
- As God's New Covenant people, Christians are inextricably related to His Old Covenant people. Together we share a common prophetic destiny.
- According to the Bible, before the Lord returns, only His true Bride from among the nations will stand with Israel.
- God uses Israel to test, reveal and refine the hearts and intents of humanity. About that, I would like to tell you a story.

Knowing Israel's God

Jesus shares a striking and prophetic parable with us in the Bible about sheep and goats. The parable, as you probably know, is about more than farm animals and good deeds. What you may not know is that it concerns Israel.

When believers gather before Him in judgment, the Lord says He will separate the righteous—those who feed, clothe, nurse and care for His needs—from those who do not. The righteous (sheep) receive their inheritance in the Kingdom of God; the unrighteous (goats) are cast from His presence. At that time, you and I will ask when it was that we saw and cared for Him—or did not. He will reply, "I tell you the truth, whatever you did for one of the least of these brothers of mine, you did for me" (Matthew 25:40).

These brothers of Mine, the Lord whispered to me years ago, *are the Jewish people.*

Instantly, my heart was gripped with grief. How many Christians did I know who seemed to love the Lord sincerely but had little, if any, inkling about His passion and purpose for the Jews? Something else always preempted their focus: a crisis with the kids, a church commitment, a more "exciting" revelation. A certain internationally known pastor, for example, once confided in me that he was sure God had called him and his congregation to minister to Israel. But whenever we talked, it was always the same: "The Lord is dealing with other issues in our church right now." The pastor died several years ago, and his church is still trying to deal with the "other issues."

Did I really hear from God? Is our destiny in Him genuinely affected by how we treat Israel? I searched my study Bibles and found in them sobering confirmation. Time and again the reference notes identified "these brothers of Mine" as the Jewish people. Said one, "Ultimately, how a person treats the Jews will reveal whether or not he is saved."[1] I have spilled many tears in travailing prayer because the Holy Spirit has persuaded me of this grave truth.

Salvation is solely by grace through faith. But true salvation is *evidenced* by love and fruits of righteousness—which are reflected in our attitude and actions toward Israel.[2]

Why? How we treat Israel reflects—and we will see why in this book—how we would treat the Lord Himself. In war or peace, Israel is a test of love.

Test of Love

Israel is not God's special pet. The Creator does not play favorites with her. He chose Israel so that people like you and me in every nation and age of history would know—through her Scriptures, her Savior and her very soul—His redemptive, holy love in all its exquisite wonder.

Do you want to give your life over fully to the One who laid His life down for you? Does your heart yearn to resonate with the beat of His? Then, my friend, He beckons you to embrace Israel. He invites you into the inner chambers of His heart for His ancient people. If there you go, there you will lay hold of blessing that cannot be obtained, I am convinced, any other way.

Be forewarned: Others may not go with you. God will allow Israel to serve as a strategic point of division in the last days—which increasingly seem to be *our* days. Some in the Body of Christ will stand with the sons and daughters of Jacob; others will turn away. As global conflict escalates between the Jews and their enemies—and sadly, it will, despite any temporary peace—your stand in the end will be less about Israel and more about *Him.* For some, perhaps, even unto death.

Why does Israel draw out the best and the worst in us? The Jewish nation is designed to test and expose the hearts of humanity. Like a threshing floor, she sifts our souls.

Long ago God picked a spot on earth to "put [His] Name forever" (2 Chronicles 33:7; see also 1 Kings 9:3). That spot—Jerusalem's Mount Moriah—originally served for centuries as a threshing floor. (A threshing floor, as you may know, is a place where wheat is sifted from chaff by repeatedly tossing both up in the air.) It was there that God halted a plague sent in judgment against Israel. King David purchased the threshing floor and, at God's instruction, built an altar on it (see 2 Samuel 24:15–25). Later, on this precise plot of real estate, David's son Solomon constructed Israel's Holy Temple. There God's Glory dwelt, unequaled in grandeur anywhere else on earth. This place is now known as the Temple Mount.

Is the Temple Mount any less a threshing floor in our day than it was when David bought it three thousand years ago? This dry and dusty hilltop sifts nations' souls through their contests over its control. And little wonder, for here our Jesus will return in splendor to rule and reign—something His enemies are scrambling to prevent. The Temple Mount will prove the ultimate testing ground, the place where Messiah and anti-Messiah, and the followers of both, will someday be exposed. The site could be called Spiritual Testing Ground Zero,[3] rendering Jerusalem and the rest of Israel a test zone surrounding it. A test God wants you to pass—because it is a test of love.

Does that mean everything Israel does is right? Of course not; the test would prove less genuine if issues involving Israel were so simple. Though matters are complex, Israel is ultimately about *Him*, and if you know *Him* as the God of Israel, your heart beating with His, you know the Answer. To help you hear heaven's heartbeat, I have written this book.

In Words of Old

God's timeless, prophetic Word on Israel pulsates with twenty-first century timelines. The New Covenant bares His burden for the Jewish people, imparting the pathos of His heart toward them. It is in Romans chapters 9 through 11 that we read His most concise, prophetic discourse on the relationship of Israel and the Church. *Why Care about Israel?* follows the general flow of that gripping portion of Scripture, matching its timeless principles with timely realities.

I have written this book for Christian readers and, therefore, it reflects a Bible-based, Christian worldview. But I also write from the unique perspective of a Messianic Jewish believer in Jesus with strong ties to Israel. While *Why Care about Israel?* is intended to inspire loving support of the Jewish nation, I dare not accuse Israel of doing everything right. But neither do I point a finger at her wrongdoings; too many others do so prolifically. My goal is to give you, as best as God has enabled me, biblical, prophetic and factual truth. In truth, Israel's call from God remains as great as her inability to carry it out on her own apart from Him. And in truth, He ensures that in His grace, she will.

A significant section of this book concerns the Arabic peoples, some of whom are our brothers and sisters in the Lord. Any denunciation of terror, Islam or enmity against Israel is not intended to reflect anything less than Messiah-like love toward the Arabs. I have tried to share a biblical picture of the Arab/Palestinian-Israeli conflict from the perspective of God's prophetic heart. Countless others have tried before me; I am not sure any of us has fully succeeded in every respect. Although this book focuses on the Jewish nation, I believe it will also give you a better grasp of the Master's love and redemptive plans for the Arabs.

Why Care about Israel? is not a scholarly treatise. Rather, as a former attorney I have researched the theological and historical works of others and distilled them into simple, easy-to-digest terms. I share that information with you from a prophetic — but not primarily eschatological — perspective based on many years of study, ministry and especially prayer for Israel.

Occasionally I use Hebrew words with translation provided. I substitute Jesus' name in English many times with the Hebrew *Yeshua*, since that is what I love to call Him. In some instances I refer to God as *Yahweh*, using the English pronunciation of His personal name derived from the Hebrew Tetragrammaton *YHVH*. I also use *Israel* interchangeably with the *Jewish nation*, meaning the geographic land or the ethnic Jewish people. The Bible makes no real distinction; neither do I. You will find there are places where I describe the Jews as God's Old Covenant people and the Church as His New Covenant people. These terms are used solely for convenience and do not reflect any particular stance or covenant theology. Lastly, where it is necessary to talk of anti-Semitism, the word refers to prejudicial hostility toward the Jewish, not Arab Semitic, people.

As you read this book, you may feel anger at times. I do not apologize for detailing important facts and incidents that may provoke your emotions, but I do grieve along with you for the fallen nature of humankind. I trust the Holy Spirit to use even disturbing truths to transform you. My hope is that as *Why Care about Israel?* brings to light compelling prophetic and biblical principles, you will experience God's passionately pulsating heart of love as you have never known. I pray that when you turn the final page of this book, you will know Him better. Because really, Israel is all about *Him*.

Come and see.

CHAPTER TWO

Blessing for Blessing

I knew instantly they had *really* been with God.

I was in a Messianic church inside the Old City of Jerusalem, celebrating Passover with Christians from abroad, when I met them—this group of ordinary-looking, slightly disheveled tourists. But tantalizingly manifest in their presence, like a magnetic field radiating holy love, was the Blesser.

One member of the group—her name was Olga—spoke singsong but otherwise coherent English. Age spots dotted well-grooved lines that, whenever Olga smiled, crinkled kindly across her countenance. The Spirit tugged on me to meet her.

"Shalom. What brings you all to Israel?" I asked.

"Ahhh," Olga replied, eyes sparkling behind bifocals, "ve came to pick up de garbage."

I smiled politely, certain I had misunderstood on account of the accent.

"Excuse me?"

"Ve're from Svitzerland," she continued. "De garbage, ve came to pick it up. Ve come here every year to clean de streets for two veeks."

Mentally short-circuited, I caught smiles and nods out of the corner of my eye from Olga's teammates. In decades of ministry, during which I had been to Israel many times, I had grown used to the eccentric. I had long ago stopped counting the Elijahs and Moseses and reincarnate John the Baptists. But here stood obviously sincere and sane, not to mention Spirit-overflowing and God-glowing, Christians.

"So . . . this project is fun for you?" I eked out.

Olga laughed, and that magnetic field around her intensified a notch.

"Ya-a-ah! It's a vay ve can bless de Jewish people. I imagine I'm cleaning de streets so de Lord can valk on dhem, like streets of gold."

I had pictured the good lady enjoying two weeks of tours and revival meetings, feasting body, soul and spirit in a first-class hotel — not bent over in the road, pelted by the past several days' wintry rain. God knew the country needed help with its litter problem, but from the old folks abroad?

"Ve vanted to bless Israel, but *ve* are so blessed. *De Lord Jesus Himself is vidh us.*"

More smiles and happy nods from Olga's comrades. None of them seemed the least bit conscious of grime embedded under fingernails, slacks shredded at the knees — or tears starting to meander down my cheeks. Olga was right; the Lord Jesus Himself was with them.

God still means it when He says, "I will bless those who bless you." These radical disciples had gotten far more than a blessing; they had found that for which God's people all over the world yearn — the abiding and manifest presence of the Blesser Himself. The humble garbage pickers from Switzerland had discovered the blessing of Israel: *To bless the Jewish people is to be blessed.*

After meeting Olga I started asking Christians — both clergy and laity who have long loved and labored on behalf of the Jews — the same question: How have you been blessed by blessing Israel? Almost without exception I heard Olga's witness rerun: "More, so very much more, of Jesus!"

They have gone beyond the place of blessing and into the Blesser Himself. Where else would *you* really want to go?

Knowing the Blesser

God never wanted the blessing of Israel kept secret. The same prophetic principle of blessing also promises cursing, and He would rather bless than curse. The choice is ours:

> "I will make you [Abraham and his chosen descendants] into a great nation and I will bless you; I will make your name great, and you will be a blessing. *I will bless those who bless you, and whoever curses you I will curse;* and all peoples on earth will be blessed through you."
>
> GENESIS 12:2–3, EMPHASIS MINE

Because I am Jewish and have studied the Old Covenant (Old Testament or Hebrew Scriptures) much of my life, this passage is familiar as well as familial to me. But I regularly meet Christians who say they do not spend much time in the Old Covenant. So I would like to ask: Have you personally ever meditated on this succinct, potent sentence for more than just a few moments? If you have not, maybe you have never noticed that *it charts the course of history.* Now since God never reneges on a promise, could the blessing of Israel—or lack thereof—still prove key in His dealings with humanity? I am convinced it does, on every level from nations to individuals.

How does blessing Israel relate to what God is doing on earth today—and in your life? Jesus said good and evil would increase simultaneously as this age draws to a close; the nightly newscast proves Him right, bringing home to our eyes and ears evidence of unprecedented upheaval and Kingdom conflict. In the Bible we see this battle focusing increasingly on Israel, but involving all nations. God wants to prepare (not scare) us so that we need not be caught off guard as tumultuous events unfold. He wants us to know that in the course of such events He is deciding destinies—of empires, nations, churches, families and people like you and me.

As surely as God promised Abraham, those who bless the Jewish people will be blessed; those who curse them or try simply to ignore them (see chapter 15) will be cursed. As my Swiss sister testified, your life, your relationship with God *will* be affected by your response to Israel.

I assume that, like me, you would rather be blessed than cursed. That is good news, because in the days and years ahead God will be giving us tangible opportunities to make that choice. We will choose . . .

Each time we meet someone who is Jewish . . .

Each time we learn (or could learn) the facts and truth about Israel . . .

Each time we speak out (or could speak out) about Israel . . .

Each time we pray (or could pray) for the Jews and Arabs . . .

Each time we expend (or could expend) tangible resources . . .

And each time we make a heart judgment about the Jewish nation.

The real question is, *Do you, like mounting multitudes across the earth, desire more of the Blesser Himself?* Do you want to *really* know God, walking with Him in the settled intimacy of holy love, even during days of distress? Is it your heart's cry to be used of Him to have an impact on people at this pivotal point in history, to glorify *Him?*

I want to see Christians shine like lights on hills, undaunted by upheaval, wars or rumors of wars. I want the Church to understand and discern these unprecedented times, abiding in peace, joyfully fulfilling the Great Commission. And I want my brothers and sisters in the Lord blessed lavishly in His most intimate love by learning how to bless Israel.

Blessing: "Kneeling to Enrich"

It is said that actions speak louder than words and, in my mind, the actions of Olga and her teammates of the Swiss trash ministry could not be silenced. What was God saying through them about blessing Israel that I had not yet grasped?

My hunt began in the Bible. Because Jesus is the Word Incarnate, I love word studies. I love to meditate on how each word of Scripture, in its *detail*, uniquely displays His splendor and beauty. I catch Him sparkling like an infinitely faceted jewel, splashing rainbows of color across the pages of my Bible. My eyes, my heart, feast on Him. The priceless and perfect detail of the Living Word allures me into His glorious depths and dimensions, patterns and pathways.

What do the word details of the Hebrew Scriptures reveal about the core concept of *blessing?*[1] Perhaps needless to say, I found our idea of a blessing in postmodern society differs dramatically from its original Hebraic meaning. In Genesis 12:3 Yahweh tells Abraham He will bless those who bless him. There He uses a word for *bless*, *barekh*, that stems from the Hebrew root word *barakh*. *Barakh*, I was surprised to find, literally means "to kneel."[2]

To bless, therefore, involves a posture of heart, if not body. At its foundation, *blessing* connotes *kneeling*. Kneeling before another implies honor, preference, deference, and/or service. It is a posture of laying down one's own life for the other. What, I wondered, does this have to do today with our use of the word *bless?* The answer was clear: Not much.

But I went on. While its root, *barakh*, refers to kneeling, the word *bless* denotes spiritual and physical enrichment.[3] We might define *enrichment* as "making rich," and *rich* means essentially "abundant in quality and/or quantity."[4] Putting *barakh* and *barekh* together, I realized that when God blesses us, He kneels (so to speak) to enrich us. It was a mind-numbing and heart-humbling construct!

Indeed, Yeshua emptied Himself of glory to dwell among us, mere dust fashioned into divinely incarnate flesh. At the near-pinnacle of His ministry, He stooped to wash twelve disciples' dirty feet. Then He hung to death, agonizing in sweat and blood on a tree. His blessing finds no end.

Try to picture holy and enormous Father God kneeling to enrich you, much like a doting dad kneeling to relate face-to-face with his small child. When our two daughters were young, my husband, Kerry, would stoop, sometimes way to the floor, to play or talk with (or scold) them face-to-face. Kerry knelt to enrich them. It was how he met his children at their level to give them whatever they happened to need—or maybe just want. Almighty Creator God does much the same for you and me. As the Hebrew psalmist rapturously acknowledges, "You stoop down to make me great!" (Psalm 18:35).

The Humility of Blessing

> Bless the LORD, O my soul: and all that is within me, bless his holy name.
>
> PSALM 103:1, KJV

> I will bless the LORD at all times.
> PSALM 34:1, KJV

> Behold, bless ye the LORD, all ye servants of the LORD.
>
> PSALM 134:1, KJV

God's people in the Scriptures speak much of blessing Him. But today when we declare "Bless God!" is the expression much more than a religious equivalent of "Wow!"? Are we genuinely seeking with wholehearted integrity to bless the Lord? The King of the universe kneels to enrich us; to what extent do we for Him? More to the point, how can we?

Personally, my spirit soars at the prospect of enriching the Creator of heaven and earth. But, alas, I have a problem: Continued kneeling hurts. After a while every muscle feels strained and I begin to ache. However much I love His presence and enjoy His affections, it is hard for me to stay on my spiritual as well as physical knees. My ache is for the great grace of humility.

Humility, it has been said, is the secret of blessing.[5] Humility means I must decrease that Jesus may increase. Humility is hard. Yet I delight to discover, over and again, that when He has increased,

I have increased as well, for He has given me more of *Him*. Andrew Murray writes, "The blessing God promises is not, cannot be any external thing apart from Himself. All that He has to give or can give is only more of Himself."[6]

Can you better grasp the tantalizing bounty of the promise "I will bless those who bless you"? Yahweh kneels to enrich all those who kneel to enrich the man Abraham and his covenant children. Through the Jews and our blessing of them, He is ready to open floodgates for fresh outpourings of His Spirit. Recall Olga and company kneeling in the littered roads of Zion, escorted, embraced and enthralled with the Blesser.

Kneeling before Abraham (or the Jewish people) does *not* suggest worshiping him (or them). It does reflect a posture of honor, deference, preference and service flowing from Messiah-like humility. It is this humility that moves the Master to bless back. An essential but often missing ingredient that God wants to restore in order to release the blessing of Israel is *humility*.

Has Israel Lost the Blessing?

Do you ask: Since Israel has failed to obey God's commands fully—and rejected Jesus as Messiah—how can Abraham's blessing still apply to her? God's answer evokes humility.

True, like all other nations, Israel has sinned. But there are two main reasons why she cannot lose the promise-blessing. First, God may spare an entire people if only a few righteous ones can be found among them. Throughout history He has preserved for Himself a faithful Jewish remnant. Since New Covenant times He has kept alive a remnant of those who trust and follow Yeshua as their Messiah. This Messianic Jewish remnant mediates redemption on behalf of the whole nation.[7]

Second and more significantly, God's promise-blessing to Israel cannot be revoked or voided, despite her sin, because it flows from the nature of covenant. A biblical covenant is a legal concept, and it can be either conditional or unconditional. If conditional, that covenant's fulfillment depends on certain prerequisite conditions being met. If God makes a conditional covenant, the person(s) with whom He makes it must do something before He fulfills His end of the deal. *But if the covenant is unconditional, then God binds only Himself to do anything.* His fulfillment of an unconditional covenant is *not* conditioned on, or affected by, human response. In other words, sin cannot revoke or void God's unconditional covenant. Amazing grace, is it not?

Yahweh's covenant with Abraham, with its promise to bless or curse, is unconditional. In it He commits only Himself, not Abraham or his descendants, to do anything. We see this enacted vividly in Genesis 15:1–21, where at God's instruction Abraham sacrifices various animals and then God passes as fire between the carcasses. This ritual was precisely the one used in Abraham's day to establish a covenant between two parties. Animals were halved and the covenanting partners walked between them. If only *one* partner walked through the slaughtered pieces, however, *only that partner* was obligated to perform anything for the sake of the other. An *unconditional* covenant was thereby established.[8] In God's covenant with Abraham, He alone passed between the animals; Abraham did not. So the promise to bless or curse through Abraham and his ethnic descendants is dramatically and unequivocally *unconditional.* This means the promise-blessing can be neither lost nor usurped—not by the Church, not by the Arabs and not by the nations. As Dr. J. Dwight Pentecost concludes, it was impossible "for God to make it any clearer that what was promised to Abraham was given him without any conditions, to be fulfilled by the integrity of God alone."[9]

The New Covenant confirms rather than cancels the unconditionality of God's promise-blessing to Israel. The book of Hebrews explains that when God made His promise to Abraham, He swore by Himself in order "to make *the unchanging nature* of his purpose very clear" (Hebrews 6:17, emphasis mine).

The story of Ruth illustrates spectacularly how the Church today is called to respond to this unconditional covenant and its unchanging truth of being blessed by blessing Israel.

"Your People Will Be My People"

Wherever I have traveled the past few years, I have found the Holy Spirit captivating believers with Ruth and her magnificent message. From a Hebraic perspective, the characters in this book portray Israel and the Church in the last days and their prophetic relationship of reciprocal kneeling to enrich the other.

As the story begins, Naomi (meaning in Hebrew "Pleasant") is married to Elimelech ("My God Is King"). Naomi is a picture of the Jewish people married to God. The names of their two sons, Mahlon ("Sickly") and Chilion ("Wasting Away") reflect the condition of the Jewish nation at the time.

Famine forces Elimelech and his family to leave their home in Bethlehem ("House of Bread") for a better life outside of Israel. Mahlon and Chilion get married, but not for long—they die after just a few years. Elimelech also dies, as if the kingship of God dies in the life of a pleasant people. Naomi is left alone except for her Gentile daughters-in-law, Orpah ("Back of Neck") and Ruth ("Clinging One" or "Friend").

When the famine in Israel ends Naomi decides to go home. She urges Orpah and Ruth to stay behind, find new husbands and start new lives. Orpah turns and goes back. But Ruth refuses. The "Clinging One" declares undying loyalty to Naomi:

> "Where you go I will go, and where you stay I will stay. Your people will be my people and your God my God. . . . May the LORD deal with me, be it ever so severely, if anything but death separates you and me."
>
> RUTH 1:16–17

Life has been so hard for Naomi and her trials so severe that she changes her name to Mara ("Bitter"). Nonetheless—and this is where the story overflows with revived prophetic unction—Ruth clings. *This Gentile who believes in the God of Israel will not let go of the Jewish people, no matter how embittered they seem.* Ruth will not be dissuaded; something tells her it is through and with this people that blessing will be hers.

The Redeemer Comes

Naomi takes Ruth back home to Bethlehem ("House of Bread") where they find physical and spiritual nourishment. Aging Naomi, for whom prolonged manual labor may have proved too strenuous, teaches the one she now calls her daughter (a picture of the Christian church) to glean leftover grain from the harvest. Ruth literally kneels in the field to enrich her mother-in-law, but thereby nourishes herself as well. Then unexpected blessing unfolds.

Because of her love and commitment to Naomi, Ruth catches the admiring eye of a man named Boaz ("Strength Is in Him"). Naomi is delighted. Boaz (a prophetic depiction of Messiah) is her near kinsman-redeemer, having been related to Elimelech. With Boaz on the scene, the hope of redemption comes into view—but only if the two women (symbolizing Christian and Jew) maintain this reciprocal relationship of kneeling to enrich the other.

Naomi details step-by-step the protocol of redemption that Ruth must follow. Ruth submits to her spiritual mother and so captures Boaz's heart. "Strength Is in Him" quickly claims her as his bride. The Jews gleefully bless their union: "May the LORD make the woman who is coming into your home like Rachel and Leah, who together built up the house of Israel" (Ruth 4:11).

Their blessing comes to pass: Boaz and Ruth have a baby named Obed ("Servant"). Little Obed so thrills and fulfills Naomi's heart that she sheds her bitterness and thus the name Mara. Through Ruth she is revived. And through Naomi, Ruth gains standing forever as a lover of God and mother in Israel, in the direct genealogy of Yeshua, God's Servant.

The Redeemer Returns

Ruth, clinging to Naomi, found favor with her kinsman-redeemer just as Christians clinging to Israel will captivate the heart of their Kinsman-Redeemer today. And through Ruth's friendship, Naomi's nature changed from bitter to pleasant, just as genuine Christian friendship with Israel will transform Jewish hearts. Across the nations, I find God raising up a "Ruth Remnant." One of them was my friend Linda.

Linda, who has since gone to be with her Redeemer in glory, was a Ruth looking to bless a Naomi. When she found me, she clung until death forced us apart. Like Naomi, I had endured a bitter pruning season in my life and ministry when Linda came along and declared unwavering loyalty. From then on—and despite my attempts to dissuade her—if I needed help with anything, Linda was there. When I needed a babysitter at the last minute, Linda showed up. If I had to construct a prop for a Jewish feast, Linda reported with hammer in hand. When I grew weary in well-doing, Linda would share the perfect prayer or word of wisdom. In return for all this she asked one favor—to be taught God's ways from the perspective of a Jewish mind, heart and soul, that is, mine. Even though at the time, like Naomi, I felt thoroughly depleted and even a bit embittered.

"When we Gentiles," Linda said, "come into God's household, a *Jewish* household, *your* household, we never even ask what the house rules are. Instead, as soon as the door opens, we trample in, make a mess and take over.

"If I invited strangers into my home," she continued, "I sure wouldn't like it if they ran me over to get in, ignored the house rules, rearranged the furniture, stole my heirlooms and then turned around and booted me out! Well, that's what the Lord showed me we've done to you—and to Him."

I had never thought of it that way.

Linda soon became my closest friend. How could I not lay down my own life for someone so willing to give hers for me? The year after we met, and to our horror, cancer was discovered in Linda's body. From then on my time and energy were given over to my Ruth. Together we sat and prayed and laughed and cried through chemo sessions, radiation blasts, herbal remedies and healing services. During those years I canceled ministry appointments; missed the kids' school plays, soccer games and piano recitals; and picked up more than a few fast food dinners late at night for my obliging family. Linda's last request of me was this: Would I please preach at her memorial service about Israel from the book of Ruth? And so I did.

The blessing that flowed between Linda and me as Gentile and Jewish believer soothed each other's souls in places that probably echoed millennia of misunderstanding between God's two covenant peoples. We were changed forever.

Maybe even the future was changed just a little bit, too. Resulting from Ruth and Naomi's relationship, Gentile and Jew together prepared the way of the Lord's first coming, through the lineage of Jesus. It will be the same, I am convinced, with His second coming. Yeshua's return will be preceded by a remnant of Christian believers who, in the spirit of Ruth, cling till death to the Jewish people. This Ruth Remnant will so captivate the Lord's heart that He, like Boaz, will come in strength for His Bride, redeeming Jew and Gentile as one in Him.

Abraham's Spiritual Children and the Blessing

In the manner of Ruth, we meet a certain Roman centurion in the New Covenant. This army commander has an uncommon dedication and love for the Jewish people and, we can assume, the Jewish God. Desperate for a healing, he sends for Jesus. "This man deserves to have you do this," the centurion's Jewish friends explain to Yeshua, "because he loves our nation and has built our synagogue" (Luke 7:4–5).

For a Gentile to underwrite the building of a synagogue in Jesus' time would have been odd enough; it would have been nearly unfathomable for this lover of Zion to be a Roman soldier. Notice how the Lord responds. He goes—immediately: "*So* Jesus went with them" (Luke 7:6, emphasis mine). Jesus goes at once, for the centurion has blessed Israel; he must be blessed in return. This humble Gentile is the only non-Jew in the gospels whose request for ministry Jesus grants without the *slightest* hesitation.

If you are a New Covenant Gentile believer, a "spiritual child" of Abraham, do you also inherit a covenant of blessing? Absolutely. God endows every believer in Yeshua with the gracious blessings of salvation. You, as part of the Church, are blessed to be a bless-ing. Those who bless the Church are blessed, those who curse the Church are cursed, and all families of the earth are blessed through the Church. Realize, though, that Gentiles have not been called to *replace* Israel in her blessing; Gentiles have been called to *make a place* for Israel's blessing. The blessings of Gentile and Jew are reciprocal. God's plan of redemption depends on it.

Do you want more of the Blesser? If so, you want to bless Israel. Let's see next what you do *not* want to do.

CHAPTER THREE

Accursed: Who, Why, When

B y nature, I am much less a historian than a visionary. Fixing on the future and how the Lord is calling us to shape it makes my heart race. Fumbling through the fossilized past makes me yawn. But a couple of years ago the Lord adjusted my attitude about what I now call the "prophetic past," the past that speaks clearly to us of the future.

I was preparing a talk that required me to research an obscure topic in Church history. My time was limited so I decided to begin at home with the Internet—presumably the simplest approach. But after navigating one search engine for about two minutes, I managed to pull up 184 websites, articles and other references to my "obscure" topic.

I cupped both hands over my face as my head fell to the desk. Groaning, I thought that maybe if I asked, the Lord would tell me which of these 184 references I should read first. He didn't. He said something more surprising. *This vast store of information can be a gift from Me. I don't just use the Scriptures as examples for you, but the full record of human events. I'm showing you the past for a reason; don't ignore it.*

The Prophetic Past

It is said that those who forget the past are doomed to repeat it. But those who remember history ("His story") are free to forge it anew.

Each of us is deeply affected by history. Whether we like it or not, and through no fault or merit of our own, we inherit both good and bad from those who precede us. As a result, we often must deal with the past before we can flow with the Spirit into the future. Many of us already know this to be the case on an individual, personal level; it is the same for families, churches and even nations.

Those of us who are parents plead with our children to learn from our mistakes so they need not suffer by repeating them. I believe our forefathers of bygone generations would do the same for us. If they could they would plead with us to reverse the curses resulting from their historical misdeeds. There are times we would do well to peek into the archives of those who have long since departed, dust off their journals and bring them to the Light.

I am convinced that God has much to say to us in the twenty-first century based on His story about His people Israel. Heaps of long-hidden facts that disclose His heart and plans are now readily accessible. The storehouse of information, however, has not been unlocked simply for us to accumulate knowledge. We are being summoned to a divine reckoning. This reckoning is associated with nothing less than the approaching climax of history and return of the Lord. I believe (because the Bible teaches it) that in the last days Yahweh will call every soul to account. This account will relate very much to our treatment of Israel. We will answer to Him for words and deeds—our own and our forefathers'—toward the Jewish people. (Remember the sheep and the goats.) We will be blessed or we will be cursed.

Today, however, is a day of grace, beckoning us to know the truth that it might set us free.

Literal Interpretation of the Bible

To start, please glimpse with me some pivotal events that affect our understanding of what the Bible teaches about Israel at the most fundamental level. I think you will be more than a bit surprised along our brief journey.

As you know, Moses was the first writer and teacher of the Hebrew Scriptures. Yeshua's teachings reflect, deepen and stamp His authority onto the Mosaic, or traditionally Jewish,[1] interpretation of the Word. (The Lord did not approve of some of the Pharisees' *application* of the Scriptures, but that is a different matter.) Following Yeshua's example, our earliest Church Fathers, the Messianic Jewish apostles and teachers, adhered to the same traditionally Jewish approach to Scripture study.

What is this "Son of God" authorized approach or, more technically, hermeneutic? Very simply, a literal one. The literal Hebraic hermeneutic assumes God's Word means what it says and says what it means.

By the third century, however, first the texture and then the text of Christianity changed. The Church had grown rapidly, shifting from mostly Jewish to mostly Gentile, and naturally so; God has always had many more Gentiles in the world than Jews. Messianic Jews had done their job well, advancing the Gospel and embracing all who believed.

As Gentiles flooded the Church, they brought with them their own traditions—many of them infused with foreign gods and pagan practices. Before long, "things Gentile" replaced "things Jewish." The Jewish approach to interpreting the Holy Scriptures, the oracles of God entrusted to them for millennia, became one of those "things" replaced. It was felt that an allegorical rather than literal approach to Bible study was more consistent with Gentile traditions. User-friendly allegory could more easily accommodate the culture and thought of pagan society. As allegory, the words of Scripture would no longer have to mean what they said; they could mean almost anything to anybody.

Biblical Allegory or Fantasy?

The allegorical approach, which still influences much of the Church today, assumes that God's words are symbolic; they are meant to have representative, not literal, meanings. Words such as *book, dog* or *chair,* for instance, do not refer to a literal book, dog or chair. Rather, they symbolize spiritual mysteries that need not be at all connected to a book, a dog or a chair. *Israel* and *Jew,* therefore, pertain no more, according to allegorist fathers, to the literal descendants of Abraham, Isaac and Jacob. Instead they symbolize the Gentile Church.

Please do not misunderstand me. The Bible is interspersed beautifully with vivid symbolism and genuine allegory. We saw earlier how the book of Ruth shines as a literal tale that contains prophetic meaning. But to grasp the symbolism of Ruth, we must first interpret the book literally. So it is with all of Scripture.

What is sad about the allegorical approach is that it stems from an erroneous assumption about God. Allegorists assume that Yahweh is so far removed and aloof from humanity that He can communicate only in language inherently difficult, if not near-impossible, for His children to understand.[2]

What fruit has this allegorical method borne? "Fantasy unlimited," according to one well-known Bible teacher.[3] Take, for instance,[4] this insight from Origen, third-century theologian, based on Jesus' triumphal entry into Jerusalem. The donkey, Origen declared, represents the Old Covenant. The donkey's colt depicts the New Covenant, while the two apostles picture the moral and mystic senses of Scripture.[5] According to Origen, a literal understanding of a donkey, its colt and the apostles is irrelevant: Jesus never actually told anyone to fetch an animal for Him and did not ride one into Jerusalem. Apparently He entered the Holy City sitting on the New Covenant—even though it was not yet written and even though the Old Covenant prophesied that Israel's King would come to her riding on a colt (Zechariah 9:9).

This sort of thinking still wends its way into seminaries and church pulpits today. How many of us have listened to sermons that take prophetic Scriptures about Zion (such as "Arise, shine, for your light has come" or "Enlarge the place of your tent") and apply them *exclusively* as allegory to the spiritual life of the Christian without regard for the literal Jewish nation? How many of us have heard this similarly misguided conclusion: All Old Covenant promises, including those pertaining to Israel's land, have been fulfilled in the Person of Jesus Christ? Such teachings can easily promote replacement theology, the erroneous doctrine that the Bible's prophetic promises and blessings pertaining to Israel now belong exclusively to the Church. They are based on an approach to the Scriptures that is essentially eisegetical and does not properly exegete the Word of God.[6] Because these interpretations leave nothing for the Jewish people (except curses), they easily foster anti-Semitism.

Walking the Emmaus Road

How ought we to interpret and apply the Scriptures to avoid such pernicious mistakes? Generally speaking, unless a biblical passage requires a symbolic interpretation in order to make sense (and some do), we are to assume a literal one.[7] If we ignore that foundation, we risk missing God Himself. Once we grasp the literal meaning of the Word, the Holy Spirit may indeed speak about symbolic interpretation. God loves to reveal His ways and means for today and tomorrow through special application of the Scriptures. I love His prophetic *rhema* as well as *logos*. But I have learned to test every revelation against sound doctrine, resisting the temptation to elevate that revelation to the status of doctrine lest I succumb to "fantasy unlimited." And I have learned not to read anything into the Bible that is not there.

I grieve that history has deprived many Christians of the richness of their biblical heritage. The issue of Israel summons us to embrace with integrity the ministry of both Word and Spirit. I want to see the Body of Messiah move forward in the fullness of divine revelation, and I thrill to watch it happen.

When my non-Jewish friend Nancy began embracing a literal view of the Bible and Hebraic roots of her faith, she described it as an "Emmaus Road" experience. I was elated along with her. "It was as if scales fell from my eyes!" Nancy exclaimed. "Jesus became so real and so—alive. I feel I know Him as I never have before. . . ." She trailed off and began weeping—and I am not sure she has ever really stopped.

God *delights* to reveal Himself. This is the original and basic belief underlying the literal approach to Scripture study. Yeshua would much rather walk the Emmaus Road intimately with you and me than confuse us along a tortuous path. The Master Communicator, He means what He says and says what He means.

When God speaks of blessing, that is what He means. When He speaks of cursing, that is what He means as well. Quite literally, He curses those who curse the literal sons and daughters of Jacob.

The Curse Verse and Israel's Enemies

In common parlance, the word *curse* refers either to four-letter expletives or occult activity. But the Hebrew Scriptures give a different, important and specific understanding of the concept of a curse. Derived from various words, the Hebrew definition is twofold: (1) to stop or impose a barrier, ban or paralysis and (2) to treat lightly or make light of; to belittle or make little.[8] A curse in the Old Covenant is much the same as a judgment.[9] When people curse, therefore, they are in essence praying for judgment. Likewise, when God curses He judges. On this basis, and given the Hebrew sentence structure of Genesis 12:3, Bible commentators suggest its "curse verse" could be translated more accurately as follows:

> "[T]he one who treats you lightly [stops you as you fulfill your calling or makes you little] I must curse."[10]

That God *must* curse is a sobering, almost chilling thought. The implications for today are critical. To learn from the prophetic past, let's telescope Jewish history and see how this principle plays out.

Soon after God promised blessing or cursing through Abraham,[11] King Abimelech of Egypt unwittingly mishandled the patriarch's wife. As a result, Abimelech's life was threatened and every woman in his household was cursed with infertility (see Genesis 20:1–18). Some years later God passed the covenant promise on to Isaac (see Genesis 17:18–21), then to Jacob and his sons (see Genesis 28:13–14). Jacob's son Joseph was favored and blessed by an Egyptian pharaoh; as a result, Egypt prospered in difficult times. Another pharaoh enslaved the Hebrews, killed their babies and imprisoned them; Egypt was laid waste and never fully recovered.

The Moabites hired a soothsayer named Balaam to curse the Israelites on their way to Canaan. Instead, God cursed the Moabites (see Nehemiah 13:1–2). Rahab the harlot came to the Jews' aid in Jericho; as a result, she was spared death and earned eternal esteem (see Joshua 2:1–21; 6:24–25; Hebrews 11:31). After their exile from the Promised Land, Jews in Persia were threatened with annihilation by an evil ruler named Haman. His sinister plan backfired and Haman was the one to hang on gallows built for a Jewish neck (see Esther 3; 5:14; 7:9–10).

Throughout the Scriptures, when Israel backslid from God He raised up nations in merciful judgment against her. But inevitably they took opportunity to mock Israel or rejoice at her downfall, and so God turned to judge *those* nations — *without* mercy. Look at the list: Those cursing the children of Israel — Amalekites, Amorites, Hittites, Perrizites, Jebusites, Gibeonites, Midianites, Edomites, Babylonians, Philistines and others — only forced God's hand against themselves.

The Pattern Persists

The pattern did not change after the close of the canon of Scripture. When the New Covenant was written, the Roman Empire loomed over a large portion of the world and continued to flourish for hundreds of years. Then Emperor Constantine came to power and made Christianity the official religion of his expansive polity. This new church-state alliance adopted virulently anti-Jewish laws. Soon thereafter, the great Roman Empire crumbled and the Church sank into a spiritual abyss called the Dark Ages. During this same period, Islam rose to the fore.

The eleventh and twelfth centuries ushered in the so-called Holy Crusades. Dispatched by popes and kings, Christian soldiers marched from England and France to liberate Jerusalem. But liberate meant liquidate. Crusaders wantonly slaughtered tens of thousands of Jews (and Muslims) all along the way in the name of Jesus Christ. What happened next? The bubonic plague decimated much of Europe; England and France re-aimed their weapons against each other in the Hundred Years' War.

A few centuries later, large numbers of Jews migrated to Spain. There they rose to prominent positions and helped transform the nation into a world power. The Golden Age of Spain ended, however, with its inquisitions against the Jewish people. In the notorious and climactic inquisition of 1492, "Christian" Spain expelled every Jew from the country. What followed? The Spanish empire plunged into "a period of unrelenting political, military, economic, and social decline,"[12] never to reclaim its previous global influence.

God says Israel is the "apple or pupil of His eye" (Zechariah 2:8, AMPLIFIED). The Hebrew word picture describes someone attempting to poke a finger into the pupils of God's eyes. But it seems the brazen individual's own eyes are injured in the process. History shows that those who mistreat the Jewish people suffer loss of visual clarity. They lose sight of truth and the grace to see right from wrong; they crumble under the curse of their own anti-Semitism.

The Twentieth Century: Coincidence or Curse?

Approximately five hundred years ago, Jewish people started settling in significant numbers in Great Britain. There they enjoyed favor and eventually support from a small but vocal Christian minority. These forerunners of Christian Zionism began taking the Bible literally again. With revived insight, they understood that prophetic promises and blessings to Israel still applied to the literal sons and daughters of Jacob.[13] By the late 1800s, British believers were playing a key role in imparting vision and practical help to European Jews in the return and rebuilding of their ancestral homeland.[14] They set the stage theologically for Christian Zionists today. In the meantime, as long as Great Britain treated the Jewish people kindly, things went quite well for her. "The sun never sets on the British Empire," it was said, for her kingdom spanned the earth. But a turning point came in the aftermath of World War I when the international community delegated to Britain a sizeable honor and responsibility. She was to supervise the official reestablishment of a sovereign Jewish state in the Middle East.

Britain, however, took nearly eighty percent of the land given her to hold in trust for the Jews and handed it over to the Arabs instead. Then, during and after the Holocaust, she blockaded the remaining twenty-percent sliver of land in order to reduce Jewish immigration to a trickle. As a result, millions of Nazi-hunted Jews found no place of escape. Why? British policy shifted specifically to appease Arab fears for the sake of petrodollars, or, in this case, petropounds. As you know, Great Britain's Empire is no more.

Likewise, Germany was left in shambles, a nation divided and humiliated after its Nazi-generated, draconian Jewish genocide.

A grand-scale drama of the twentieth century played out in the once-formidable Soviet Union. Throughout the history of the USSR, documented reports of unbridled, murderous anti-Semitism made their way to the Jewish community worldwide. Demand was made for decades, inside the Soviet Empire and out: "Let my people go!" The Communists stubbornly refused until suddenly the fearsome USSR fell to its knees, releasing from its chokehold an exodus of nearly one million Jews.

"Those who curse you I will curse." To curse, you recall, is to stop or make little—as history records of the Romans, the French, the Spanish, the British, the Germans, the Soviets and someday, apart from repentance, the Arabs. For a century their collective cry has not subsided: "The Zionist State must be destroyed!" I fear the Arabs may reap the very curse they relentlessly revile against Israel.

Reversing Cursing

If a curse has been reaped due to anti-Semitism, can it be reversed?

I have watched it happen many times in many places, and it always begins with humility — that secret to blessing. When Christians discover the Scriptures about God's heart and plans for Israel, the Holy Spirit often convicts them deeply. I first learned this in a church near my own home in Southern California.

The pastor had invited me to speak at a Sunday service about Israel. I prepared a general, introductory sort of talk and arranged for a brief altar ministry in case some folks wanted prayer. At the end of my message the Lord impressed on me to provide opportunity for repentance from the sin of anti-Semitism. Because that had not been the topic of my message I felt rather embarrassed to bring it up and expected at most a handful of those present to respond obligingly. Instead, I was stunned to watch virtually every person in the church — including a few personal acquaintances — scramble to the altar. Through their tears, many confessed the startling realization that they secretly despised the Jews. Others wept over their lovelessness or disinterest toward the Jewish people. The heart of the church changed that day. The congregation stayed committed to praying for Israel, and their local and international outreach ministries have borne more fruit than ever.

Even more dramatic are the radical renunciations of anti-Semitism I have witnessed in the former Soviet Union. When we co-labor with indigenous churches in Jewish evangelistic outreach (see chapter 10), the need to repent of Jew hatred always comes up — from the local believers. In one city, government officials threatened at the last minute to shut down our entire outreach. A local pastor told us he believed the problem stemmed from a spiritual stronghold

of anti-Semitism. He called for churches citywide to repent immediately of this evil. It would take too long to tell the whole story,
but the outreach went forward and thousands of Jews—as well as
Gentiles—professed faith in Yeshua as their Messiah. The formerly
hostile officials asked us to stay and prolong the mission, which
they now felt had brought much-needed unity to the city. The local
pastor who had so boldly stood for the Jews suddenly received a
city permit for a new church building for which he had applied and
tediously waited many, many months.

Yes, a curse can be reversed.

And in America?

Since I am an American citizen, I would like to share a little about
my country's unique relationship with Israel. I love and pray for
the United States and our leaders. I am extremely thankful to have
been born in this special nation.

"Your country has to be blessed," said my friend Yossi, almost
matter-of-factly. "America is Israel's best friend."

Yossi is an Israeli and a Holocaust survivor. He spoke those
words to me almost twenty years ago. But when I last saw Yossi
in 2001, he had a different opinion. "Does a friend handcuff you
and slice out your heart to feed his dog? This is what America is
doing, tying our hands and carving up our heartland—our *home*—to
feed terrorists."

The comment was painful to hear. How could Yossi say such a
thing?

When Israel was miraculously reborn in 1948, America rose
first to recognize her officially and bless her as a sovereign state.
Since then the two countries have been closely allied. Many regard
the United States as Israel's best friend—although the friendship
is definitely reciprocal, with Israel serving U.S. interests in the
Middle East (and thereby the world) and helping fight America's
war against terror. Unequivocally, God has blessed America for
her support of Israel.

But in 1993 things changed. Alongside an American president smiling proudly on the lawn of the White House, Israeli Prime Minister Rabin shook hands with PLO Chairman Arafat. The United States had charted a new course of coercion against Israel: the relinquishment of her land for a promise of peace. The world applauded.

Since then, piece by piece—yet never achieving peace—the United States has pressed persistently upon the Jewish nation to sacrifice more land, and more of her sons and daughters, to an enemy that cannot be appeased. Israel's security has been so dramatically compromised that she has suffered thousands *more* incidents of terror within her borders than before the land-for-peace process began. Not unpredictably, when we refused to let Israel quell terror on her own turf, it eventually made its way to American soil.

It bears repeating: To curse is to belittle—as in make tiny Israel even littler. A local politician, a Christian, recently said, "We've no right anymore to say 'God bless America' if we aren't saying and meaning 'God bless Israel.'"

A chronology of domestic events corresponding with our nation's role as prime mover in the land-for-peace process was compiled in a book published in 2002.[15] The side-by-side tracking of major political pushes toward peace correlates in a sobering fashion with different disasters befalling the United States. Widespread devastation, treacherous weather aberrations and colossal accidents—including the tragic space shuttle crash that spilled its wreckage around Palestine, Texas—seem to occur as America takes steps that endanger Israel.

I do not draw a definitive cause-and-effect relationship from these phenomena, but I cannot deny the portentous parallels. I see these calamities as evil-induced events through which God desires graciously to wake us up and warn us. Those who claw capriciously at the apple of God's eye will experience His retribution. He does not desire to curse America, a nation with many who faithfully love and serve Him. On the other hand, I cannot agree with those Christian leaders who say that America has blessed Israel too much ever to be accused of cursing her. God says that to whom much is given, much is required. He has invested enormous physical and spiritual resources in America. With our resources come great responsibilities, together with weighty choices. In the Bible we sometimes see whole nations suffering on account of the choices of their leaders. We must pray that America's leaders do not follow the precedent set by Egypt, Spain, Great Britain, Germany and other countries that, having first set on a course of blessing the Jewish people, later turned to cursing them.

A Word to Messianic Jews

May I take a moment to share some private words with my fellow Jewish believers in Yeshua? Dear brothers and sisters, can we arise to forgive? Messiah tells us to bless those who curse us and pray for those who mistreat us. Can we humble ourselves to follow in His footsteps? Or would we rather grieve God's heart and in so doing, curse even ourselves? You and I are called to exercise spiritual authority in Messiah to bless the nations, including non-Jewish believers who have wounded our people. Whatever personal offenses we might hold against Gentiles, it is time to let them go. The Lord wants us free to be used to propel the nations into their destinies in Him. It is part of our calling. Israel may not have fulfilled this call consistently, but we have a world-changing opportunity to do so today.

A resurgence in Christian Zionism has taken place before our eyes in recent years. Believers all over the world stand ready to aid and abet our people. God is moving on their hearts in ways we may not now fully understand, but they have and will play a key part in the restoration of Israel. Our privilege is to serve them, kneeling to enrich these righteous Gentiles.

Also, I believe we Messianic Jews have a role of repentance to assume on behalf of the ungodly influence that segments of the unsaved Jewish community have had on America—or whatever country in which we live. The Jews have tremendously blessed the United States—and other nations—but we are not without sin. Remember the words of the prophet Jeremiah who urged us to pray for the peace and prosperity of the place to which we are dispersed; if it prospers, so will we (see Jeremiah 29:7). Messianic brothers and sisters, will you stand with me in the gap, praying for our host nation and perhaps quelling a curse?

Speaking now to all, Yahweh's promise to bless or curse, tied inexorably to Israel, pulsates from His heart of pure love. He so loves the world, He so loves *you*, that He is using Israel to prove it. Let's see how.

PART 2

Father's Heart

For I am convinced that neither death nor life, neither angels nor demons, neither the present nor the future, nor any powers, neither height nor depth, nor anything else in all creation, will be able to separate us from the love of God that is in Christ Jesus our Lord. I speak the truth in Christ—I am not lying, my conscience confirms it in the Holy Spirit—I have great sorrow and unceasing anguish in my heart. For I could wish that I myself were cursed and cut off from Christ for the sake of my brothers, those of my own race, the people of Israel.

ROMANS 8:38–9:4

CHAPTER FOUR

Through the Lens of Love

O n what began as an otherwise routine and uneventful day in 1981, God changed the course of my life. I was at home dusting furniture, the clothes dryer puffing dutifully and rhythmically in the background. Suddenly shattering the mundane, God's breathtakingly sacred, sovereign presence filled my home. I don't know how else to describe it.

I had given my life to Yeshua several years earlier. But I had never experienced Him like this before—so palpably, potently close that I was afraid to open my eyes lest I literally see Him and His glory wipe me out. *He* was in the room; *I* was on the floor, undone in His presence. Then (it seemed) the Father tore open His heart and spoke one sentence: *This is how I feel about Israel.*

Instantly I doubled over and began to wail—loud, piercing cries I had never heard come out of me before. I grabbed a pillow to stuff over my mouth, thinking my startled neighbors might call the police. A dull, throbbing weight pressed on my heart with an ache that exploded into tears of liquid despair. I lay writhing on the floor, engulfed by both a horrifying awareness of sin that separated my people from God and His consuming anguish over that wretched separation. Then His love—His boundless, all-conquering, ever-comforting love—enfolded me. I could not talk; words would have seemed a desecration. But every ounce of my being pleaded, "Father, forgive us!"

I knew next to nothing about travailing intercessory prayer or supernatural manifestations of the Holy Spirit. Neither was I particularly concerned about Israel at that point in my life. But in that otherworldly encounter with Love Himself, I felt willing to give up my life—even my eternal life—for the salvation of my Jewish people. I understood how the apostle Paul said he "could wish that [he himself] were cursed and cut off from Christ for the sake of . . . the people of Israel" (Romans 9:3–4).

The Burden of the Lord

When God drenched me in divine love that unforgettable day, He transformed my heart toward the Jewish people. Only years later did I realize that is more or less how it is supposed to happen.

Most Christians are familiar with the comforting conclusion of Romans 8: "[Nothing] will be able to separate us from the love of God that is in Christ Jesus our Lord" (verse 39). That power-packed verse has strengthened the Church for two thousand years. Despite life's difficulties, you and I can cling to the truth of His unwavering love. Nothing, *but nothing*, can separate us from it.

How many of us, however, have made the connection between God's love in Romans 8:38 and Paul's inspired words about Israel in the very next sentence of Romans 9:1? The flow of Scriptures is strategic by the Spirit. Right after we are assured of Yahweh's unconditional love, we are reminded of the unquenchable flame in His heart for the Jews. There is a reason that the New Covenant's keynote message on Israel—that is, Romans 9 through 11—comes in the context of God's love in Romans 8. Bear in mind the original letter to the Roman church had no chapter breaks; they were added later for our convenience. The biblical context for a Christian understanding of Israel, therefore, is *love*.

As Paul trumpets the triumph of God's love, the Spirit turns his thoughts naturally to Israel. Not only is this divine design, it is logical. Birthed from Yahweh's love for humanity, Israel was created as an object of His affection and ardor—to love Him back and mediate His love to others. Yet for the most part, she does not. Like other nations, she is lost in her sin. So the anointed apostle spills before us his secret and unshakeable grief: Israel's lostness. The same Paul who exhorts us to rejoice always (see Philippians 4:4) confides in us that he carries "unceasing anguish" over Israel.

Why does his sorrow never end? Paul is gripped by the *Spirit's* unending burden, the *Spirit's* unending love for the Jewish people. Not once, but three times, he affirms the veracity of this passion: "I speak the truth in Christ—I am not lying, my conscience confirms it in the Holy Spirit—I have great sorrow and unceasing anguish in my heart . . . for the sake . . . of the people of Israel." Paul's lament echoes that of Moses, who centuries earlier cried out to God on Israel's behalf: "Please forgive their sin—but if not, *then blot me out* of the book you have written" (Exodus 32:32, emphasis mine). Paul, like Moses, carries the unchanging heart cry of God. Do you want to know the "burden of the Lord" today? It is Israel.

The Greatest Is Love

Does this exclude other nations from a special place in the Father's heart? On the contrary, the Spirit's burden for Israel is central to His plan of salvation for all peoples. God purposed with Abraham that through his progeny all nations would be blessed, His love for the world would be revealed. In keeping with His unconditional covenant, both the Scriptures and the Savior came to us through the Jewish people. And millennia after the Messiah, His love story remains on display for global observation as the eyes of the world focus increasingly on Israel. His heart's desire is evident in the ancient as well as the modern nation's day-to-day existence. *To understand God's love, understand Israel. Conversely, to understand Israel, understand God's love.*

Many believers with little grasp of God's heart for the Jewish people undeniably love Him, and through the millennia countless numbers of such saints have laid their lives down for Yeshua. In no way do I intend to impugn their spirituality. Still, to fully understand God's love as revealed in the Scriptures, we must understand Israel. To accurately understand Israel today and in the years ahead, we must understand Love Himself. Thus Israel serves as a testing ground of sorts for the nations—a test of love.

What is love, exactly? Bible scholars tell us that while love is the "first and last word in Christian theology," it is also "an exceedingly ambiguous term"[1] because the Bible never defines it. Instead, God tells us what love looks like and what it does. He declares He *is* love (see 1 John 4:8, 16), and that foremost of love's qualities is patience or, according to some translations, longsuffering (see 1 Corinthians 13:4, KJV). Indeed, God suffers long and He is patient, giving of Himself to the point of dying on a tree.

I believe we are born—and born again—craving God's love. Humanity, however "sophisticated," needs His love today no less than in eras gone by. You and I need His love in our churches, families and individual lives as much as ever. The more wholly we abide in His love, the more wholeheartedly we love Him back; we become whole.

This past century the Holy Spirit has lavished *charismata*, or supernatural gifts, on the Church worldwide. He has released and revived anointing and empowering long believed to have ceased with the first-century apostles. But despite all our *charismata*, to paraphrase 1 Corinthians 13, without love we are nothing. Without love even the priceless gifts of the Holy Spirit do not add anything to our worth. If we speak in tongues or prophesy without love, we make only noise. If we have faith to move mountains but have not love, we are nothing. If we give all we possess to the poor or surrender ourselves as martyrs for Messiah, we gain nothing without love. Love is the greatest gift and most excellent way. It never fails; it lasts forever. It is the most valued element of the universe, spiritual or tangible, next to Love Incarnate Himself.

Jesus said that in the last days clashes between good and evil would increase. As a result He cautioned that the love of many will grow cold (see Matthew 24:12). I am convinced this is one reason why, in recent years, the Spirit has so generously poured out His affections on the Church. You and I are being "loved on," not just because it is our Father's nature, but because He is preparing us for Kingdom conflict—and ultimate victory—such as we have never seen before. Israel will stand at the center, a testing ground of love. In these unprecedented days God wants us to remember this: The greatest is love.

Blessing Israel releases the blessing *of* Israel. Now, blessing for blessing is not a bad motive. But the more excellent way—the highest and noblest—is love. Unconditional love without ulterior motive is the ultimate substance and test of our faith. It is that which the Lord most radically requires of us. So the question becomes, Do you want yours to be a life of love?

Followers of Jesus Christ are called to love like Him. Genuine Christlike love for Israel, I am convinced, is destined to catapult the Jewish nation into revival. Ask just about any Messianic Jew you know and you will probably learn that the love of a Gentile believer was pivotal to his or her turning to faith. Even unsaved Jews admit that during these increasingly anti-Semitic times, the steadfast love of Christian Zionists is melting their hearts.

The Bible through New Lenses

God can transform anyone's life into a life of love. Not long ago at a conference of Messianic Jews and Christian Arabs, I met a former member of the PLO who had snuffed out more than one Jewish life. Taysir ("Tass") Abu Saada used to train children to kill Israelis. But then this ex-Muslim *Fatah* fighter had a dramatic encounter with the Holy Spirit. Now he loves and serves the Lord Jesus Christ, the Arabs—and the Jews. How was Tass's heart transformed from one of hate to love?

Someone told Tass that to know God he would have to love a Jew, namely Jesus. When this person set a Bible before Tass, he suddenly began to shake, violently. Tass did not know if he was shaking from anger, fear, the awesome awareness of Israel's God or all of the above—but he did know the book was about his enemy. Tass says that when he eventually read the Word, and through it came to know God's love for Israel, he felt love for the first time in his life. "I grew up hating—and especially hating Jews. When I was willing love *them,* God filled me with His love for *me.*"

Have you ever read the Scriptures, like Tass, from this perspective—through the lens of Yahweh's love for His covenant people Israel? Through Israel, God wants to unveil new dimensions of His vast, magnificent heart for you. Because Yahweh so faithfully loves His Old Covenant people, He faithfully loves His New Covenant people.

Do you desire to love the Lord with your whole heart, mind and strength? To wholly love your God, I am convinced, will usher you into new dimensions of His holy love for Israel. You will find, then, that holy love for Israel magnetizes you deeper and deeper into Holy Love Himself. However well you know the Lord, as you read the Bible through the lens of His covenant love for the Jews, I think you will know Him even more. An ardent adventure awaits you.

Why Does God Love Israel?

We hear Yahweh speak directly of His love for Israel for the first time in the book of Deuteronomy. Try to picture the scene: The children of Israel are gathered expectantly before Moses, their beloved leader of more than forty years. The great lawgiver, prophet and friend of God is saying good-bye to the Israelites as they stand at the precipice of the Promised Land. Moses is about to die, and so (I imagine) the hushed crowd clings to his every word. Nobody pays heed to the punishing desert sun, crying babies or unending demands of life-on-the-go. Here and now, for the first time, Moses tells the Israelites that God loves them:

> "The Lord your God has chosen you to be a people for His own possession out of all the peoples who are on the face of the earth. The Lord did not set His love [*khashaq* in Hebrew] on you nor choose you because you were more in number than any of the peoples, for

you were the fewest of all peoples, but because the Lord loved [*ahav*] you and kept the oath which He swore to your forefathers."

DEUTERONOMY 7:6–8, NASB

Why does God love Israel? He says simply that *He loves Israel because He loved Israel.* Yahweh does not say Israel is loveable; He does not even say her forefathers with whom He made covenant were loveable. He offers no explanation conforming to human logic for His love for the Jewish people. This does not mean His love for them is illogical or irrational; it does mean His love is according to perfectly divine reasoning and sovereign purpose.

God hints that His love for His chosen people exists for its own sake. Peer into the chambers of His heart; He loves because He *is* love. He loves because love is His nature and character. In the same way, He loves *you* for His own sake. He cannot *not* love you. "Thou art Thyself the reason for the love wherewith we are loved," summarized A. W. Tozer.[2]

God ties His love for the Jewish people to the oath He swore to them. He binds Himself by His word to Abraham, Isaac and Jacob. It has been said that love is spelled c-o-m-m-i-t-m-e-n-t. Sovereign God loves Israel because of His covenantal commitment to her. At the same time, His commitment stems from His love. God loves Israel because He loved Israel, because He committed to love Israel.

Bear in mind and heart that God is greater than, and not equal to, love. His attributes are many; He is holy, faithful, just, merciful, true, powerful and infinitely more. Yet it seems love is uniquely attributable to His very essence—who He is, what He does and why and how He does it. Indeed, love is the greatest.

Love in Hebrew: Ahav

If you go to church, you have probably heard more than one sermon about the nuances of the different Greek words used in the New Covenant for *love.* But have you ever studied the fascinating Hebrew concept of love? It is in Hebrew that God gives us a foundational knowledge of His love, and solid foundations are key to good constructs of any kind. So let us momentarily revisit Deuteronomy 7:6–8, where we first hear, straight-out and plain, about God's love for the Jews:

> "The Lord . . . set His *love* [*khashaq*] on you . . . because the Lord *loved* [*ahav*] you and kept the oath which He swore to your forefathers."
>
> NASB, EMPHASIS ADDED

In this pivotal passage, where two different but related Hebrew words for *love* are used, we learn how God's word choice reveals one of the secrets of His heart. The Hebrew Scriptures employ three different words to convey love.[3] The first and most significant word, *ahav,* is used where Moses explains that the Lord loves the Israelites "because the Lord *loved* you." *Ahav* also appears in the related verse "because the Lord *loved* your fathers." *Ahav,* a primary root, is the most frequently used word for love in the Hebrew Scriptures. *Ahav* means "to love, have affection, be attached to, delight in." *Ahav* is also used to convey "to lust" and "to breathe after."[4]

The second word for love, *khashaq,* is found where Moses says the Lord has "set His *love* on you." *Khashaq* means "to love, long for, desire and delight in." It also implies "clinging."[5] (A third word that conveys love, *keenah,* is not found in this passage but is used elsewhere to denote Yahweh's ardor, zeal or jealousy.)[6] Based on the above, we could paraphrase our passage: "The Lord set His longing, clinging desire, delight and love on you because of His affectionate attachment, panting delight and love for you."

Why take so much time with definitions? *The point is the passion!* God is absolutely amorous toward Israel. Israel is the object of a divine love affair, the longest romance on record—which never ends.

Love Letters

Listen to Yahweh's heartbeat for His people not only in the words of Scripture, but in the very *letters* that comprise them. According to certain Jewish schools of thought, each letter of the Hebrew alphabet carries with it a deposit of the divine. Since God is the Author of language and Hebrew is the original language in which He spoke to His people, some rabbis say that not only every word but *every letter* of every word communicates something of His nature. When defining a word in the Old Covenant they consider the meaning of the individual letters in that word.[7] I applied this intriguing concept to the three Hebrew letters that comprise *ahav* (to love) and was dazzled all over again by Father's heart.

In the word *ahav*, the first letter is *aleph*, which is said to designate sacrifice, strength and servant leadership. *Hey*, the second letter, connotes an opening or open window. It is also used as a substitute for writing God's name. The third letter, *vet*, is a modification of the letter *bet*, which means "house" or "family," and implies covenantal, affectionate relationship.[8]

By its three component letters, *ahav* communicates sacrifice, strength, open intimacy with God and familial relationship. In *ahav* we catch nuances of the all-powerful One sacrificing so His people can relate openly and freely to Him as members of His family. J. I. Packer, in *Knowing God*, describes the intimacy implicit in the word *ahav*: God's "love reaches its highest form in personal fellowship in which each lives in the life of the other, imparting to the other, and receiving back the outflow of that other's affection."[9]

I am not suggesting that these somewhat mystical musings be elevated to the level of Bible doctrine, but they mirror gorgeously Yahweh's universal, prophetic reach into human affairs. He is big beyond imagination. He sovereignly and lovingly invades creation and all that concerns us with patterns of His presence—even, perhaps, in the very letters of His words.

Special Spots in God's Heart

Christians beginning to understand God's heart for Israel sometimes ask me for pointers on witnessing to Jewish neighbors, co-workers or friends. My answer always starts with, "Love them."

Jewish hearts will resonate and respond to God's love, but we must never forget that love is patient.

It was God's patient love that won my own heart to Yeshua many years ago. The glaring and persistent love of a Christian friend named Ann provoked me to jealousy. I had read and prayed about God's love since I was a small child in synagogue. I grew up reciting daily the cornerstone Jewish Scripture: "Love [*ahav*] the Lord your God with all your heart and with all your soul and with all your strength" (Deuteronomy 6:5). The problem was, I did not love the Lord anything like that; in fact, I did not know anyone who did. It was troubling: If even the rabbi could not love the Lord with all his heart, soul or strength, what chance did I stand? What was wrong—and what was the solution?

As a young adult I finally found someone—Ann—who loved God as the Scriptures command. I puzzled, "What is that woman doing with *our* God?" This Gentile believer provoked me to jealousy; I wanted that kind of relationship with Him, too. "There's a special spot in God's heart for you," Ann would say, "that matches the emptiness in yours for Him." There is more to the story, but not much later Ann led me in prayer to dedicate my life to Messiah.

Indeed, from the moment Yahweh created Israel she held a special spot in His heart. He moved heaven and earth to *ahav* her. With doting care He raised her and called her His treasure (see Exodus 19:5). Whenever she strayed, off He went in hot pursuit to win her back. God is the ultimate lover and the Jewish nation still resonates to His love.

Of course, if you are a Gentile Christian, God's love for you is no less than His love for Israel. While there is a special spot in His heart for the Jewish people that only they can occupy, there is a special spot in His heart for you *that only you can occupy*. Read on; His love calls you there.

CHAPTER FIVE

Love Calls

God is the Master of story. He loves to capture our attention and arouse our passion through parabolic spin, only to catch us off guard with a finale so surprising it cannot be forgotten. Story enables us to know Him better, which of course is why He uses it. In Ezekiel 16, we are told a rapturous tale of love that invites us to explore the enormous, inner and intimate chambers of Father's heart for the Jewish people. There is nothing else quite like it in all the Bible.

The story starts with Yahweh recounting His adoring, doting care for Israel. On the day she was born, He says, she was despised. She was thrown into a field, unbathed, helpless, naked and alone. Her umbilical cord was not cut. Not a soul had pity or compassion on her. But He passed by and saw her kicking in her blood. As she lay there, He said, "Live!"

God grew her like a lovely plant of the field. Over time she developed into "the most beautiful of jewels." Later He passed by again, and saw that she was "old enough for love." So He spread the corner of His garment over her, covering her nakedness. He gave her His "solemn oath"; she became His. He dressed her in fine linen and costly embroidery, fitting leather sandals onto her feet.

He adorned her with jewels, silver and gold. He placed a crown on her head. He nourished her with fine flour, honey and olive oil. "You became very beautiful and rose to be a queen," God said. "And your fame spread among the nations on account of your beauty, because the splendor I had given you made your beauty perfect" (Ezekiel 16:13–14).

In return, Israel took her beauty and fame and with them ran off to become a whore:

> "You lavished your favors on anyone who passed by and your beauty became his. You took some of your garments to make gaudy high places, where you carried on your prostitution. Such things should not . . . ever occur. You also took the fine jewelry I gave you . . . and you made for yourself male idols and engaged in prostitution with them. And you took your embroidered clothes to put on them, and you offered my oil and incense before them. Also the food I provided for you—the fine flour, olive oil and honey I gave you to eat—you offered as fragrant incense before them. That is what happened, declares the Sovereign LORD."
>
> EZEKIEL 16:15–19

How does God respond to Israel now that she has spurned His attention and affection only to disgrace herself?

> "Yet I will remember the covenant I made with you in the days of your youth, and I will establish an *everlasting* covenant with you."
>
> EZEKIEL 16:60, EMPHASIS ADDED

Do you hear the long-suffering passion and pain, the ache despite anger in His voice? Father's heart is ravished yet forever faithful. In spite of her despicable sin, He loves Israel unconditionally. He will save her, and she will love Him back. The message gets repeated over and again by all the Old Covenant prophets and Yeshua Himself.

Through the ages, love calls from God's heart to Israel. In the Scriptures He sounds at various times like a long-suffering husband, father, shepherd and more. Let's begin by listening to one biblical portrayal—Yahweh as Israel's husband—that is downright scandalous: the story of Hosea and Gomer.

Israel's Long-Suffering Husband

In extraordinary fashion, the prophet Hosea dramatically plays out God's covenant love for all Israel to see (together with you and me). Here it is more than mere story; it is flesh-and-blood reality. At the outset God startles us, and no doubt Hosea, by telling him to marry a harlot, a sex addict whom He warns will repeatedly prove unfaithful. Despite his wife's rebellion, however, Hosea must love and keep covenant with her. So the prophet finds and marries a prostitute named Gomer, and their marriage proves a technicolor picture of Israel's tragically adulterous relationship with Yahweh (see Hosea 3:1).

From this vivid demonstration of infidelity comes the word of the Lord to His people: Israel, like Gomer, is hopelessly (so it seems) prostituted to sin. But jealous God will not stand for it. He will do whatever it takes to win her back—if not the easy way, then the hard way. He "will be like a lion" to the Jewish nation. He plans to "tear her to pieces," then hide Himself and make sure nobody comes to her rescue. In the meantime, He will wait patiently for her to admit her guilt, turn back and then earnestly seek Him (see Hosea 5:14–15).

I see in this story the tough love of an incomparably compassionate God. In wrath, He remembers mercy; His own love constrains Him. Hear His heart pounding with anticipation for the hour of His beloved's return:

> "In that day," declares the LORD, "you will call me 'my husband'; you will no longer call me 'my master.' . . . I will betroth you to me forever; I will betroth you in righteousness and justice, in love and compassion. I will betroth you in faithfulness, and you will acknowledge the LORD. . . . I will plant [you] for myself in the land."
>
> HOSEA 2:16–23

The book of Hosea closes with some of the most beautiful, romantic poetry in the Bible. Our long-suffering Creator, knowing the end from the beginning, stoutly refuses to give up. Rest assured, says Hosea, the Jewish nation *will* be transformed in glory and grace:

> "I will heal their waywardness and love them freely, for my anger has turned away from them. I will be like the dew to Israel; he will blossom like a lily. . . . His splendor will be like an olive tree, his fragrance like a cedar of Lebanon. Men will dwell again in his shade. He will flourish like the grain. He will blossom like a vine, and his fame will be like the wine from Lebanon."
>
> HOSEA 14:4–7

Hosea loved and therefore Hosea suffered long. Consider the honor—and the horror—to which this otherwise little-known servant was called. Could anyone besides the Lord relate to the betrayal, grief and shame Hosea endured for Israel's sake? The prophet knew the cross, in essence, long before it ever existed.

Countless times Hosea must have poured out his pained soul to God who had called him to such intimate identification with His own heart. As together they communed, great grace must have flowed from heaven to earth. Between these two friends deep called unto deep (see Psalm 42:7). In Hosea, Yahweh found a man willing to share His agony as well as ecstasy. In return, I believe Hosea knew God as few others have experienced Him.

Someone who has known God's love a bit like Hosea is my friend Rick Lunsford. Rick is a prophetic intercessor who directs a ministry to Israeli Messianic believers. I met Rick when he was leading a prayer mission in Israel, despite ongoing threats and episodes of terror. He shared with me how one day, many years earlier and through tears, he had to tell his wife he had fallen hopelessly in love with another woman—Gomer. By Gomer, of course, Rick meant Israel. The Lord had captivated and enraptured this Gentile believer's heart for the salvation of the Jewish people. Now Rick is a robust fellow full of the joy of the Lord, but like Hosea and the apostle Paul, he carries "unceasing anguish" for Israel. Rick does not complain; he would say the burden is bittersweet—bitter because of the Spirit's travail, but deliciously sweet because of His intimacy. (And by the way, Rick's faithful wife is right alongside him in ministry to Israel.)

Deep down, do you yearn to have a relationship like this with your long-suffering Lord? Does your innermost being cry out to know and have more and more of Jesus? Then allow me to ask, are you willing to abandon yourself to Him like Hosea or Rick—even if it means "unceasing anguish"? If you give yourself wholly to the Most Holy, He will entrust you with a bittersweet secret of His heart: His unquenchable love for Israel. Embrace her as if she were your own Gomer. Let Him find in you a heart, like Hosea's, willing to carry His burden for her. And don't be afraid; He is not likely to tell you to marry a prostitute!

It has been said that the supreme fruit of the Christian life is loving the unlovable. Not many attain it, for such fruit is borne from the cross of long-suffering. Yet, as Rick would attest, it yields intimacy and joyful knowledge of the Perfect Lover obtainable in no other way. God is looking for prophetic intercessors for Israel so driven to know Him, they are undeterred by the fellowship of His long-suffering.

Old Covenant Grace

God's grace is resplendently manifest in the Old Covenant. This I discovered many years ago during a very trying time in my life. Perplexed and disappointed by various circumstances, I began to wonder if I had fallen from grace or out of favor with God. Somehow, I needed to be reminded of His grace and compassion, so I decided to compile a list of His most stalwart assurances of love for Israel. Through that exercise, the Lord unveiled something that has helped sustain me in my walk with Him ever since. Consistently, I found, it is in the context of *Israel's failure and sin*—and His judgment—that He shockingly interjects, "I love you."

Just when it seems the Lord is about to disown His people (and rightly so), He declares instead His undying love. When it appears all fair and legal grounds for dissolution of the relationship finally exist, He renews His vows. In the midst of deserved chastisement, God deals out compassion. Israel spurns the Creator—again and with impunity—and receives an engraved invitation to repent. His grace is appalling; His kisses are outrageous.

There came a time when sin so screamed for justice that God exiled the Jews temporarily from the Promised Land. After their brutal defeat, the Israelites lay broken and bleeding, disgraced and displaced on foreign soil. Surely they—like me at the time—wondered if God would ever favor them again. In this extremely unlikely context of misery and despair came a dizzying word from the Lord. Like a windfall, hope from heaven descended upon the Israelites. Never before had He spoken explicitly of it—this "New Covenant":

> "The time is coming," declares the LORD, "when I will make a *new covenant* with the house of Israel and with the house of Judah. . . . I will put my law in their minds and write it on their hearts. I will be their God, and they will be my people. . . . For I will forgive their wickedness and will remember their sins no more."
>
> JEREMIAH 31:31–34, EMPHASIS ADDED

Holy God is wholly in love with Israel; therefore, Israel must and will be made holy. The New Covenant guarantees it. Next, as if this all-surpassing prophetic promise were not enough, God reaffirms His commitment to sustain Israel as a nation *forever:*

> This is what the LORD says, he who appoints the sun to shine by day, who decrees the moon and stars to shine by night, who stirs up the sea so that its waves roar—the LORD Almighty is his name: *"Only if these decrees vanish from my sight,"* declares the LORD, *"will the descendants of Israel ever cease to be a nation before me."* This is what the LORD says: "Only if the heavens above can be measured and the foundations of the earth below be searched out will I reject all the descendants of Israel because of all they have done," declares the LORD.
>
> JEREMIAH 31:35–37, EMPHASIS ADDED

Have the sun, moon or stars stopped shining? Have the waves of the sea stopped roaring? If not, then the Jews have not stopped being a chosen nation before God. Have men measured the heavens or plumbed the deepest bowels of the earth? Then neither has God rejected Israel because of her sin.

Because we are assured God will not reject His Old Covenant people, we can trust He will not reject His New Covenant people either. And I could rest assured He had not rejected me, despite my fears, failures and distressing circumstances.

The Shepherd of Israel

Some of you may chuckle at this, but God reaffirmed to me the truth of His everlasting, faithful love through an unusual means: one of our family pets, a Shetland sheepdog named Misha.

Now, our Misha can't *not* herd. The poor fellow is obsessed with herding anything that moves, from the postal service truck that rolls by daily, to each member of our household (including the hapless cat), to his own shadow—which he encircles and pounces upon with true dogged determination. Even at this very moment, as I write, Misha barks. And so I know surely something, somewhere is moving—and Misha's instincts summon him to service. The dog trainer, the vet, the library books all tell me the same thing: Our Misha has been bred to shepherd, it is just who he is; do not expect him to change.

Our Yeshua has been bred (so to speak) to shepherd Israel; it is just who He is; do not expect Him to change.

As Israel's Good Shepherd, He serves and cares for her endlessly, extending loving-kindness and direction to His flock through thick and thin. With all *His* heart and all *His* soul and all *His* might He longs to do good for His people. David the psalmist knew the Shepherd of Israel so well he wished for nothing else: "The LORD is my shepherd, *I shall not want*" (Psalm 23:1, KJV, emphasis added).

Even when the flock is unwilling, Yeshua gathers His lambs in His arms, carrying them close to His heart (see Isaiah 40:11; Matthew 23:37). The Good Shepherd seeks and finds His straying sheep, laying His life down for them. He does it for Israel and He does it for you.

Father's Heart for a Prodigal Nation

A friend of mine was praying about the Jewish people one day when the Lord flashed a memorable picture across her mind, reminiscent of the famed parable of the Prodigal Son. She saw a large house with a ranch-style veranda built on a lovely, estate-sized parcel of property. Inside the house a festive party was in full swing. But the father of the family was not celebrating. He stood alone on the veranda, his eyes fixed far on the horizon, waiting for the return of a long lost son. He did not object to the party; occasionally he popped in and smiled at the bubbly crowd that remained oblivious to the son's absence. But the master of the house simply could or would not join in the festivities until his beloved boy came home.

The interpretation? My friend knew instantly that the father represented the Father; and the house, His Church. The long lost son whose return He awaited with long-suffering was the prodigal Jewish nation:

> "Is not [Israel] my dear son, the child in whom I delight? Though I often speak against him, I still remember him. Therefore my heart yearns for him; I have great compassion for him," declares the LORD.
>
> JEREMIAH 31:20

Could some of us be rejoicing in our own salvation to the point of forgetting all about the Father's fervent, impassioned longing for His lost son?

Do some happy celebrants ever take a moment to stop, seek out the Master and ask what is on His heart? Actually, I think many are now doing just that.

Intercessory Reconciliation

The Spirit is fueling fresh passion for God across the globe. He is opening our twenty-first-century eyes to gaze upon His dazzling splendor and majesty, healing and freeing us to behold and delight in the only One who satisfies. This deepening intimacy with the Creator begets holy zeal to participate in His prophetic plans. It births a compulsion to impact people for the Kingdom and the coming King. It stirs our souls toward that fragrant offering, "Not my will, but Yours be done." The presence of His Holiness changes us—and makes us want to be more like Jesus.

If we are committed to being more like Jesus, *Ahav*[1] Incarnate, we will find ourselves desiring to mediate His love. The Spirit's strategy of love, as we have seen in the Scriptures (Romans 8 and 9), points directly to Israel. Once we fathom the fullness of Father's heart, He invites us to stand in the gap for His ancient covenant people, prevailing upon Him to close it. Thus I take time to relate—and pray the Spirit will impart—new vision through the lens of His love.

The ministry of reconciliation begins with prayer, and need not be complicated. I am convinced that *who* we are *in* the Lord is strategically more important than *how* exactly we pray *to* Him. As we come into the presence of Creator God Almighty, we find that being clothed in His character is more effective and pleasing to Him than recitations from any cache of Bible bullets, prophecy charts or conference notes. The character of love and the intimacy it invokes is the greatest—the greatest tool, strategic weapon, pathway to prayer and Kingdom representation. Add tears to love, and heaven *really* takes heart.

The prophet Ezekiel says God looks for someone to stand before Him in the gap on behalf of Israel, to avert her destruction (see Ezekiel 22:30). Intercession is standing in the gap between God and the one(s) for whom we are mediating reconciliation. Intercession is fixing our feet on earth while arching our arms to heaven, not just in prayer, but in *life*. Intercession also requires identification. Identification with God and with those for whom we stand in the gap (in this case, His covenant people) gives us authority for a platform in the Spirit. It provides spiritual standing with both God and man. It enables us to mediate and communicate conciliatory love between heaven and earth. In so doing the Beloved shares with us the secrets of His heart, and we will not be the same.

Surrendered to and filled with the Spirit of Love, you may find yourself living out, through circumstances ordered by God, your own intercession. You may find the Lord wants your life itself, surrendered to the Holy Spirit, resounding as an unending prayer—and one that avails much. He wants your prayer issuing from the pathos of life shared with Him in the crucible of what He is doing on earth today. Since He is doing much with Israel, the nation on whom His eyes are ever fixed (see Deuteronomy 11:12), expect your life as well as your prayers to touch her.

But please, touch her only in love.

Love in the Last Days

January 1, 1989, I was awakened by a phone call. On the other end was my friend (let's call him Neil), a sincere believer and avid student of Bible prophecy. Neil was obsessively interested in Israel and always up on the latest news concerning her. So I shuddered to think of what might have occurred overnight (terrorism?), about which he felt compelled to inform me at 6:45 A.M. on my—and just about everyone else's—day off.

"It didn't happen. Nineteen-eighty-eight is over and Jesus didn't come back," sighed the voice on the other end.

Neil sounded quite depressed. He had been tracking the prophetic Scriptures, as he interpreted them, with events that had taken place in Israel since her rebirth as a state in 1948. According to his calculations, by 1988—Neil's interpretation of one biblical generation later—Jesus would have to return. But Jesus did not return, and it was not long before my disillusioned friend lost interest in the Jewish people altogether.

Since Israel's modern-day restoration, many people like Neil have viewed her as an exciting prophetic timepiece. Indeed, that is an aspect—albeit a secondary one—of her existence. As a prophetic people through whom Yahweh speaks to all nations, Israel inherently and uniquely reflects the hour of world history. God intends this to be so.

But Jesus did not die for prophetic timepieces. Neither is the Father's heart ravished over some cosmic hourglass. Israel is His nation of treasured souls, most of whom still desperately need salvation through faith in Messiah. In the twenty-first century, believers will arise who so know the heart of God, they will stand for and with the Jews as never before—out of unconditional love, no ulterior motive.

Plenty of good reasons exist for serving Israel, like fulfilling prophecy, getting a blessing or seeing Jews saved. But good reasons can turn into ulterior motives, and they will likely not survive in the crucible of complex global events in the years ahead. When the pressure is on, only those moved by love will endure. And so God is raising up believers who love and stand with Israel:

Not because Jesus will return there;

Not because her land is holy;

Not because a Temple is being rebuilt there;

Not (even) because most Jews need to get saved; and

Not (even) because they want to get blessed by blessing the Jewish people;

But because *God loves Israel,* unconditionally, uncompromisingly.

The divine irony is that through the unconditional and uncompromising love of believers who *really* know their God, blessing will flow back, Jews will come to Yeshua, their land will be preserved and prophecy will be fulfilled. Then we shall see what Israel's identity has been about all along.

PART 3

Israel's Identity

Theirs is the adoption as sons; theirs the divine glory, the covenants, the receiving of the law, the temple worship and the promises. Theirs are the patriarchs, and from them is traced the human ancestry of Christ, who is God over all, forever praised! Amen.

Romans 9:4–5

CHAPTER SIX

The Purpose of Service

Nobel laureate Elie Wiesel, Jewish author and Holocaust survivor, once compared modern Jewry to a messenger who had been hit on the head and knocked out. When he woke up, he could not remember the message, who had sent him, to whom he had been sent or the very fact of his being a messenger.[1] Using Wiesel's analogy, I would like you to meet some special messengers in recovery.

Since the 1990s, we have ministered several times in the former Soviet Union to reach Jews with the Gospel. After seventy years of state-sponsored, brutally enforced atheism, we found that ex-Soviet Jews were spiritually starved. When it came to faith, they, like everyone else, were officially atheists. Jewish identity meant nothing more than the stamp "Jew" on a government-issued identity card required to be in their possession at all times. Like Wiesel's messenger, Soviet Jewry had been hit on the head, knocked out by the club of Communism.

My husband, Kerry, and I were visiting an elderly Jewish couple in their tiny flat in Kiev the first time we came face to face with this perplexing question of ex-Soviet Jewish identity. Alex and Luba had invited us over for tea, to spend an afternoon telling them about God. Like other well-educated professionals, they had grown up indoctrinated with atheism. But for some years now, Alex and Luba had secretly suspected that God might, after all, exist. We told them about the Bible and its Author, sin and salvation, Jesus and Jewishness.

Alex's and Luba's eyes popped wide when they heard what being Jewish was actually about. They kept us sitting and talking and going through countless cups of superbly blended Ukrainian tea all afternoon. At one point, however, Alex slowly stood up and carefully maneuvered around the cramped living/dining/sleeping quarters (all one room per standard Soviet specs) in which we sat. Gingerly, he opened a glass hutch, stooped over to reach the bottom shelf and gently plied out from under a stack of papers a little black book. He carried the object in both hands with gentleness akin to affection and placed it before Kerry on the table.

"Maybe you know what is it?" Alex asked in broken English. "It was belong to my grandfather. . . . Maybe is it something about Jewish?"

The book's timeworn title had completely faded. We turned to the first page, its browned edges crackling. Alex hovered over Kerry's shoulder with anticipation. We easily recognized it as a Yiddish[2] *Tenakh*, the Old Covenant Scriptures. It had been published a full century earlier, during the pre-Soviet era of the Russian czars.

"Alex, God has kept His Word with you all this time!" we assured our delighted host. For whatever reason, the dusty, tattered book had survived both czars and Communists, preserving Jewish identity far more than any government-stamped document. Alex and Luba were like Wiesel's legendary amnesiac messengers, once knocked out, now coming alive. Tearfully they gave themselves to Yeshua.

What is Alex and Luba's Jewish identity about—besides owning government-issued pieces of paper and a Yiddish Bible they cannot read anyway? In other words, what is the purpose of Israel?

Israel on Purpose

Paul's words in Romans 9:4–5 open up for us Israel's purpose in the New as well as Old Covenants. Here he pours out his heart for Israel, giving us one reason after another why he cannot shake his "unceasing anguish" for the Jews. For many years I read this passage largely as a lamentation. It sounded much like a gut-wrenching sigh, as if the apostle were mourning the colossal tragedy of the Jews—who were given so much—missing their Messiah and day of His visitation.

But this is not Paul's main point in these two all-important verses. Paul is not bemoaning anything here as much as he is splendidly describing Israel's treasured heritage and prophetic destiny. He is enumerating blessings still resident in her, profiling for us Israel's identity and purpose. Now, the apostle is not in fanciful awe of the Jewish people. He is burdened both for her national loss and for the fulfillment of her role in world redemption. Invested in her is blessing for the nations; God's irrevocable gifts and His call on her (see Romans 11:29) are for the benefit of *others*. Israel's purpose on earth relates to God's strategy for reviving all peoples. Israel's identity destines her uniquely to glorify God in the earth by serving as a light to the nations (see Isaiah 49:6) through the Light of the World.

Prophetic Names: Disclosing Destiny

You probably know that names are very significant in the Bible, often conveying a person's or place's calling or destiny. Names disclose identity or the essence of character and personality. The name *Yeshua*, for example, means "God Is Salvation" or "God Saves," and it communicates Messiah's nature and mission. Similarly, names in the Scriptures referring to the Jewish people are prophetically revealing. These names communicate a destiny that still lays claim to the lives of people like Alex and Luba, and Jews all over the world. So to better understand biblical Jewish identity, let's look at some foundational names and their meanings.

Hebrew: Crossing Over

We turn first to the heritage of the great patriarch Abraham. He is introduced to us as Abram the Hebrew or *Ivri*,[3] a tribal name that may be derived from his ancestor Eber or *Iver* (see Genesis 11:16–27). Is there something about this word *Ivri* (meaning "Hebrew") that charts Israel's destiny?

Ivri and *Iver* both stem from *avar*, a root word laden with meaning. *Avar* means "to cross over" or "pass through, by or over." The main idea is one of movement, of crossing boundaries from one place or state of being to another. So a Hebrew is literally "one who crosses over."[4] Our patriarch is Abraham, the One Who Crosses Over; our Savior is Jesus, the One Who Crosses Over; and your Jewish friend is, let's say, Esther Gerstein,[5] the One Who Crosses Over. The implication is that the Hebrews are a *missionary* people. Their foundational identity bespeaks an anointing to reach the world.

It should not surprise us, therefore, that God's first recorded word to Abraham is "Leave." Yahweh's number one order to Abraham is to *leave* his people and home in Ur (modern-day Iraq) *and go to* another land (see Genesis 12:1). From then on, the patriarch becomes a traveler of the Middle East. Much of his life is spent coming and going as the Lord directs. But Abraham is no mere sojourner; he traverses not just geographic but spiritual boundaries as well. He leaves a pagan civilization to worship the one true God. The rabbis teach—and there is good reason to believe—that Abraham made many proselytes to his faith along the way.[6] He served as God's first missionary, the prototype Hebrew who crosses boundaries.

Abraham: Father of Many Peoples

Abraham means "father of many peoples." True to his name, Abraham's children include not only ethnic Jews and Arabs but the patriarch's "spiritual" progeny as well—those from all nations justified by faith in Jesus (see Galatians 3:7). God appoints Abraham's son Isaac to inherit His covenant—the call and anointing to cross boundaries. This claim on Isaac is resident in his physical DNA and, also, his "spiritual" DNA, what we might call his *Divine Nature Anointing*. In turn, and by Sovereign choice, Isaac passes the calling down to Jacob, and Jacob to his children, the Jewish people.

What are the implications for the Jews today? The unique *Divine Nature Anointing*—the covenant blessing and call to cross boundaries—is still with them. Now, by the term *DNA* or *Divine Nature Anointing* I do not imply any racial or ethnic superiority or inferiority of any people group. Neither do I suggest that a greater or better measure of God's Spirit resides in, with or on the Jews than any other people group. I believe *every* nation is endowed uniquely with redemptive gifts to serve the Creator and mediate His character on earth. These gifts (*Divine Nature Anointings*) are suited to each nation's redemptive destiny in the Lord. But concerning the Jewish nation, they have inherited from Abraham's loins—and carry in them—his flesh-and-blood as well as spiritual genetic code. The Hebrew people today remain prophetically programmed to cross over. By nature, Israel is a missionary nation whose appointment is irrevocable—for the benefit of others. God will not be revealed fully in the earth, therefore, until He is revealed as He intends through *them*. The clearest example and culmination is in Yeshua's return; He will not reveal Himself in fullness to this groaning planet until the Jewish people yield themselves to Him as Messiah King (see Matthew 23:39).

Can you imagine what it will be like when, someday, Israel as a whole crosses over into the Kingdom of God's Son through *His* cross? I believe the Jews will be transformed into a nation of insuppressible firebrands. They will *cross* the earth, igniting it with the power of the Gospel as never before!

Jews: Missionaries of Praise

Does it surprise you to discover there is no universally accepted meaning in modern Jewry for the word *Jew?* Not even the State of Israel has put to rest the question, Who is a Jew? Debates and treatises abound among the descendants of Abraham, Isaac and Jacob in search of self-definition. Let's see what God has to say.

The word *Jew* comes from *Judah*, one of Jacob's twelve sons and progenitor of the tribe of Judah (into which Yeshua was born). The name *Judah* means "thanks" or "praise." Judah's *Divine Nature Anointing* is to thank God and praise the Lord. After the first exile, the word *Jew* is used in the Bible[7] synonymously with *Israel* to refer to the physical descendants of Abraham, Isaac and Jacob. The connotation is that the Jews are a people created for God's praise.

Multitudes of Jews are coming to faith in Yeshua and beginning to recapture Israel's ancient mission. Is it coincidental that Yahweh is also being revealed to Gentile nations of the earth as never before? Not according to the ancient understanding:

> May God be gracious to us and bless us and make His face shine upon us, *that your ways may be known on earth,* your salvation among *all* nations. . . . God will bless us, and *all* the ends of the earth will fear him.
>
> PSALM 67, EMPHASIS ADDED

When God blesses Israel, He reveals Himself to the ends of the earth. As more and more Jewish people join in the global chorus of God's praise, expect worldwide awakening. If Israel's corporate disobedience and rejection of Messiah has resulted in salvation for the nations, "what will their acceptance be but life from the dead?" (Romans 11:15).

Israel: Striving and Overcoming

As explained in chapter 1, I use the word *Israel* to refer either to the Jewish people worldwide or the Jewish State in the Middle East. My intended reference should be clear from the context. In any case, exactly what does *Israel* mean? What can we discern about God's call on this people from this name?

The identity *Israel* is given initially to Abraham's grandson Jacob. In his unredeemed nature, Jacob does not always behave honorably, scheming and deceiving his older brother Esau out of his birthright.

When Esau seeks revenge Jacob flees for his life. Frankly, the young man strikes us as an unlikely candidate for Yahweh's everlasting favor.

Many years pass and the time comes for Jacob to go home—and face Esau's wrath. He is understandably worried. I imagine Jacob spends the night before their reunion reckoning his soul with his decades-old, self-made troubles. But Jacob's struggle is really less with Esau than with God, and physically it becomes so when he encounters a mysterious figure, the Angel of the Lord, who wrestles with him all night long. The Angel is most likely Yeshua Himself, and Jacob will not quit struggling until He blesses him.

The Angel indeed blesses the man—displacing a joint in the process so that thereafter he walks with a limp, as if humbled by God's touch on his life. At the same time Jacob is given a new name, *Yisrael*. *Yisrael* has two related meanings. The technical meaning derives from the roots *sara* ("to strive, persist or exert oneself") and *El*, referring to God. Jacob has striven with God all through the night of his life. But at daybreak his striving comes to an end and he overcomes. Jacob's striving *with* God has been transformed to striving *toward* God. Jacob's overcoming is in allowing himself to *be* overcome by Yahweh.[8] This striving toward Him is what is rewarded; the man's struggle with the Creator climaxes in submission to Him. And so it remains for *Yisrael* today.

Second, *Yisrael* stands for "prince with God," from a play on the Hebrew words *sar* meaning "prince" and *El*. Combining both meanings, we could say that *Yisrael* is a prince who has striven with God and men, and overcome (see Genesis 32:28).

Embracing an Identity

An amusing children's movie was produced several years ago that I enjoyed at least as much as my kids. *The Lion King*, though not meant to be biblical, contains fascinating nuggets of spiritual truth reminiscent of *Yisrael*. The story revolves around a lion named Simba who as a young cub is foolishly intent on disobeying his parents.

In one of Simba's mischievous escapades, his father, Mufasa the King, must come to his rescue. Mufasa is killed in the process and Simba despairs of his misdeeds. An evil lion persuades the guilt-ridden prince—and rightful heir to the throne—to punish himself and slip quietly into exile. With Simba gone, the evil lion crowns himself king.

Simba, suppressing memories of his past, learns to live happily in a distant land. Meanwhile, the deceitful king wreaks havoc with the kingdom, bringing it to the brink of disaster. All the while it is assumed Simba is dead—until one day Rafiki, a saga-cious monkey, learns that the prince is alive. Simba represents the only hope for deliverance from the evil king, so Rafiki sets out to find him. But Simba no longer thinks, acts or looks much like a prince.

When the monkey locates him, the lion is looking toward heaven, talking to his dad—something he has not done for a long time. "You said you'd always be there for me, but you're not . . . and it's because of me. It's all my fault," Simba bemoans.

At that moment Rafiki confronts the lion, affectionately egging him on until Simba stops and asks, "Who are you?"

Quips Rafiki, "The question is, Who are *you?*" Now the real dialogue begins.

"I suppose you know who I am," Simba mutters, annoyed.

"Sure do! You're Mufasa's boy!"

Rafiki has captured Simba's attention. "Hey wait! You knew my father?"

"Correction—I *know* your father!"

"Aw, he's dead," laments Simba.

"No, he's alive! I'll show him to you. Come with me."

Monkey and lion romp through the jungle and stop at a pond, where Simba gazes down at the water and sees only himself. "That's just my reflection," he sighs, disappointed.

Instructs Rafiki, "Look harder. You see? . . . *He lives in you!*"

Next we hear the thunderous yet tender voice of Mufasa. "Simba, you've forgotten me."

"No-o!" the prince retorts, sounding hurt by the truth.

"You have forgotten who you are," persists Mufasa, "and so forgotten me. You are more than what you've become. You must take your place."

Visibly shaken, Simba asks, "How?"

"Remember who you are! You are my son! Remember . . . remember . . . *remember!*"

Having heard from his father, Simba indeed remembers. He heads back to the kingdom, overthrows the wicked ruler and takes his rightful place. Everyone rejoices and the kingdom thrives again in peace and prosperity.

Without intending any irreverence, if we substitute the Triune God for Mufasa and Israel for Simba and then view Rafiki as a Christian, we have a script that is practically prophetic (loosely speaking). With help from praying, loving believers, the Jewish nation is about to remember whose she is and where she belongs. She is about to join brothers and sisters around the world who have found their places in the Kingdom and long for her to find hers as well. May I ask, like Rafiki, Do you know who you are? If you are a Gentile believer, do you know how unconditionally beloved you are of the Father, and how as co-heir with Christ (see Romans 8:17), He has graciously bestowed princely status on you? Will you then answer His call to help bring home to the Kingdom the Old Covenant prince with God?

In the world's eyes, the children of Israel may look less like Kingdom heirs and more like Jacob in his nightlong struggle as Yahweh draws them to submission to Him. But in their trials and tribulations, many Israelis are crying out to Him as never before. Like Jacob, Israel's greatest overcoming will take place in being overcome by Him. And when that happens, the whole Kingdom will benefit.

Lest we grow critical of Israel's recalcitrance, it has been said that the Jewish people are just like everyone else, only more so. Jacob's unredeemed nature is much like the rest of humankind's; how else could everything written about Israel in the Scriptures be an example for you and me (see 1 Corinthians 10:6)?

The Jewish nation typifies all nations, truly turning princely only when submitted to God.

If I could speak again to my fellow Messianic brothers and sisters, let us remember that the prototype Messianic Jewish apostle Paul cautions us to put *no* confidence in the flesh—and we must not. May we exalt only our Jesus, not our Jewishness. Our example is Paul, who calls himself "a Hebrew of Hebrews" (Philippians 3:5) yet glories in Yeshua alone. He urges us to "consider everything a loss compared to the surpassing greatness of knowing Christ Jesus" (Philippians 3:8). The divine irony is that if we dare *glory* in our DNA—which gives us no superior standing before God or man anyway—we will never truly *walk* in that *Divine Nature Anointing.* We will miss altogether the essence of our humble call—to sacrificially serve God and the nations.

The Suffering of God's Servant

"You are My Servant, Israel, in Whom I will show My glory" (Isaiah 49:3, NASB). Whether or not she knows it, or even wants to, Israel serves God's purposes. She serves Him when she loves and obeys Him—and she serves Him when she does not. Though she herself may be blind and deaf spiritually, God still calls her His servant: "Who is blind but *my servant,* and deaf like the messenger I send?" (Isaiah 42:19, emphasis added).

How does Israel serve the Lord in disobedience? First, since much of the Bible is a record of her failure to serve in obedience, her history serves as an example from which you and I benefit (see 2 Timothy 3:16). Second, Israel's corporate rejection of the Messiah serves the nations. Because of her hardness of heart, the Bible says, the Gospel has gone to the Gentiles (see Romans 11:11–12). Even in her disobedience she serves, and in her service she suffers—for the benefit of others.

Called the "Suffering Servant" in the Scriptures, Yeshua stands alone as *the* Servant of the Lord and *the* High Priest. He alone atoned for the sin of humanity. Yet the prophetic Scriptures also apply the term *servant of the Lord* on another level to the corporate nation of Israel.[9] In 1958 Basilea Schlink wrote about Israel's Messiah-like, sacrificial service in her book *Israel, My Chosen People:*

Israel, unintentionally and unwittingly, has become a spectacle before heaven and mankind, because she bears the features of the Servant of God. The sight of her should continually remind Christians of Jesus, despised, destitute, covered with bruises, afflicted, hated, persecuted, tormented, and hounded to death. . . . We as Christians are to hold in high esteem this people who bears such a close resemblance to Jesus.[10]

The same One who appointed and anointed Israel to serve the Gentiles watches and weighs our response to this ransom nation that, in or out of obedience, serves. God is looking for believers who will honor Israel the same way they honor those who serve in the Church—with esteem for their ministry for the Kingdom's sake.

I believe Israel's sacrificial service will be recognized someday by those who have been the recipients of it. The result will be unmatched blessing, especially for those who lovingly extend grateful honor in return for her sacrifice.

The Scapegoat

I suspect that since you are reading this book, you, like most folks who care about Israel, have given at least some thought to the issue of Jewish suffering. The historical enormity of my people's pain is staggering and perplexing; tomes have been written about it from countless perspectives.[11] I am guessing that you would agree that Israel's suffering seems highly disproportionate to her sins. The anguish of the Jews appears a mystery, an ongoing puzzle that defies human logic. At this writing, terror attacks in the Jewish State are at an all-time high, and many Jewish communities around the globe face anti-Semitism at levels not seen since just before the Holocaust. Why? Why does the world so hate the Jews?

The mystery of Israel's suffering, though comprehendible this side of eternity only in part, points ultimately to the existence of evil and Satan himself. The devil despises and opposes who and what God loves and does. God loves Israel and through her chose to redeem humanity; the devil despises and opposes every step of His redemptive plan. The devil's opposition is so intense it is illogical.

To illustrate, during one trip to Moscow I received many irate scoldings for coming to minister to the Jewish people: "Don't you know the Jews are the reason for all our troubles!" One person would chastise me because the Jews left Russia and emigrated to Israel with their skills and money-making abilities. The next person would reprimand me because the Jews *stayed* and caused problems with their skills and money-making abilities. Of one thing I became certain: The Jews, once again, were the scapegoat.

The notion of the scapegoat is an interesting one. It is a psychological concept that originates in the Bible, based on the Day of Atonement (see Leviticus 16). On that most solemn of days, the high priest followed prescribed steps to achieve atonement, confessing and vicariously laying all of Israel's sins on two different goats. The fate of the goats would be determined by lot. One would be killed as Israel's sin-bearer; the other—the scapegoat—went free. While the scapegoat served as a tangible sign of forgiveness through the sin-bearer, it was also a reminder of the fact of sin in the world.

I believe that to some degree Israel's suffering at the hands of the nations has somehow been in service to those nations. I am not suggesting, of course, that Israel's suffering atones for anybody's sins; Yeshua alone accomplished that once for all. But, still, there is evidence for the notion of vicarious suffering. Recall, for example, how Israel suffered under Egyptian slavery. The Bible makes clear the Hebrews did not suffer under Pharaoh's bondage because of their own sins. Rather, their suffering was related to the sins of the Egyptians and the Amorites, the people then living in Canaan. God did not deliver the Hebrews out of Egypt until the time came for Him to judge the Amorites (see Genesis 15:13–16). Israel bore no responsibility for the sins of these people, yet she suffered as a result of them. "As it is written: 'For your sake we face death all day long; we are considered as sheep to be slaughtered'" (Romans 8:36, quoting Psalm 44:22).

I have also come to believe that to an extent Israel absorbs, in some mysterious manner, the impact of the world's depravity. She suffers not only for her sins, but as a nation of priests, for the sins of humanity. The concept is not as strange as it might at first sound. What parent has not suffered for the sins of his or her child? Do we not at times absorb, even gladly, the impact of our kids' problems and misdeeds? Similarly, the Bible calls Christians to bear one another's burdens. Jesus, we are reminded, suffered for us as an example to follow (see 1 Peter 2:21). In suffering for others' sake, believers mysteriously "fill up" what is "lacking in regard to Christ's afflictions" (Colossians 1:24). Israel's blessings, extended through the New Covenant, include the gift of suffering!

In their service, Jews have a message for the world. Actually, it is said the Jewish people *are* a message; their very existence bespeaks a sovereign and faithful God who has miraculously preserved them. A Jewish presence, like the biblical scapegoat, is an ongoing reminder to the kingdoms of this world of the King to whom someday every knee will bow. It is a message the world hates; true to the adage, it seeks to kill the messenger.

But it can never completely do so, despite millennia of effort. For Israel's calling and God's preservation of her are irrevocable.

CHAPTER SEVEN

An Irrevocable Calling

As a former attorney, I remember rather painfully President Clinton's infamous focus on the word *is*. In the course of his impeachment, international attention was brought to bear on the significance in the president's mind of this heretofore uncontroversial form of the infinitive "to be." To the rest of the English-speaking world, *is* seemed pretty clear. It refers to present tense existence. If something is, then it exists now.

In Romans 9:4, Paul writes that Israel's "is" the "adoption as sons" and more. As it "is" in English, so it "is" in the Greek,[1] in which *is* refers to something that currently exists. If God says Israel's "is" the adoption as sons, He means it is in an ongoing sense. The adoption as sons is still theirs — as well as the other surprising blessings of Romans 9:4–5, as we will now see.

They all still pertain to Israel — not so much for her blessing, but for that of all nations. In this chapter we will see how Paul's prophetic profile of Israel's *Divine Nature Anointing* that "is," shapes our relationship to her and promises good for humankind.

The Adoption as Sons

God says the Jewish people retain an irrevocable birthright as His *adopted firstborn son* (see Exodus 4:22–23; Romans 11:29). Now, all who trust Messiah for their salvation are God's adopted children in "a community of the firstborn" (Hebrews 12:23, *Complete Jewish Bible*).[2] But only Israel as a *nation* is God's adopted firstborn.

In our family we understand the difference. Our two daughters are both adopted. Like other parents, we adore our children. Though we do not love one more than the other, we do love them differently, because they *are* different. But both girls have all the privileges — and problems — that come with being a Teplinsky.

Our older daughter, the firstborn, has a unique place in the family. Kasey is generally the first to experience new challenges. She simply encounters them sooner in the course of growing up. Now her younger sister, Tasha, has some trouble with this. Tasha manages to take diligent note of Kasey's privileges but never her problems (including the "You're older, you should know better" drone she invariably gets when sparks of sibling rivalry fly). In any case, I am often reminding Tasha that the sensible — as well as godly — thing for her to do is cheerfully bless and gladly let her older sister go first. She stands to learn and benefit much from Kasey's experience — and mistakes. Their birth order is no accident, I reassure her (again); it is God-given for their mutual blessing.

As Yahweh's firstborn son, Israel typically is the first to get whatever He has in store for the rest of us. This is one reason the nation serves as a prophetic microcosm of His larger dealings with humanity. Israel was the first nation on earth to experience God's immanent presence; the first to know His love and learn faith and obedience; the first to experience corporate worship, receive prophetic direction and reap divine judgment.

Keeping with this pattern the New Covenant says the Gospel is "first for the Jew, then for the Gentile" (see Romans 1:16). All who do good receive a blessing, "first for the Jew, then for the Gentile" (see Romans 2:10). At the same time, tribulation and distress come to all who do evil, "first for the Jew, then for the Gentile" (see Romans 2:9). When the Spirit moves anew on the earth, Israel typically reverberates first — first blessed and first distressed. And typically, as firstborn, she gets a double portion.

In the ancient Near East, the firstborn son received greater honor than his younger siblings. We see this when the infant Jesus is consecrated to the Father in the Temple. His dedication does not occur because He is the Messiah but to comply with biblical law pertaining to firstborn sons (see Luke 2:22–24; Exodus 13:1, 12–13).

The firstborn son was also respected as family leader[3] and priest.[4] Preferential status, authority, responsibility and the right of succession rested with him. He was said to embody the soul and character of the whole group, bearing responsibility for its survival and welfare.[5]

In postmodern Western society, certain privileges and problems still rest with the firstborn. They are likely to be responsible for younger siblings, their actions set the household tone, and they may have the most impact on the family reputation. The firstborn typically is the first to be blessed for good choices — and the first to suffer for bad ones. In a sense, the double portion is still theirs.

As God's firstborn, Israel gets a double portion. She gets a double portion of blessing, but she gets a double portion of cursing, too (see Isaiah 40:2; 61:7; Jeremiah 16:18). For to whom much is given, much is required (see Luke 12:48). Israel has been given very much, and very much is required of her. I encourage Christians to remember, like my daughter Tasha with respect to Kasey, that great benefits come from Israel's experience. No need for sibling rivalry; birth order is God's blessing.

Divine Glory: Shekhinah

Israel's is the divine glory, continues Paul in his Holy Spirit-inspired prophetic profile of Israel's *Divine Nature Anointing.* Notice that he says this well *after* Israel's leaders have rejected Jesus as Messiah. Despite her disobedience, a divine glory — a dimension of God's presence — still resides on the Jewish nation.[6]

Theologically, the divine glory (*Shekhinah* in Hebrew) is the manifestation of Yahweh's presence and display of His attributes.[7] Experientially, it is what all of us who know and love Him crave. And in Israel, God's splendor seems to materialize uniquely in the tangible realm, intersecting with the spiritual into an explosive dimension of His divine presence.

In the Israeli nation I catch glimmers of God's glory in myriad ways, starting with the miraculous fact of her modern-day existence. In her biblical faith, prophetic archaeology, creative arts, science and technology, Israel radiates the glory of God. His *Shekhinah* shines tenderly on the faces of His beloved covenant people. Though Israel's collective countenance is understandably worn with fatigue, God's spirit of grace and supplication is stirring her battle-weary soul. Interacting in the Spirit with the Israeli people manifests a glory all its own. Last but far from least, I experience His glory on a very personal level, as if portals to the realm of the Spirit were posted throughout the land that reach right into my heart.

Israel's unique history bespeaks an incomparable glory.[8] To her forefathers appeared the theophanies, God's visitations in human or angelic form (such as the Angel who wrestled with Jacob). Day and night the *Shekhinah* led Israel through her forty-year wilderness wanderings, a cloud by day and fire by night. After the nation settled in Canaan, Solomon's Temple became its sacred resting place. Less dramatic in appearance but not effect were God's glorious interventions on Israel's behalf throughout her history. Time and again, He miraculously sustained her, parting bodies of water, engraving laws on stone, crumbling city walls and more. The Holy Scriptures themselves, God's Word with which Israel has been entrusted, reflect His glory (see 2 Corinthians 3:7–11).

While Yahweh does not share His glory with anyone (see Isaiah 42:8; 48:11), a dimension of the divine has been imparted to Israel, and the nation's heart still beats, however faintly, to heaven's rhythm. She is imprinted by and to the *Shekhinah*. God is preparing her to respond to a future glory that will strategically bless all peoples on earth (see Isaiah 44:23; 60:1–2). At the apex of that glory, Israel will serve as host nation to all others when Messiah returns and takes up residence in His Temple in Jerusalem (see Ezekiel 43:1–5). In that day the earth will literally and spiritually be filled with the knowledge of the glory of God (Habakkuk 2:14).

The Covenants

To Israel belong the covenants. The Spirit stirs Paul to pen this reminder in his revelation of Israel's identity because Roman Christians were beginning to believe they had replaced the Jews as God's chosen people. The predominately Gentile church in Rome already wielded significant influence in the fledgling Christian world. Eventually it gave rise to Roman Catholicism—for centuries a powerful and dominant force against the Jewish people—and then Protestantism, which sadly inherited much of the same erroneous doctrine of supersessionism. Romans 9–11 pleads the Spirit's case against replacement theology, urging believers to posture themselves to bless Israel, that they, too, may be blessed.

Speaking in their defense, I must say that the Roman church did not have the same background in the Hebrew Scriptures as did churches in other cities with heavier Jewish populations, and therefore greater numbers of Jewish believers. As a result, the Romans naturally questioned how they could trust God's Word when it seemed to have failed the Jews, as most of them had rejected Jesus as Messiah. In calling attention to the covenants, Yahweh confirms that His Word can be trusted because it—or rather He—has *not* failed the Jews.[9] The covenants contained collectively in the Old Covenant, as well as the New, still belong to them—and as He goes on to say, the *Jews* still belong to Him.

Assuredly, future fulfillment of the covenants pertaining to Israel (including the granting of her land) will occur. But—and herein lies the challenge of our day—*I believe these fulfillments are keenly connected to Christian intercession.* God's Word stands poised to prosper His ancient covenant people. But the intermediary ingredient of intercession is essential.

> I have posted watchmen on your walls, O Jerusalem; they will never be silent day or night. You who call on the LORD, give yourselves no rest, and give him no rest till he establishes Jerusalem and makes her the praise of the earth.
>
> ISAIAH 62:6–7

The unconditional nature of Yahweh's covenants does not diminish our call to stand in the gap and petition heaven until they come to pass. On the contrary, principles reflecting His heart and plans are therein revealed to keep our prayers and labors on sovereign track.

The Law

"The law!" The term conjures up images of servitude and bondage; something to cower under if we are going to relate to it at all. Better not try, we conclude, for we've been set free from its oppressive condemnation. Yet, continuing our study of Romans 9:4–5, we find the Holy Spirit saying the Jews are *blessed* for receiving the law. Paul asks and answers: "What advantage, then, is there in being a Jew . . .? Much in every way! First of all, they have been entrusted with the very words of God" (Romans 3:1–2).

An anointing "is" on the Jewish people to love, comprehend, teach and mediate the law. The Scriptures are their heritage; their call to minister the oracles of God is irrevocable. We owe our Bible to the Jewish people who scrupulously wrote and guarded its integrity, at times paying for it with their very lives. The issue of the law is important because our mind-and-heart understanding of the Jewish law affects our mind-and-heart understanding of the Jewish God, and therefore the Jewish people. Through history, whenever and wherever the Old Covenant has been disdained, so inevitably have the Old Covenant people.

When he was alive, my beloved Jewish father used to spend evenings with the law. He worked hard at various bookkeeping jobs in order to keep the family afloat. When he came home he would sink into his easy chair after dinner, open up his *Tanakh* (Old Covenant) and rabbinic commentaries, and spend hours poring over them. This was no dutiful chore or task for him; Dad found obvious pleasure and enjoyment in studying and meditating on God's Word. Without realizing it, I absorbed this same love of *Tanakh* into the fiber of my being. Now that I love its Author, must I disregard what He wrote? I think not; let me tell you why.

Fulfilling the Law

"Christ is *the end of the law*," Paul writes, so that there may be "righteousness for everyone who believes" (Romans 10:4, emphasis added). The salient question is, What exactly is "the end" of the "law"?

The word translated "law" is the Greek word *nomos*. But—and this is critical—*nomos* is the same word used in the New Covenant for *Torah*. The Hebrew word *Torah* means "instruction" or "teaching." The Torah technically constitutes the first five books of the Bible, but can *also* refer to *all* the Hebrew Scriptures. Indeed, when the Jewish writers of the New Covenant speak of Torah, they are often referring to the *whole body of Old Covenant teaching.* In using the term *nomos*, they are not speaking strictly of the commands and statutes, or list of do's and don'ts that we today might think of as "the law." They are speaking of the supernatural means by which believers grow, in Holy Spirit anointing, to appropriate and mediate *God's instruction* in holy love. They refer to His Word engraved on our hearts. This is why Paul writes, "All Scripture is God-breathed and is useful for teaching, rebuking, correcting and training in righteousness, so that the man of God may be thoroughly equipped for every good work" (2 Timothy 3:16–17). While the New Covenant is as inspired as the Old, the New Covenant Scriptures did not exist in canonized form in Paul's day. So the "all Scripture" he is referring to—and affirming—is the *Old* Covenant.

Now if "the law" refers to Old Covenant teaching as a whole, what is the "end" of it? The answer is not what we might think at first. Yeshua Himself clarifies He will not do away with the Old Covenant: "Do not think that I have come to abolish the Law or the Prophets" (Matthew 5:17). Instead He *encourages* Torah teaching for New Covenant believers: "Every teacher of the [*nomos*] who has been instructed about the kingdom of heaven is like the owner of a house who brings out of his storeroom new treasures *as well as old*" (Matthew 13:52, emphasis added).

A little more linguistic digging: The Greek word translated "end" (*telos*) does not mean cessation or termination. God's teachings are not over and they have not come to an end. Rather, *telos* means "completion" in the sense of goal fulfillment or maturity. We can very simply think of the goal of the Old Covenant as Yeshua filling it full of Himself. Because we love Him, we are enjoined to love the fulfilled or filled-full-of Yeshua, Old as well as New Covenant teaching. Again, recall the promise, "I will put my law in their minds and write it on their hearts" (Jeremiah 31:33).

An eye-opening, revised translation of Romans 10:4 is found in the *Complete Jewish Bible:* "For the goal at which the Torah aims is the Messiah, who offers righteousness to everyone who believes."

Bursting Out of Bondage

These critical days cry for a cure from the law of God. The rotten fruits of lawlessness—killing, immorality, terror—threaten to shred the fabric of society. We have rebelled against God's laws under the false pretense of freedom and reaped death. We have abused amazing grace, shirking at the prospect of "the law" and "coming under it," as if the Word were a thing of bondage rather than beauty. In essence, Dietrich Bonhoeffer compared this to cheap as opposed to costly grace:

> Cheap grace is grace without discipleship. . . . Costly grace is the sanctuary of God; it has to be protected from the world. . . . It is therefore the living word, the Word of God.[10]

Would you allow the Lord to dispel a myth mistakenly taught about the Torah? Somehow we have nurtured the notion that a New Covenant believer embracing the Old Covenant has "lapsed" into "legalism." As we will see in chapter 8, this same thinking gave rise to the Church's self-destructive chopping off of its Jewish roots—its much-needed support system.

Obedience to the law justifies or saves no one, and under the New Covenant we are not obligated to follow all the dictates of the law the same as if living solely under the Old Covenant. Jesus, our atoning sacrifice, achieved salvation once for all. But we are not to dismiss the Old Covenant as irrelevant to our lives, either. The New and Old Covenants are inextricably connected. It has been said, the Old is the New concealed; the New is the Old revealed.

In contrast to shouldering a load of legalis.n, hear how the Hebrew psalmist exults in the law (or more accurately, Torah). The fervid worshiper does not sound bound up by statutory restriction; I hear free and intimate, grace-full high praise:

Blessed are they . . . who walk according to the law of the LORD.

Open my eyes that I may see wonderful things in your law.

I remember your ancient laws, O LORD, and I find comfort in them.

I delight in your law.

The law from your mouth is more precious to me than . . . silver and gold.

Oh, how I love your law!

I stand in awe of your laws.

Blessed is the man who[se] . . . delight is in the law of the LORD. . . . He is like a tree planted by streams of water.

PSALM 119:1, 18, 52, 70, 72, 97, 120; PSALM 1:1–3

In my Messianic experience, the Torah is Jewish root—and route—to intimate knowledge of the God of Israel. His Holy Word carries His Holy Presence. The New Covenant describes the "ministry" of Torah as "glorious" (2 Corinthians 3:8–11). My prayer is that you will be lovingly and graciously led of the Spirit to a fresh embrace and nourishment from the treasure that is Torah.

Am I suggesting we all don black skull caps (which is not in Torah, by the way), keep rabbinically kosher kitchens and line up the men for covenantal cutting? Rest assured, I am definitely not. I do, however, encourage believers to view Torah as a positive rather than negative spiritual reality. It represents a holy document that unveils Yahweh's expectations for His cherished ones, offering prophetic direction and instruction for our lives. The Torah serves as an instrument and act of grace to His already delivered-from-bondage (out of Egypt) people. It describes lifestyle principles for a redeemed, holy community—principles we cannot afford to ignore.

From another perspective, Torah serves as a type of sacred marital agreement with God's covenant people. Its structure and contents parallel the marriage contract of the ancient Hebrews, reflected even today in Jewish bridal vows.[11] Yahweh is in love with Israel, the people He redeemed for Himself out of bondage. If you have been redeemed from a metaphorical Egypt, you are being sanctified as His Bride—by the ministry of the Word. Yeshua prayed, "Sanctify them by the truth; your word is truth" (John 17:17).

If you disagree about the relevance of God's Old Covenant teaching, allow me respectfully to ask how you feel about the Ten Commandments. Does the Creator still expect us not to worship other gods? Not to murder, steal or commit adultery? Is bearing false witness wrong? Is coveting okay? Let's go a little further. Do you feel He favors bribes and unjust scales? What about fulfilling your vows? Remembering the poor? Being kind to animals? Has God not engraved such things on your heart? I think you get the idea—and I think you will enjoy the exciting endeavor of embracing His whole Word.

Perfectly Legal

There is coming a day in which "the law will go out from Zion" to all nations. Christians will visit Jerusalem's Temple for the greatest teaching on earth (Isaiah 2:3). It will be a time of unprecedented peace, when lambs snuggle up next to wolves, calves cuddle with lions, kids play with cobras and weapons of war till the soil. The knowledge of God will cover the planet. The Bible tells us this idyllic and quite literal reign lasts a thousand years. Christians call it the Millennium. The Jews have traditionally understood this age to come as the Messianic Kingdom rule of God.

I think you will agree that the Kingdom, though already here to an extent, is not yet manifest in fullness. The Kingdom has, we could say, broken into present reality, but it is not manifest in totality. Consequently, my kids do not play with cobras and "peace on earth" is mostly to be found on Christmas cards. Many godly saints still die of disease, while others are marvelously healed. Some are delivered from evil; others are delivered through evil. In short, this present, transitional age is one of overlapping kingdoms, an "in-between" time. You and I live in between the time Yeshua first came—the Kingdom of heaven breaking into earth's realm—and the time He will come again. For now, heaven's rule and reign is at hand; but on the other hand, so is the world's. Not until the King Himself returns will the Kingdom come in all its glorious fullness.[12]

What does all this have to do with the law and Jesus' fulfillment of it? God is going to ensure that His laws are followed and enforced on this earth. The Scriptures prophesy it; the Kingdom of God is—and will be—governed by it. That His law will go forth from Zion to all nations shows us how highly He values Torah—so much so, that by it someday all humanity will ultimately experience the liberty of perfect love.

The Promises

The promises of God are associated with His law. Both are part and parcel of His Word. Paul writes in Romans 9 that God's promises still belong to the Jews, even though the nation as a whole has rejected the New Covenant.

God's promises can be like life itself; they sustain and nourish us, they offer us hope, they strengthen our faith. All believers are entitled to claim and enjoy God's bountiful promises. But, we must never deny that there remains a future and literal fulfillment of many promises that pertain to ethnic Israel. Anyone who tries to usurp those promises — denying their unique, prophetic application to the Jewish nation — will likely suffer for it.

I know of a church on the East Coast that disintegrated, in large part, because of such a misunderstanding. The pastor and elders decided to construct a new church building to accommodate the rapidly growing congregation. They picked Isaiah 2:3 as a personal promise for them from God: "The law will go out from Zion, the word of the LORD from Jerusalem."

Now, this church did not accept the truth that such prophetic promises still apply literally to Israel. They had decided that the words *Zion* and *Jerusalem* referred in this present day to their new church building. I tried to reason with the pastor. He seemed to love the Lord sincerely, but he insisted just as sincerely that the passage had no relevance to Israel. Such promises, he felt, were now solely for Christians — and, in particular, church-builders.

He and his congregation did construct their new building, and it was beautiful. But, sadly, only a few years later the congregation split on account of financial problems, the building went up for sale and the pastor left the ministry. If only they had understood God enough to make room in their hearts and minds for Israel, the fiasco may have been avoided.

The Temple Worship

Israel's is the Temple worship, says the Holy Spirit through Paul in Romans 9:4–5. Yet the Jewish Temple in Jerusalem is no more; perched in its place sits the Muslim Dome of the Rock and Al Aqsa Mosque. Maybe you wonder if that matters: Isn't worship in spirit and truth the pinnacle of praise on earth? And what about the God-breathed, international movement establishing round-the-clock houses of Davidic-style worship and prayer: Don't these adequately substitute for Israel's Temple worship? Not according to the Word, which tells us their Temple worship is still important to God. David's true house of homage will not be completely restored without it.

God has graced the Body of Christ with magnificently anointed worship giftings. I love to praise Him with my Gentile as well as Jewish brothers and sisters in the Lord, certain that at times I am tasting heaven on earth. Yet I ache for that greater glory ahead—the one that will envelop the earth when the literal descendants of the ancient Levites and priests join us in worshiping the King in Spirit and Truth.

Religious Jews—still God Praisers by name—have never ceased their longing to rebuild the Temple and have forged elaborate plans for its construction. Indeed, the Scriptures prophesy a third Temple will be erected before Yeshua returns, and then a fourth. (See chapter 16.) Temple worship flows in Israel's *Divine Nature Anointing*.

A Nation of Priests

Israel's Temple worship, in both Old and New Covenants, refers to much more than music, singing and dancing. Trying to convey the whole concept, different Bible translations use different terms for Paul's words, such as the "service of God" (Romans 9:4, KJV) or "temple service" (NASB). The notion really relates to Temple worship together with service.[13] The two are so inseparable that even in the New Covenant, the Greek word for *worship* also refers to the service ritual of Temple sacrifice. Taken together, Temple worship and service reflects Israel's destiny as a nation of priests. Says Yahweh, "You will be for me a kingdom of priests and a holy nation" (Exodus 19:6).

That destiny goes back to Abraham, who serves prophetically as priest when God instructs him to sacrifice Isaac. The progenitor of the Gospel proves willing to give up his son, dramatically foreshadowing Jesus' Messianic sacrifice. At this early stage in the history of redemption, the patriarch's faith response mediates between heaven and earth. His actions release the next stage of redemption history between God and mankind—the creation of the Jewish nation. Abraham's virtual sacrifice can be seen as an intercessory act, a priestly oblation—on behalf of all humanity—even though Yahweh intervenes and prevents the slaying of his son.

Later in history, God limits the priesthood to one lineage in the tribe of Levi, which then ministers to Israel at large. At the same time, the whole Jewish nation functions, on another level, as a nation of priests. Yahweh anoints corporate Israel to mediate His Kingdom on behalf of all other nations. This is in keeping with His promised plan to bless all nations through Abraham.

Ancient Israel's ministry of combined intercession, sacrifice and worship—offered on the basis of the Messianic Lamb that God would someday provide—has had enduring effect. These priestly intercessory acts all pointed to Yeshua and served a role in His first coming. I believe that in some mysterious manner Israel continues to serve God and man as a nation of priests, and together with the Church, is playing an integral intercessory role in Yeshua's second coming, as well.

Observant Jews have never forgotten Israel's Temple service on the nations' behalf,[14] as I was reminded by one of them. The recent scene was Jerusalem during the Feast of Tabernacles, a time historically when the Old Covenant priests sacrificed animals not just to bless Israel but all nations (see Numbers 29:12–38). I was traveling and ministering with Gentile Christians, to whom the Israelis were extending a warm and hearty welcome. "This feast is very much for you," said my smiling friend Rabbi Shlomo—speaking not to me, but to my non-Jewish companions.

The good rabbi proceeded to outline for them (insisting that they know to his satisfaction) both the historical and future significance of this feast. "When the Messiah comes, all the Gentiles will be here for this holiday. But it's good that you're here now . . . maybe it helps *Him* to come."

Our group smiled, sensing that Rabbi Shlomo was getting a Holy Ghost tug toward faith in Yeshua as that Messiah.

Gesturing dramatically with anticipation, Rabbi Shlomo read Zechariah 14:16 from his Hebrew Scriptures—though my friends could not understand a word of it: "The survivors from all the nations that have attacked Jerusalem will go up year after year to worship the King, the Lord Almighty, and to celebrate the Feast of Tabernacles."

Something inside Rabbi Shlomo still resonated to the priestly call. God chose him—and all Israel—to be a nation of priests, not as His pets or favorites, but to serve and minister to others. He set Israel apart as a "light to the nations" (Isaiah 42:6, NASB) and "holy nation" to mediate prophetic revelation of God to all peoples. Like our forefather Abraham the *Ivri*, my people are destined to cross boundaries, even priestly boundaries between heaven and earth. The Jews are—and will increasingly become as they are born anew and anointed of the Spirit—an evangelistic missionary nation, a prophetic-teaching nation and a nation of intercessory priests.

The Family Tree: Patriarchs and Jesus Christ

Paul finishes his profile of Israel's identity in Romans 9:5: "Theirs are the patriarchs, and from them is traced the human ancestry of Christ, who is God over all" ("the Christ according to the flesh," NASB). Out of this people, from a promise made millennia ago to their patriarchs, comes the God-Man Messiah. Could any greater honor (and responsibility) be given any nation?

The next time you talk with a Jewish friend, you might just wonder if he or she is related to Jesus Christ. Jesus' identity—and Israel's—goes back to God's covenantal investment in the patriarchs, inherited by their children and children's children forever. The Savior of humankind was birthed from a Jewish womb with Jewish DNA, grew up in a Jewish home with a Jewish family and observed Jewish traditions. I suppose Jesus played Jewish games, ate Jewish food and had a Jewish sense of humor. According to the Scriptures He had Jewish half-brothers and sisters, who themselves presumably had children of their own. Some of their children's children may still be around—perhaps in the form of your Jewish neighbor or co-worker.

God Forever Praised

After spelling out for us the identity of Israel, Paul bursts into praise: "Christ, who is God over all, forever praised!" (Romans 9:5).

He revels in God's plan to make known the Creator of the universe to the ends of the earth, even to you and me. He rejoices in God's sovereign design for the spread of the Gospel to the Gentiles.

Paul's understanding of God's plan was no secret. The Jews were well aware they had been called to make Him known to all nations. When they failed to do so, it was not so much because of ingrown exclusivity, but on account of a larger failure to obey God. Even so, Yahweh raised up His Jonahs and Obadiahs to prophecy to non-Jewish peoples, as well as His Isaiahs and Ezekiels to minister not only to Israel but also to her Gentile neighbors.

One Messianic Israeli writer looks forward to the time when Israel's identity is fully revived and restored to bless humankind:

> There is a people on earth for whom the Bible is their own history, and not merely spiritual allegories; there is a nation who tasted real freedom as they crossed the Red Sea, who knew the flavor of the original manna in the wilderness, and who let out a loud shout and saw Jericho's walls collapse before them in a heap of rubble. There is a people who . . . slew real giants, who claimed and possessed a tangible land, and who beheld the glory come down upon and fill the temple of their God. There is a nation on earth today which carries deep within its blood and bosom a purpose and a call which must be rediscovered, cultivated and perfected, yet one last time!
>
> What will it be like when such a people come alive unto God? What hidden treasure will then explode within the church . . . as these ancient brethren are quickened again and revived into their true identity, "Hebrew" and "Israelite"?[15]

Pray for Israel to embrace her irrevocable calling and for Messianic Jews to fulfill their destinies in God. Pray for Gentile believers to rise to the challenge of helping restore biblical Jewish identity—and the Church's own Jewish roots.

PART 4

The Salvation of Israel

If some of the branches have been broken off, and you, though a wild olive shoot, have been grafted in among the others and now share in the nourishing sap from the olive root, do not boast over those branches. If you do, consider this: You do not support the root, but the root supports you . . . for God is able to graft them in again.

ROMANS 11:17–18, 23

Brothers, my heart's desire and prayer to God for the Israelites is that they may be saved. . . . How, then, can they call on the one they have not believed in? And how can they believe in the one of whom they have not heard? And how can they hear without someone preaching to them?

ROMANS 10:1, 14

CHAPTER EIGHT

Rejected Roots, Broken Branches

Flash back with me, if you would, to a childhood experience that seared my soul about "Christianity":

I stare in puzzled horror at a parade of living skeletons, sunken cheeks and bulging eyes, the subjects of macabre Nazi "medical" experiments. Seconds later, corpses—countless piles of them—are bulldozed and dumped into a gargantuan pit, like refuse heaped in a junkyard.

Then the film stops. The rabbi fumbles with the movie projector, an old reel-to-reel, and switches on the lights. He shuffles slowly around to share with the youth group from my synagogue in Chicago. Everyone is very quiet, and I can tell he has something important to say.

"This is what Christians will do to you, if you let them," he warns. "You must never let them; no, never again!"

"No . . . *never* again," I vow silently. I am five.

From then on, I land in more than one schoolyard scruff after being jeered a Christ-killer. I must fight back to survive; for whoever this Christ was or is, I am certain He wants me dead. His people keep telling me so.

I am ignorant, and so are they.

Ignorance of the Word Is No Excuse

At different times the Holy Spirit, through the Scriptures, cautions you and me not to be "ignorant" or "arrogant." These warnings flash and bleep like red alerts—meant to be read, alert. They appear only half a dozen times in the whole New Covenant, their infrequency suggesting to me their importance. When I come to these passages I hear the Lord saying, in that tender but firm voice of His, *Sandy, this is very important. You need to know what I'm about to say. So don't be arrogant, listen up, and for your own good, remember.*

Sometimes Deity lovingly demands our attention because the passages are going to prove critical. God's children need to know there is a test—and what is required to pass it. Such a test and such a warning come to Christians about Israel.

In this book we have listened to Paul speak in Romans about God's love for His ancient covenant people and their irrevocable, prophetic destiny. Now he turns to the monumental matter of the Church's hardening heart. He pauses to plead, *"I do not want you to be ignorant of this mystery, brothers, so that you may not be conceited"* (Romans 11:25, emphasis added). In other words, "Listen up, and for your own good, please don't be conceited; if you are, you'll likely miss what God has for you!"

As we saw earlier, there is important background to this passage. The church in Rome and Gentile believers at large have begun to believe God is finished with the Jews and so, bottom line, His reputation as Faithful Father is at stake. The anointed apostle, his heart bursting with compassion and prophetic purpose for both Gentile and Jew, is setting the record straight.

"Do not be arrogant," Paul cautions, "but be afraid. For if God did not spare the natural branches [that is, unbelieving Jews], he will not spare you either" (Romans 11:20–21). Here's how serious the

stakes are: Consider God's kindness toward Israel—and continue in it—*otherwise, you also will be cut off* (see Romans 11:22).

Does Paul imply that our right-standing with God, maybe even our salvation, is linked to our treatment of the Jewish people? (Remember the parable of the sheep and the goats?) Perhaps you have never understood the urgency of the matter. Much of the Church knows grievously little of the very issue about which we are enjoined *not* to be ignorant or arrogant!

Can we honestly deny the centuries of documented ignorance— and arrogance—of Gentile believers toward Israel? Ignorance in itself is not sin. But concerning Israel, ignorance easily breeds arrogance, and arrogance of heart feeds further ignorance. In other words, if I know nothing about Jewish people, I am simply ignorant about them. But if I am reading the Bible with a humble spirit, I must know something about them; if not, I dare say I am arrogant. And if I am arrogant, I will likely stay ignorant: "Why bother; I know it all."

But if I love the Lord and beseech His blessing, that is not what I want.

Severing Jewish Roots

Sadly, much of our ignorance about Israel has been handed to us historically. To a large extent, our lack of knowledge stems from a long-ago, institutionalized severance of the Jewish roots of Christianity. Many of our most influential, early Church fathers rejected the spiritual roots that supported them. Instead of sharing in the "nourishing sap" God intended, they turned away and tapped headlong into the deadly poison of anti-Semitism.

Vast volumes have been written on this sordid subject. As a Jewish believer writing primarily to non-Jews, I would rather you hear in the words of other non-Jews how the Church failed to heed God's "red alerts" about Israel. Here are a few condensed comments that reveal how ignorance and arrogance have robbed Gentile believers of their inheritance. My hope is that you will accept His offer to restore to you personally this tragically lost treasure.

> Paul's warning to gentile believers about pride went unheeded. The church had become overwhelmingly gentile, so it reasoned that there was no more need for the support of the root (Israel). What presumption! . . . Gentiles claimed to have replaced Israel. . . . Church fathers taught that the unfaithfulness of the Jewish people resulted in a collective guilt which made them subject to the permanent curse of God.[1]

As a result Christians renounced their Jewish heritage:

> The so-called "parting of the ways" between Christians and Jews would take place gradually over two or three centuries. . . . Church fathers, well into the fourth century, warn against Christian participation in Jewish observances . . . [and] carried the idea of supersessionist "fulfillment" [replacement theology] to its logical conclusion, arguing that the Jewish Scriptures no longer had validity as the revealed Word of God. . . . It would be impossible for a believing Jew to accept a Jesus whose meaning, by definition, involved a *de*meaning of the Jewish Scriptures. . . . A Jew could accept Jesus only by rejecting—betraying—everything Jesus himself believed.[2]

Shortly after the close of the New Covenant canon, the Jews lost most of their civil and religious rights. Sermons against the Jewish people, often inciting violence, were routinely preached. Accordingly, Saint John Chrysostom left no margin for misinterpretation: "As for me, I hate the synagogue. . . . I hate the Jews."[3]

Emperor Constantine made Christianity the official religion of Rome in 312 A.D. In so doing, he married church and state, injecting "theological" anti-Semitism throughout the polity:

> Overnight, Christianity was given the power of the Imperial State, and the emperors began to translate [to political reality] the concepts and claims of the Christian theologians against the Jews.[4]

With Constantine's Christendom, the notion of portraying Jews as the killers of Jesus originated—never to vanish.

> The very presence of the Jewish people in the world, continuing to believe in the faithfulness of God to the original covenant . . . puts a great question against Christian belief in a New Covenant made through Christ. The presence of this question, often buried deep in the Christian [subconscious] mind, could not fail to cause profound and gnawing anxiety . . . leading to hostility.[5]

> At first glance Christian anti-Semitism would appear to be an oxymoron, something totally contradictory. Unfortunately, it is *not*. The seeds were sown early in Christian history. . . . Replacement theology and/or supersessionism also had its beginnings in early church history.[6]

In 1543 the beloved herald of the Protestant Reformation, Martin Luther, instructed his followers with these words:

> Wherever they [Jews] have their synagogues, nothing is found but a den of devils. . . . What shall we Christians do with this rejected and condemned people, the Jews? . . . First set fire to their synagogues or schools. . . . I advise that their houses also be razed and destroyed. . . . I advise that their rabbis be forbidden to teach henceforth on pain of loss of life. . . . I advise that safe conduct on the highways be abolished completely for the Jews. If this does not help we must drive them out like mad dogs.[7]

Luther's words set a dark tone in Germany—one that, five hundred years later, Adolf Hitler exploited to unimaginable horrors. Summarizes one Christian commentator:

> The missionaries of Christianity had said in effect to the Jews: "You may not live among us as Jews." The secular rulers who followed them from the late Middle Ages then decided: "You may not live among us;" and the Nazis finally decreed: "You may not live."[8]

Did They Pass the Test?

As we saw earlier, God highlights certain passages in His Word because there is going to be a test. One test for the Church involves Israel.

Thankfully, since the Holocaust many Christians have demonstrated sincere repentance on behalf of their spiritual predecessors. They have initiated God-breathed endeavors to reclaim the Church's Jewish roots and heritage, as well as relationship with Israel. Some of them write as follows:

> That such a great man of faith and the Scriptures as Luther could be seduced by Satan to write such a monstrous thing . . . proves the anti-Jewish propaganda within the Church.[9]

> Why was the church unable to resist the Nazi regime? We saw very well that the church had lost its connection to its roots in the Old Testament. . . . We understood that taking root again in Jewish ground was a condition for regaining the [Christian] content.[10]

> The vast majority of Christians, even well educated, are all but totally ignorant of what happened to Jews in history and of the culpable involvement of the Church.[11]

Throughout Church history, wherever and whenever the theological stance on the Jewish Scriptures is that they are irrelevant, unnecessary or harmful to the Christian, the stance has inevitably followed that the Jewish people are irrelevant, unnecessary in their existence or harmful to the Christian. Yet as one contemporary Church leader writes, the days ahead can be different:

> We can learn from the mistakes of the past and prevent history from repeating itself. . . . Our faithful prayers and righteous deeds must provide proof that we have recovered from our spiritual bankruptcy and now have more than enough of God's love to extend . . . to the Jews. . . . We can no longer afford to look the other way. Our Master just will not have it.[12]

To my Gentile brothers and sisters, I say that these matters are just as hard for me to write about as (I assume) they are for you to read. Yet we delve here into only a minuscule fraction of the problematic past. To the extent our churches have inherited even forgotten vestiges of anti-Semitism, cursing can remain on us. If so, God wants to deliver us. The truth will set us free; therefore, we must creak open to Light yet another doleful door of our shared, haunting history. Our hearts and hands joined by His Holiness, let us go on.

Outlawing Messianic Judaism

In rejecting its Jewish roots, Christianity took aim at one segment of the Church in particular—Messianic Jews. Before the Body of Christ can fully reconcile with the Jews—and *itself*—it must deal with its historic rejection of the Messianic Jewish community. So in the power and love of the Holy Spirit, let us look into this legacy and purpose never to relive it.

To my fellow Messianic Jewish believers, I ask you to join me in opening your hearts to the repentant Church, the universal Body of believers to which we belong and for whom Yeshua died. Now is the time for forgiveness and love to cover a multitude of sins. If we have clung to arrogance of our own, it is time to let it go. The Master will not have it any other way.

The following is an abbreviated list of official canon and decrees imposed on the Church throughout history, which, at this writing, have never been formally repealed.[13] Because they have not been revoked, these directives still carry spiritual force and effect to varying degrees.

- First and second century Church fathers issue various anti-Jewish statements that are binding in regions where they hold authority.
- Pope Victor condemns use of the Bible's Jewish calendar for dating Christian holy days; A.D. 175.
- Council of Elvira, Spain, forbids Christians to marry Jews on threat of excommunication (Canon 16), forbids Christians from

receiving Jewish prayers or blessing (Canon 49), and prohibits Christians from eating with Jews (Canon 50); A.D. 306.

- Council of Nicea I rejects the biblical date for celebrating Resurrection Day, for the specified purpose of severing Jewish connections to Passover; A.D. 325.
- Council of Antioch excommunicates any Christian celebrating Passover with a Jew, and defrocks any cleric who communicates with such Christian (Canon 1); A.D. 345.
- Council of Laodocia forbids Christians from attending Jewish festivals (Canon 37), or receiving unleavened bread from them (Canon 38); A.D. 360.
- Council of Agde, France, prescribes strict rules for the baptism of Messianic Jews, "as it is well known that they return easily to their vomit" (Canon 34), and again prohibits clerics from taking part in Jewish festivals (Canon 40); A.D. 506.
- Council of Toledo IV prevents Jews, and specifically Messianic Jews, from holding public office, and authorizes excommunication of noncomplying Gentile officials, an edict that is reissued over the centuries; A.D. 633.
- Council of Nicea II requires Jews who fellowship with or join the Church first to reveal names of other Jews who openly or secretly follow the Old Covenant, observe the Sabbath or honor other biblical festivals. Baptized Messianic Jews must formally renounce and condemn all such forms of worship, and then be watched to ensure "that they depart from Hebrew practices" (Canon 8); A.D. 787. (From this point on, Jesus and His disciples would have been banned from the Church.)
- Pope Gregory IX authorizes investigations against Messianic Jews allegedly embracing their Jewish roots; A.D. 1231.
- Spain expels all Jews, including Messianic Jews, who do not renounce Judaism and all Old Covenant practices. Those who do not comply, including many Messianic Jews, are burned at the stake. Converted Jews are forced to sign pledges that state curses against unconverted Jews and to vow not to interact with them; A.D. 1492.

- Congregation of the Holy Office tortures and burns at the stake Messianic Jews who follow Old Covenant practices; A.D. 1542.
- Germany's National Reich Church requires pastors to take oaths of allegiance to Hitler and expel from churches all Messianic Jews or Christians of Jewish descent; A.D. 1935.[14]

A historical review of the love and mercy of Jesus Christ? Little wonder that in hacking away at their Jewish roots, Gentile believers in the Church all but demolished any Jewish routes to the faith. (A remnant of non-Jewish Christians, however, refused to relinquish Old Covenant practices and also suffered martyrdom.) Could any Messiah-loving Jewish person of integrity have joined or identified with this fellowship of scorn?

If you are a Gentile Christian, you have been grafted into an olive tree, *the root of which supports you.* Paul says that God intends to graft the natural branches back in. Please don't let centuries of anti-Semitic training poison your heart and lead to your own branch being cut away. God wants you sharing in the roots' nourishing sap and blossoming instead. Let's see how.

Gentile Branches Save the Tree

When Paul penned his vivid olive tree metaphor, a horticultural practice in Israel was to invigorate an olive tree that had stopped bearing fruit by grafting wild olive branches into it.[15] The fresh sap, or life-blood of the wild olive branches, would revive the cultivated tree, so the original branches could begin bearing fruit again. Meanwhile, the wild branches, formerly untended and unwieldy, flourished beautifully. What's more, with both wild and cultivated branches intermingled, the whole tree yielded such good and plentiful fruit as would otherwise prove impossible. When Gentile branches grafted into a Jewish-rooted tree function as God intends, the fruit is spectacular.

I have seen some gargantuan olive trees in Israel, hundreds or perhaps thousands of years old. Their gnarly roots span maybe half a city block, sturdily protruding above ground and firmly entrenched (as I suspect with my "city girl" understanding) until Messiah comes. Breathtaking in appearance, they grow knotty, wild and alone, bearing little fruit compared to the carefully planted and tended olive groves that dot the land.

I can imagine the Divine Husbandman gently lopping off a few branches from one of these untamed trees and hand carrying them to a failing cultivated tree. Next He cuts off some of the natural, cultivated branches, protectively setting them aside for future use. I picture Him lovingly linking the foreign branches onto the host, oozing a good dab of humility between them for His grafting agent. Then He blesses the branches and waits. Will this transplant "take"?

Jewish roots support new Gentile branches—but these engrafted branches are needed with their fresh vigor and vitality to save the whole tree. Now what if, for some reason, things go wrong and the Gentile branches sap rather than save the life of the tree? I suppose the Master could stand idly by, watching wistfully as the branches perish along with the tree they have choked. But that is not His nature; He will not let the tree die. I imagine He will have no real choice but to slice off and toss away those unruly engrafted branches.

Meanwhile, if the original tree is to bear fruit again, it must accept foreign, transplanted branches and freely share every bit of life it has with them. The two must become one for their mutual survival. God's grafting agent, *humility*, makes the miracle possible.

Jews and engrafted Gentiles must serve one another in a reciprocal flow of life not only to survive, but to bear "fruit that will last" (John 15:16). To put it more practically, Messianic Jews represent today's original, once-broken-off but now re-grafted, branches. We need lovingly reciprocal relationships of integrity with Gentile Christians. Just as much, Gentile churches need relationship with Messianic congregations and ministries. To produce fruit pleasing to the Master, we must learn (if that is what it takes) to serve one another in humility, for our destinies in Him are inextricably intertwined as one body.

Theologians have different—and good—interpretations as to the "root" of the olive tree. Some say the root refers to God

Himself, some say the patriarchs, others say the faithful remnant of the Jewish nation, and still others say the Jewish Scriptures. I say, Why not *all* the above? If you are grafted into the olive tree, God Himself is your portion, the Jewish Scriptures sustain your spirit and the Jewish patriarchs and people (most of all Jesus) offer you their legacy of truth. God wants the words of the Jewish Scriptures spoken to Jewish patriarchs and prophets to flow like nourishing sap through *every* branch in the tree.

Nourished Anew

I recently caught an interesting view of this timeless truth from, of all things, my daughter Kasey's first science fair project. For her topic she chose plant nutrition. Kasey started out with three identical, healthy green plants, but she nourished them differently. To one plant she gave water. To another she gave a high-powered nutrition drink. To the third she gave a kids' product described dubiously as a "fun drink" (euphemism for "liquified junk food"). Kasey's results were predictable—only one healthy, happy plant by experiment's end. Neither the junk juice nor the exotic extract produced nourishing sap. The branches from those plants looked sick, and before long they died.

Similarly, what have we in the Body of Messiah been drinking—junk juice, exotic extracts or living water? If, for most of our history, the original Jewish "nourishing sap" has not fed the Church, what has? More practically, what can be done about it?

First, let me point out that many Christians all over the world have begun embracing their biblically Jewish roots. They have been nourished anew and are being used by the Spirit to revive the remnant of Israel. Christian Zionists and lovers of the Jewish people have risen from the ranks of those who truly know and love the God of Israel.

A marvelous place to begin restoring your Old Covenant heritage, if you have not already, is with the biblical feasts. "Feasts" are not big, happy meals; they are accurately translated from the Hebrew as "appointed times." Every biblical feast foretells something of the first or second coming of Messiah. I see these appointed times, in Holy Spirit anointing, as intimate dates with Deity—kisses from heaven and prophetic, intercessory acts that usher in His Holiness. Kerry and I often lead Passover celebrations for churches. Time and again, we witness eye-opening wonder expressed by our brothers and sisters participating for the first time in a Spirit-filled "appointed time" with Jesus. Almost inevitably, they find themselves eager for more.

But for multitudes of other believers bereft of their Jewish roots, the story is different.

The New Christian Anti-Semitism

Tragically, smoldering embers of hate for the Jews have assumed a new form of acceptable expression in the twenty-first century. "The new anti-Semitism," as it is called, is based on anti-Zionism. We will look further into this phenomenon in later chapters of this book. For now, it is enough to know that anti-Zionism has become the catchall term for the world's mounting, irrational castigation of Israel, or anti-Israelism. Anti-Zionism allegedly stems from Israel's treatment of Palestinian Arabs—but has gone well beyond a local fight about land rights.

Israel is being blamed in our day for everything from airliners crashing into skyscrapers to germ warfare jitters, tremors on stock exchanges and new mystery diseases. Many are even pointing their fingers at Israel for the spread of Islamic terror. If the Jewish nation is responsible for such acts of world terror, however, I cannot imagine what she did to encourage Syria's overtake of Lebanon, Saddam Hussein's unleashing of the bloodbath against Iran and invasion of Kuwait, the Taliban's overrun of Afghanistan, the slaughter in Sudan, bombings in places like Bali, Indonesia and Pakistan—or Muhammad's invasion of Spain—all involving Muslim terror.

Furthermore, who is this "Israel"? Ask the hundreds of European Jews who have been brutally beaten, the thousands across the globe whose synagogues, shops and loved ones' graves have been torched or vandalized, or the American Jews whose family members were gunned down at the Israeli airlines counter at a Los Angeles airport—all at the inception of this present "enlightened" century. The people of Israel are the children of Jacob—the Jews—wherever they happen to live. Anti-Zionism is today's socially and politically correct resurgence of plain old anti-Semitism.

How has institutionalized Christianity responded to these re-stoked flames of Jew hatred? The World Council of Churches, the largest operating international church fellowship, repeatedly misrepresents and denounces Israeli, but not Palestinian, policy. It regards the creation of the modern Jewish State as problematic.[16] The organization initiated an international movement in 2002 called Ecumenical Campaign to End the Illegal Occupation of Palestine—a vigilante committee reporting on Israel's (not Palestinian terrorists') "violations of human rights."[17] The World Council of Churches claims to represent 400 million Christians, including Catholics, Episcopalians, Lutherans, Methodists, Presbyterians and Eastern Orthodox believers in more than 100 countries.[18] Does it also represent the new *Christian* anti-Semitism?

The National Council of the Churches of Christ in the USA, composed of 50 million believers in 36 different Protestant, Anglican and Orthodox denominations, calls itself the leading force for cooperation among Christians in America. In 2002 this Council condemned Israel for her treatment of Palestinians,[19] but did not censure Palestinians for their murderous terror against Israel. Meanwhile, certain Baptist, Brethren, Episcopalian, Evangelical Lutheran, Friends/Quaker, Mennonite, Presbyterian, Reformed, United Methodist and United Churches of Christ groups have joined with Arab Christian churches to form Churches for Middle East Peace—to help create a Palestinian state. The problem with their initiative is that it does not address the well-documented and terribly obvious Palestinian goal of annihilating Israel once that state is established.

So many church groups have rallied around pro-Palestinian endeavors that threaten Israel's survival, that it is no exaggeration to say the twenty-first century has generated an Islam-influenced, new Christian anti-Semitism.

Evangelical Ignorance or Arrogance?

Many mainline believers, including evangelicals who formerly were among Israel's staunchest supporters, have taken a theological turn. Once emphasizing the literal and unconditional nature of the Abrahamic covenant, they have altered their theology to conclude that Israel's biblical rights to the land are merely symbolic or entirely conditional.[20] Some point out that in the Bible, when the Jewish nation was disobedient to God's law, she was exiled from the land. Since the Jews are not following God's law today, He has every right to cast them out. (See chapter 15.)

God, of course, has every right to do what He pleases with Israel. Certainly He wants her, as well as her Arab neighbors, to repent and turn fully to Him. But He warns the nations that disciplining Israel or taking away her land is His business alone. The excuse, "We are not guilty, for they sinned against the Lord" (see Jeremiah 50:7) did not go over well for the Gentiles in the Bible—and will not for the nations of today. Such thinking runs dangerously close to that used historically to justify despising and punishing the Jews for rejecting Jesus.

Others discern that only when a church denies its Jewish or biblical roots can it fall prey to the new anti-Semitism, however cleverly cloaked. Such Christians are casting their lot with the Jewish nation in unconditional love, prayer and support. Their focus is not only on Israel's relationship to the land but on her relationship to the Lord. These saints and their ministries have had a tremendous impact on the Jews worldwide. Of them, former Israeli Foreign Minister Moshe Aumann, not a believer in Yeshua, has said:

> With Christians now reaching out to the Jewish people in genuine contrition and love, we are witnessing a remarkable phenomenon: The baseless hatred of Christian anti-Judaism that was so prevalent in the world for so many centuries is gradually being replaced

by unconditional love . . . that will, please God, usher in the final redemption of the Jewish people and of all humankind.[21]

The final redemption of the Jewish people and of all humankind is what, in a sense, this book is about. We look next at the exciting manner in which that redemption has already begun.

"I will restore you . . . and heal your wounds," declares the Lord, "because you are called an outcast, Zion for whom nobody cares."

JEREMIAH 30:17

CHAPTER NINE

The Jews and the Gospel

The Lord has called me to intercede for the Jewish people, and that calling is a high priority in my life. I pray in and out of the closet, and in and out of the land of Israel. I keep apprised of current events affecting Israel and seek the Spirit's prompting on how to pray strategically concerning them. I also stay in touch with trusted Israeli friends who love and serve Yeshua, such as Avner and Rachel Boskey. The Boskeys are well known for their informed and biblically balanced, prophetic perspectives on Israel. Over the years I have asked Avner countless times what he believes the most critical prayer need is for the Jewish nation at that hour. His answer is always — and I mean always — the same: "Israel's salvation."

And I always say back to him: "That's what I hear from the Spirit, too."

At this writing, the political situation in the Middle East is dire and more rapidly changing than ever. When Israelis awaken tomorrow morning, it is anybody's guess who will land in the wrong place at the wrong time and be blown into eternity by a devilishly driven terrorist, or who will get handed a final paycheck as the country's war torn economy gasps for breath.

But if I were to call Avner today and ask for his take on Israel's most urgent need, I know what he would say. And I would tell him, "That's what I hear from the Spirit, too."

The prayer is nothing new; Paul stated it succinctly two millennia ago: "My heart's desire and prayer to God for the Israelites is that they may be saved" (Romans 10:1).

Certainly it is important to pray specifically for Israel's peace and protection, wisdom for her leaders, healing for her wounded and jobs for her poor. These are compelling issues, for which I encourage you to petition heaven passionately. But top priority in the Spirit is prayer for Israel "that they may be saved." If you want to know God's heart intimately, hear it beating through Paul's words. Yahweh's burden is for Israel to be saved.

How Are Jews Saved?

It may surprise you to learn that Jewish people are saved the same as anyone else, by grace through faith in God's Son. The day before His execution, Yeshua said to a roomful of Jews, "I am the way and the truth and the life. *No one* comes to the Father except through me" (John 14:6, emphasis added). Later Peter declared to a gathering of Jewish leaders, "Salvation is found in no one else, for there is no other name under heaven given to men by which we must be saved" (Acts 4:12). Only the Jewish Messiah Jesus fulfills the Jewish hope for Jewish redemption.

The Bible says there is one way to enjoy a saving knowledge of God, whether you are Jewish or Gentile, Israeli or Arab, black, brown, yellow, red, white or any combination thereof. God loves you so much He gave you His Son, so that *whoever* you are, if you believe in Him, you may receive eternal life. His Son Jesus is the name by which any of us gets our sins forgiven, our relationship with the Creator made right.

To many of you I am stating the obvious. But some Christians take exception with me on this point—at least as it applies to Israel. They say something like this: "Because the Jews are God's chosen people, they don't need Jesus. God already has a covenant with Israel through Abraham by which He loves and saves them."

This so-called dual covenant doctrine teaches that Yahweh has two different means of salvation: one for the Jews, one for the Gentiles. To simplify, the Jews get saved via the Old Covenant while the Gentiles get saved through the New. In other words, Jewish people gain eternal life through the law of *Tanakh*, and non-Jews, through the Gospel. Friend, forgive me if my words sting, but this thinking presents a classic—and tragic—case of a road to hell paved with good intentions.

Dual covenant teaching reflects an attempt, developed in the past century, to remedy and compensate for past theological error about Israel. The heretical teaching of contempt, canonized by highly esteemed leaders in the early centuries of the Church, urged fellow Gentile believers to relate to Jews with "divine disdain." Not surprisingly, centuries of institutionalized contempt gave way to outright hate, then inquisitions, pogroms and eventually ground-level "justification" for the Holocaust. By then, bad fruit growing in the Church could no longer be denied; *something* had to be done about "Christian anti-Semitism," a tragic oxymoron. The time was ripe for bold truth and bold love. But the solution was yet another mistruth regarding God's beloved people.

The Dialogue of Dual Covenant

After the Holocaust, God moved on the hearts of church leaders in a spirit of repentant self-examination. Courageously facing their indirect (if not direct) roles in the horrific slaughter of European Jewry, Christian ministers began reaching out in fellowship to the Jews, giving rise to a Jewish-Christian movement known as interfaith dialogue. As the name implies, dialogue involves Jews and Christians talking together in a formal setting, usually a church, synagogue or educational institution, in a spirit of mutual respect for each other's faith. (But it has practically nothing to do with Jewish Christians, who are rarely, if ever, permitted to participate.) In dialogue, everybody agrees not to try to change anybody's faith, typically because nobody necessarily *believes* anybody's faith needs to be changed. The aim is mutual acceptance.

I am not against interfaith dialogue. Much benefit can result from people of different beliefs communicating in an atmosphere of mutual respect and friendship. I have non-Christian friends whom I respect and enjoy, and hope you do, too. But if we are not careful, mutual respect and acceptance can become subtle substitutes for unconditional love and truth. In certain cases Jewish-Christian dialogue has fostered friendship at a high price: In search of a more compassionate way to relate to the Jews, some believers have compromised the essential tenet of the Gospel—salvation solely by grace through faith in Christ. Is this withholding of eternal life the fruit of unconditional love?

The dialogue of dual covenant has had such a significant impact on segments of the Church that mainline denominations and institutions, one after another, have issued formal statements exempting the Jews from the need for evangelization. An example of a typical platform, signed by 21 representatives of different Christian—including evangelical—denominations in 2002 concludes, "In view of our conviction that Jews are in an eternal covenant with God, we renounce missionary efforts directed at [them]. . . . Christians need new ways of understanding the universal significance of Christ."[1]

Have we gone from one extreme to the other—from condemning Israel for her rejection of Yeshua to condoning that rejection because, supposedly, she no longer needs Him? Have churches acquiesced in unsanctified mercy to the Jewish tradition that prescribes Jesus "for Gentile use only"? The desire to demonstrate loving sensitivity to the Jewish people for all they have suffered is noble, right and good—but not at the expense of their salvation.

Is there an alternative way to relate to the Jews?

God has fresh strategies from heaven to entrust to those ready to respond. In recent years, many believers have reached out to Israel and the international Jewish community in humble repentance for

Christian anti-Semitism. Jews worldwide, including Messianic Jews, have been deeply swayed by these conciliatory words and deeds. The Gospel is not overtly preached in every instance, but Christian belief in its universal truth is never concealed. These God-breathed breakthroughs exist at all levels, from large, international Christian Zionist networks, to the efforts of Jesus-filled folks like my Swiss friend Olga who cleans streets every year in Israel. Once these bridges are built, gateways to the Gospel open—and must be stepped through. Friend, it is a matter of eternal life or death.

Times of the Gentiles

Some believers have another reason for not sharing the Gospel with the Jews: It's not time.

Personally, I read the New Covenant for the first time in 1975, and when I came to the verse in 2 Corinthians that says "now is the day of salvation," I believed it. Imagine that—I, a Jew, believed God wanted to forgive my sins right then and there! Not until I went to church did I find out that according to the timetable, I was not supposed to believe in Jesus until after something called a rapture. Now, if anything is disconcerting to a new believer, it is discovering you are an unplanned, inappropriately conceived, celestial mistake!

I trust you know that I am poking a little fun. But I was indeed raised by the Church to believe that you and I live in "the time of the Gentiles." We supposedly must wait, according to Romans 11:25, until the "full number of the Gentiles has come in" before giving attention to Israel's salvation. Meanwhile, Israel must experience a "hardening" or "blindness" to the Gospel.

Now, this was quite troubling. My own heart's desire and prayer to God for Israel was that they be saved; like Paul, I had an unceasing sorrow in my spirit for the sake of my people. As time went on I met others—Gentile as well as Jewish believers—who carried the same unquenchable fire in their souls. We wondered why we could not shake the burden. Had something gotten lost somewhere in the translation?

Apparently, yes. I discovered that more traditional versions of Romans 11:25 convey a radically different, and more literal, view of Israel's salvation:

Blindness in part is happened to Israel, until the *fulness* [not *full number*] of the Gentiles be come in.

KJV, EMPHASIS ADDED

The distinction between *full number* and *fullness* of the Gentiles is critical; it means the difference between eternal life and death. Here is why: If Israel is Gospel-blind until the *full number* of Gentiles comes to faith, there is no point sharing the Lord with them now or tomorrow or the day after that. So not until that last Gentile way over, let's say, on the island of Tuvalu finally gets saved, is it time to turn to the Jewish people.

On the other hand, if Israel's blindness is removed when the *fullness* of the Gentiles comes in, the strategy of the Spirit is different.

What does "fullness of the Gentiles" mean? Romans 11:11 says that "salvation has come to the Gentiles to make Israel envious." We can think of fullness, quite simply, as Spirit-fullness. From a practical perspective, fullness is that quality of mature Christ-likeness, or sanctification, that provokes Jewish people to godly envy for the Gospel. It is another way to describe the full regenerate life to which you and I are called as followers of Messiah. God's will for every believer since the inception of the Church has been the attaining of this fullness.

Fullness or *full number* is translated from the Greek word *pleroma*. *Pleroma* appears seventeen times in the New Covenant, and the King James Bible consistently translates it "fullness" all seventeen times. The New International Version, perhaps the most widely used contemporary translation, does the same—*except* for Romans 11:25. Nowhere else in the NIV is *pleroma* given the meaning "full number." Especially odd about this lone exception is that only a few verses earlier, in the same letter to the Romans on the same topic, the NIV translates *pleroma* as "fullness": "But if their [Israel's] transgression means riches for the world, and their loss means riches for the Gentiles, how much greater riches will their *fullness* bring" (verse 12, emphasis added).

With all due respect to the NIV and other Bible translations that make this distinction, I join the growing ranks of those who believe the Romans 11:25 exception for *pleroma* reflects the translators' theological bias.[2] As New Covenant scholar Mark Nanos points out, "There is certainly no linguistic reason why 'fulness' [*pleroma*] should take on a numeric quality, as it has to do with 'that which is brought to fulness or completion.' "[3]

It is the *quality* of Christianity that Jewish people encounter that impresses them more than the *quantity* of Christians they encounter.

Why do I spend so much time on one little word? It communicates a concept vitally significant to both Israel and the Church today. Our (mis)interpretation of the time in which we live—our appointed watch—will affect whether we focus ministry on the Gentiles, the Jews or both. The Bible says God is willing that none perish; now is the day of salvation, with the Gospel going to the Jew first and then the Gentile (see Romans 1:16). Not only is it time for Jewish evangelism, but, as we have seen, Israel's salvation affects evangelization of the nations. In fact, right after we are told that the Gentiles' fullness will cause Israel to be saved, the very next verse reminds us that at Israel's salvation "the deliverer will come from Zion" (Romans 11:26). Jesus will literally return—to Zion—at a time related to the salvation of the Jewish people.

Israel's "Hardness" and "Blindness"

Maybe you desire to see Jewish people come to Yeshua but feel they are too hardened or blinded to believe. I confess I, too, was tempted to think this way, even toward my father. Dad was raised Orthodox, and when I came home one day proclaiming faith in Yeshua, he hung his head low and went to his father's grave to apologize.

For sixteen years I prayed for Dad, during which time he would not even utter the name *Yeshua* or *Jesus*, utilizing instead an insulting Hebrew acronym that stands for a curse against the Savior. I agonized over his seeming hardness of heart and spiritual myopia.

But then my father got sick. His condition was incurable; good medical care could only buy him a little extra time. As Dad languished on his deathbed, thinking about the conversations we had had over the years, he surrendered his heart to Jesus. When he phoned me in California to tell me the news, his voice was weak, his speech a little slurred, but his intention clear. The next day I flew to his bedside in Chicago, but by then he had fallen into a coma. The following morning Dad awoke in heaven with his Messiah. From then on, I purposed never to resign any Jewish person as too hard or blind to surrender to Yeshua, given enough prayer, love and sensitive witness.

The New Covenant never ascribes Gospel resistance to all of Israel. Hardening and blindness is not over the whole Jewish nation; it is only in part:

> Israel has experienced a hardening *in part* until the . . . [fullness] of the Gentiles has come in.
>
> ROMANS 11:25, EMPHASIS ADDED

> Blindness *in part* is happened to Israel, until the fulness of the Gentiles be come in.
>
> ROMANS 11:25, KJV, EMPHASIS ADDED

> [Israel's] elect [obtained grace.] *The others* were hardened.
>
> ROMANS 11:7, EMPHASIS ADDED

Part of Israel responds to the Gospel; part of Israel does not—just as some Gentiles respond to the Gospel and some do not. If we forget this and consciously or subconsciously assume that all Israel—or even all but a teensy fraction—is presently hardened or blinded to Yeshua, will most of us even try to reach them with the Gospel? Could withholding the Good News prove the most deadly form of anti-Semitism of all?

Israel's Twofold Restoration: Physical and Spiritual Aliyah

I frequently meet Christians who want to minister to Israel but say they don't know how. They feel unequipped or too intimidated to evangelize, so they are drawn to humanitarian and political endeavors instead. I thank God for every Christian Zionist ministry to the sons and daughters of Jacob. These organizations shine as bright lights to Israel in an increasingly dark world, and I encourage you to stand with them. At the same time, I encourage you not to neglect Israel's need to know her Savior, or the Spirit's burden for her salvation.

I once met a sweet Christian Zionist who loved the Jewish people (let's call her Megan) in an evangelical megachurch. Megan had studied Romans 9 through 11 and understood the importance of Israel being saved. She was considering supporting one of several organizations that help transport Jews to Israel from remote regions of the earth for the purpose of *aliyah* (Hebrew for "immigration," but literally meaning "going up"). Megan sparkled with enthusiasm as she told me her story. I commended her heart of compassion and generosity.

But Megan seemed a little starstruck, and I felt prompted to ask if she knew this organization prohibited evangelism. No, she said; she had never imagined that would be the case.

Megan stared back at me rather blankly, so I asked another question. "Did you know they will not take to Israel any Jew who trusts in Jesus?"

The blank look did not budge. I could tell Megan was having a hard time believing that what I had said was true. After all, respected evangelical leaders endorsed this organization and it seemed such a laudable labor. So we sat down and talked.

"Megan," I continued, "I truly appreciate what these people are doing. But as evangelicals, we must not forget to ask how much eternal value there is in bringing Jewish people to Israel, only to have them live and die in their sins on Jewish, as opposed to, say, Russian soil, separated eternally from God."

"Well . . . it's important to help the Jews escape anti-Semitism," she replied. "And don't they need to get back to the land before God does His sovereign work there to save them?"

I hugged Megan. Her heart was right and she genuinely wanted to bless the Jews. "Yes, God will do a sovereign work with Israel. But in the meantime, what about those countless Israelis who live a hard life and then die without that sovereign work?"

I showed Megan how the Scriptures prophesy that Jewish people will turn to the Lord even while in exile, scattered among the nations. In fact, more Messianic Jews live outside of Israel than in the land. She need not worry about God being unable to save His people unless they first get to Israel:

"If they [Israel] have a change of heart *in the land where they are held captive,* and repent and . . . turn back to you [God] with all their heart and soul . . . [then] forgive your people, who have sinned against you; forgive all the offenses they have committed against you."

1 KINGS 8:47–50, EMPHASIS ADDED

Wherever the LORD your God disperses you among the nations, and when you and your children *return to the LORD* your God and obey him . . . *then* the LORD your God will . . . gather you again from all the nations where he scattered you. . . . He will bring you to the land that belonged to your fathers, and you will take possession of it.

DEUTERONOMY 30:1–5, EMPHASIS ADDED

"You will seek me and find me when you seek me with all your heart. *I will be found by you,*" declares the LORD, "*and will bring you back from captivity.* I will gather you from all the nations and places where I have banished you," declares the LORD, "and will bring you back to the place from which I carried you into exile."

JEREMIAH 29:13–14, EMPHASIS ADDED

Megan caught a new perspective that day. She decided to pray and rethink how best to support God's restoration of Israel.

In our Zionist fervor, sometimes we forget this restoration is twofold. It is taking place in the physical realm, in the Jews' return to the land. But it is occurring simultaneously in the spiritual realm—in the Jews' return to the *Lord*—which can occur anywhere. The Spirit is doing both at the same time. I appreciatively bless every believer who ever aided in the physical restoration of Israel or lent the nation political support. Such sacrificially loving Gentiles have been counted as some of Israel's dearest friends and their ongoing efforts are greatly needed. But now is *also* the time to undergird the *spiritual* restoration of the Jewish people, the modern-day miracle unfolding this very hour.

Life from the Dead

Romans 11:11 says that if you are a Christian, you have been saved to make Israel jealous. He wants you to love Him enough to provoke the Jewish people to godly jealousy. (As I shared earlier, it worked for me!) The Lover of Zion has enlisted your help in the greatest romance on record, the wooing of His ancient covenant people back to His heart.

Witnessing to unsaved Jews need not be intimidating. Most Jewish people have much less familiarity with their Bible than you do. Most have never read the Messianic prophecies that point clearly to Yeshua. And most have deep, unspoken questions about spiritual reality. If you know and love the Lord, and love Israel, you have no reason not to prayerfully follow His leading in telling them about the Source of that love. If you feel you need guidance with cultural sensitivities, plenty of Messianic ministries and resources are available to help.[4]

The devil fights hard against Jews coming to faith, and for good reason. Besides the fact he hates who and what God loves, Israel's corporate, national salvation is destined to bless the Gentiles in untold proportion, ushering in life from the dead: "For if their rejection [of Messiah] is the reconciliation of the world, what will their acceptance be but life from the dead?" (Romans 11:15).

When the Jewish nation *as a whole* is saved, the world will experience a profound release of life that practically defies description. Israel's embrace of Messiah will trigger an explosion of vitality that will propel our planet to new planes of existence. At its climax, life from the dead will invoke the resurrection of deceased humanity—and the Lord's return. Recall Jesus' words to Jerusalem: "You will not see me again until you say, 'Blessed is he who comes in the name of the Lord'" (Matthew 23:39). Messiah will return when Israel corporately welcomes Him back.

In the meantime, it seems that as the remnant of Israel revives in stages, so, too, does the Church. The past century alone is punctuated with parallels—remarkable coincidences (or God-incidents?)—of progressive life from the dead. The following is a sample of striking correlations from the past century alone:

- Modern-day Zionism and Messianic Judaism take hold at the turn of the twentieth century; the Azusa Street revival follows, giving rise to a worldwide Pentecostal movement.
- Israel becomes a sovereign state in 1948; healing revival breaks out in the United States.
- Israel regains Jerusalem in 1967; the Jesus Movement and charismatic renewal begin.
- Jewish people from the former Soviet Union embrace Jesus and immigrate to Israel en masse in the early 1990s; Church renewal originates in Toronto and spreads internationally.

The apostles may have been anticipating this parallel of Israel and the Church's restoration when they beseeched their Jewish brethren:

"Repent . . . that times of refreshing may come from the Lord, and that he may send the Christ. . . . He must remain in heaven until the time comes for God to *restore everything*, as he promised long ago."

ACTS 3:19–21, EMPHASIS ADDED

The Messianic Jewish leaders in the New Covenant knew that while God loves all nations, Israel's repentance in particular would open ancient gates of righteousness for the King of Glory to come in. I trust you are catching that vision by now, too. As we will see next, those ancient gates have already begun creaking open in preparation for the day they will fling wide apart—and heaven hears the prophetic cry, *"Barukh haba b'shem Adonai!"* "Blessed is He who comes in the name of the Lord!"

CHAPTER TEN

Revival of the Remnant

An electrifying revival is under way: Jews are embracing Yeshua in numbers not seen since the days of the book of Acts. I have witnessed it personally, and it is supernaturally intoxicating.

The prophet Jeremiah foresaw a day of Israel's restoration in which multitudes of Jews broke out of captivity from "the land of the north" and then all other nations (see Jeremiah 16:14–16; 23:7–8). The land of the north refers to land north of Israel—including in particular the former USSR. As Jeremiah prophesied, in the late nineteenth century two major movements took root in the land of the north at the same time: Zionism and Messianic Judaism. Then, one hundred years later in this land of the north, multitudes of Jews burst out of bondage and started flocking in droves not only to the State, but to the Savior of Israel.

Revisiting the Book of Acts

In the 1990s Kerry and I joined our Jewish evangelist friend Jonathan Bernis for our first mission trip to the former Soviet Union. In faith, Jonathan had rented the largest stadium in Moscow and invited every Jew in town to come hear about Jesus. He had persuaded us that the Jewish community there was unusually open to the Gospel.

I have to admit I had moments of doubt. When, the day before the outreach, I stepped inside the colossal stadium and eyed its thousands upon thousands of empty seats, I wondered just how many "unusually open" Russian Jews Jonathan thought were out there. I steeled myself for the next day. I suspected we would find ourselves ministering to maybe a couple of rows of Muscovites, plus our obliging team members, an ocean of empty chairs behind them.

But that is not how it happened. Crowds materialized and surged toward the stadium from every direction. Jews and non-Jews appeared from all strata of society, some decked in furs and fancies, some staggering with Vodka bottles in hand. As worship began, a mass of stoic Soviet faces seemed to thaw out of a collective, veritable frozen stupor. Throughout the arena, tears trickled irresistibly at the Son's warm glow. I had never seen anything like it.

At the altar call only a sprinkling of folks did *not* respond. Thousands of Russian Jews and Gentiles stood together to profess faith in the God of Israel and His Son, their Messiah. The place was awash in tears. I was witnessing a sweeping return of a prodigal nation and our Father's ecstatic welcome home. It was delightfully dizzying.

Afterward we researched both Church and Jewish history to discover that we had witnessed a historic, apparently unprecedented move of the Holy Spirit on the Jewish people. In future missions to different ex-Soviet republics, we would see crowds literally break down stadium doors to hear about Yeshua. We would see newly saved Jews off on their way to Israel, taking their fiery faith with them. We would see churches blessed with new life after laboring with us to take the Gospel to their local Jewish communities. And we would see Messianic congregations take root and flourish. The revival in Russian lands says to the world that now is the day of Israel's salvation.[1]

In recent years multitudes of Jews have responded to the Gospel in not only the former Soviet Union but the Americas and elsewhere. As Jeremiah prophesied, from the land of the north and all nations God is restoring His people. For many reasons, specific numbers are impossible to obtain, but some estimate that up to two million Jewish people believe in Yeshua worldwide.[2]

Israel's Softened, Seeing Part

Israeli Jews have softened significantly to the Gospel. Christian news services report that while Israel claimed an estimated total of 250 Messianic Jews in 1967,[3] the number, at this writing, has increased to 7,000:[4]

In Israel . . . amid ongoing and recently escalating acts of terrorism, the body of Messianic believers . . . is growing. As secular Israelis grow increasingly frustrated with the violence and apparent failure of the political peace process, Messianic congregations are reaching out to those who are seeking some meaning in life amid all the unrest.[5]

Collective disillusionment with manmade peace is echoed in cries across the country to turn to the God of Israel's fathers. An editorial in the *Jerusalem Post* by Michael Freund, a former official in the Prime Minister's Office, summons the people to repentance and prayer:[6]

Israel's best defense is the power of prayer, and it is time we unleash this weapon. . . . Israel should launch an international campaign, Operation Shield of David, which would bring together Jews, Christians, and others to pray on the country's behalf. . . . Now is the time to give God a chance, for unlike politicians, He can always be relied upon to keep His word.

The writer is not a believer in Yeshua; nonetheless, does he sound hardened or softened, blinded or at least open to see? Mr. Freund articulates a traditional Jewish perspective, reflecting spiritual qualities that are on the rise among many seeking Israelis today.

For the first time in Israel's modern history, her rabbis have gal-
vanized Jews worldwide for focused prayer for the nation. Their
words give evidence of God's drawing the people to Himself: "At
this hour . . . how can we not tremble and our hearts not melt?
How can we not raise our prayers in supplication to our Father
in Heaven?"[7]

What is the state of the Gospel in the State of the Gospel? Waves
of Russian Jews immigrating to Israel ablaze with faith in Yeshua
are changing the spiritual climate of the land. As early as 1999,
the *Jerusalem Post* ran its story, "Russian *Olim* [new immigrants]
Swell Ranks of Messianic Jews."[8] The article described a burgeon-
ing Messianic Jewish revival, estimating a total of five thousand
Israeli Jewish believers.[9] At this writing, Messianic Israeli leaders
say that salvations are at an all-time high. Here is what some of
them report:

> Almost every [Messianic] congregation is experiencing so much
> growth that they don't have enough seats.[10]

> The conflict in the region is opening people's hearts to the Lord.
> The past few months we have seen young people coming to faith
> almost every week.[11]

> The seekers are many, the workers are few.[12]

More and more Israeli heartstrings are being tugged tenderly by
the Holy One. "In their affliction they will seek me," the Scriptures
prophesy (Hosea 5:15, KJV).

With so many seeking and coming to faith, how can we write off
the Jewish people as too hardened and blinded, or too offended by
anti-Semitism, or too set aside for God's future sovereign work to
share Yeshua with them? Israel is hardened and blinded in part—but
she is also softened and seeing. Whatever the times of the Gentiles
means eschatologically, it is coming to a close; God is turning Jewish hearts back to Himself in these days just as He is moving on
Gentile hearts.

Opposing the Salvation of the Jewish People

As with any breakthrough move of the Holy Spirit, the devil is disturbed enough to organize opposition against Messianic Jewish revival. When a Jew comes to Jesus, it can sometimes seem that spiritual havoc is wreaked all around him or her. Family and friends may feel betrayed, even enraged. But our enemy is *the enemy,* not our loved ones, associates or religious community. When Messianic Jews face opposition based on the premise that Jesus is not our Messiah—which usually comes from other Jews—we pray in love for those who persecute us. Often we get to welcome them into the Kingdom of God some time later, as I did with my dad.

The most "fascinating" array of opposition to Jewish evangelism I have encountered personally arose in Moscow. There we found ultra-Orthodox Jews, neo-fascist terror groups, neo-Nazis and Communists—all normally at odds with each other, to put it mildly—strangely allied to keep us from preaching the Gospel. By our sheer existence as Messianic Jews, we had managed to incite not just the anti-Semitic groups but also the anti-Christian forces to near-violent resistance. We prayed; their efforts backfired. Some of the protestors who picketed the outreach, with their hodgepodge of placards, costumes and causes, ended up staying well after the event to ask questions about Yeshua. ("Does the Old Covenant really describe what He will be like?")

The staunchest opposition to Jewish evangelism, however, is the so-called anti-missionary movement. Anti-missionaries are Orthodox and ultra-Orthodox Jews whose *raison d'etre* is to prevent other Jews from believing in Yeshua. Very much "anti" missions, they resemble the Pharisees[13] who opposed Yeshua and His followers. Anti-missionaries tail Jewish evangelists around the globe, passionately dedicated to undermining all efforts to introduce their brethren to Messiah. Today's anti-missionaries trace their religious traditions back to rabbis of the post-Middle Ages who embraced *Kabbalah* (Jewish mysticism/witchcraft). Of them, Paul's words seem especially appropriate:

They are zealous for God, but their zeal is not based on knowledge
. . . [b]ecause they pursued [righteousness] not by faith but as if
it were by works. . . . As far as the gospel is concerned, they are
enemies on your account; but as far as election is concerned, they
are loved on account of the patriarchs.

ROMANS 10:2; 9:32; 11:28

I urge you to pray for the salvation of those among my people
who are so feverishly anti-Messiah, remembering the apostle Paul
formerly counted himself among them. God loves anti-missionaries,
in all their misguided zeal. At the same time, these inflamed anti-
Yeshua people would proudly stand up and be counted as Israel's
"hardened part" toward the Gospel and have fostered outright
persecution against some Israeli Messianic Jews.

Discrimination against Israeli Messianic Jews

Fueling anti-missionary fervor is the historical misunderstanding that one cannot be both Jewish and Christian. According to
this conventional—but illogical and biblically incorrect—stream
of thought, any Jew believing in Jesus is no longer Jewish. He
is disdainfully deemed a deserter of his people. Tragically, millennia of church sponsored or supported anti-Semitism probably
constitutes the single most significant tool the enemy has used to
entrench this untruth.

What I share next is not to level criticism against God's chosen
people. His heart is big enough to love Israel unconditionally despite
her imperfections, and ours must be, too. Those of us who love her
must also uphold her weaknesses in prayer, which means we must
be aware of them. My purpose in making you aware of discrimination against Messianic Jews in Israel is to inspire strategic prayer
and proactive strategies to bless the Israeli body of believers. In so
doing you will bless the whole nation.

For decades Israeli anti-missionaries have firebombed Messianic
congregations and believers' homes, physically assaulted believers,

vandalized their property, boycotted their businesses, hurled death threats, and published libelous news reports about their individual countrymen who trust in Yeshua. Israeli police are notoriously slow to respond to anti-missionary crime, for which prosecutions practically never occur.[14]

Israel is a freedom-loving and democratic society, not a repressive regime. Nonetheless, insidious anti-missionary opposition is worked through political and religious propaganda aimed at the population as a whole. Jewish ultra-Orthodox (*Haredi*) political parties, though a national minority, wield significant power in the country.[15] Easily recognizable, *Haredim* dress in the same black layered garb as their forerunners in the Jewish ghettos of Eastern Europe hundreds of years ago. Swayed by anti-missionaries, the *Haredim* have so affected various institutional processes that Israeli policy—which is not in line with the Bible on this point—regards Jewish believers in Yeshua as no longer Jewish.

Believing Yeshua is the Messiah is no crime. But as a result of their faith, Israeli believers risk losing full protection under the law. Messianic Jews immigrating to Israel (making *aliyah*) bear the brunt of this discrimination; many have been refused citizenship, others have been deported. As to sharing the Gospel—which Israelis do boldly—the Messianic community faces proposed legislation that could outlaw even talking informally about Yeshua.[16]

Jobs can be lost—or never obtained—because of anti-missionary intimidation aimed at employers otherwise willing to hire believers; consequently, poverty among Israeli Messianics is a chronic problem. The situation is made worse by the fact that charitable Christian and Jewish relief funds rarely reach Messianic hands. The government, which regulates and disperses most private funds, precludes Israeli Messianic organizations from receiving charitable monies that they themselves have not raised.[17]

Meanwhile, it is socially and politically acceptable in Israel for Jews to believe in any *other* messiah—so long as it is not Jesus. Some ultra-Orthodox, including anti-missionary groups, openly profess and proselytize faith in an assortment of alleged messiahs—most notably one Rabbi Menachem Schneerson who died in Brooklyn,

New York, in 1994. The deceased Schneerson's picture remains plas-
tered about Jerusalem, where his adherents still await his return.
Worship of not just Schneerson, but Buddha, Mother Earth and
even Satan are not only legal but practiced by some in Israel—who
are regarded as full-fledged citizens of the Jewish State.

Weep with me for those entangled in error, but please do not
begrudge them. "As far as election is concerned, they are loved on
account of the patriarchs" (Romans 11:28). Remember, most are
reacting to centuries of institutionalized persecution by the Church
that forced an artificial split between Old and New Covenant faith.
I can say, thankfully, that serious persecution against Messianic
Jews is not widespread at this writing. Despite obstacles, the Holy
Spirit sweeps across the Jewish nation and the church in Israel
will thrive, nothing able to ever prevail against it.

Let me mention that the Israeli Messianic community includes
Christian Arabs, even Palestinians, who genuinely love the Lord. They
also endure much persecution, not at the hands of anti-missionaries,
but of their nonbelieving Arab brethren. We must remember them
with compassionate prayer and ministry as well.

The Remnant of Israel

A large, lifelike statue of Elijah the prophet stands on Mount
Carmel near the city of Haifa. Sword in hand, the imposing figure
with its piercing eyes appears ready to strike once more at Baal's
prophets—or any who dare exalt another above the God of Israel.
I am always moved at this statue to pray for Israeli firebrands to
arise, tear down false altars, dethrone false messiahs and proclaim
Yeshua as King. Convinced it is what He wants to do (see Malachi
4:5), I beseech the Lord to raise up indigenous believers in the spirit
of Elijah throughout the land.

Now, being human, Elijah had a down side. Following his most
stunning spiritual victory, the great seer temporarily lost perspective.
With a sigh, he once told the All-Knowing, "I am the only one left"
(1 Kings 19:14). According to Elijah, there was not another soul in

all Israel still serving God. But Elijah did not see the whole picture, and so Yahweh set his friend straight: "I reserve seven thousand in Israel—all whose knees have not bowed down to Baal and all whose mouths have not kissed him" (verse 18).

God had a remnant of seven thousand in Elijah's day; He has a remnant in our day; and throughout history He would have a remnant of faithful Jewish worshipers. He points out that, as with Elijah, "So too, at the present time there is a [Jewish] remnant chosen by grace" (Romans 11:5). While this remnant obtained grace, "the others were hardened" (verse 7).

Who, what, where is the biblical remnant chosen by grace today? Messianic Jewish followers of Yeshua all over the earth. As long as the Church has existed, so has the remnant of Israel. The remnant constitutes a needed but often missing link in the Church's relationship with Israel. Though we have often seemed invisible to much of the Body (this was Elijah's problem), that is changing.

The remnant of Israel belongs to the universal Body of Messiah. We are your brothers and sisters in the "family of believers" or "household of faith" (Galatians 6:10, NIV, KJV respectively). Jew and Gentile as "one new man" is God's "mystery" turned to reality:

> You who are Gentiles by birth . . . were separate from Christ, excluded from citizenship in Israel and foreigners to the covenants. . . . But now in Christ Jesus you who once were far away have been brought near. . . . His purpose was to create in himself *one new man out of the two.* . . . Consequently, you are no longer foreigners and aliens, but fellow citizens with God's people and members of God's household. . . . This *mystery* is that through the gospel the Gentiles are heirs together with Israel, *members together of one body* . . . which for ages past was kept hidden in God.
>
> EPHESIANS 2:11–3:9, EMPHASIS ADDED

Christian friend, you and I need each other. The Body of Messiah will never be complete without Jews and Gentiles reciprocally loving and blessing (kneeling to enrich) the other. God has invested irrevocable gifts and callings on every *ethnos,* or nation, destined to uniquely reflect His glory. You need to remain the Gentile He created you to be, with the special *Divine Nature Anointing* He has invested in you. Gentile conversion to Judaism is not required to enter into the beauty of relationship, in all its spiritual dimensions, with Israel's God.

I want to see you blessed in the fullness of your authentic identity in Christ. Perhaps we Jewish people have too long neglected this aspect of our call to bless the nations. In that case, I humbly ask you to accept my heart's prayer for God to undergird and propel you in Yeshua's name, in Holy Spirit power, toward all heaven has for you and your nation!

As we Messianic Jews seek to bless you, we seek to honor what the Bible says about Gentile-Jewish protocol for "one new man" in the Spirit.

Jewish-Gentile Protocol for "One New Man"

Protocol relates to proper order and respect of divine and del-egated authority in the Body of Christ. Following protocol in the Spirit pleases Him, makes for more fruitful ministry, and helps us steward our resources effectively. Examples of biblical protocol relate to administering the Lord's Supper (see 1 Corinthians 11:17–34) and exercising the Holy Spirit's gifts (see 1 Corinthians 14:27–33). In addition, there is also strategic protocol pertaining to Gentiles and Jews in the Church. The Bible tells us that family comes first: "As we have opportunity, let us do good to all people, *especially to those who belong to the family of believers*" (Galatians 6:10, emphasis added).

You and I are to do Spirit-led good—especially to our brothers and sisters in the household of faith. How many of us, however, think this way when it comes to Israel? Do we remember to do good to the remnant first? Or do we skip protocol and hone our love, prayers, resources and service exclusively onto the unbelieving part of the Jewish nation? Of course we are to continue our sincere support of Jews who do not—and may never—believe in Yeshua. But we must not forget to do good to Jewish, and especially Israeli, believers who typically receive nothing from mainline Christian or Jewish ministries to Israel.

A second point of protocol is this: "For if the Gentiles have shared in the Jews' spiritual blessings, they owe it to the Jews to share with them their material blessings" (Romans 15:27). Put this directive together with that above, and think of the fruit that will be borne when Christian resources — both tangible and intangible — are aimed strategically at strengthening the remnant of Israel. Missions experts say the most effective way to penetrate any people group with the Gospel is to empower indigenous believers to minister to their own. Messianic Jews are called to catapult their countrymen to faith but often lack the necessary tangible resources.

How can we respond in right protocol? We can pray for, befriend and co-labor with Messianic Jewish individuals and outreach organizations. We can support Messianic ministries with relief programs designed specifically to benefit Israeli believers. These ministries collect and distribute funds to the Jewish church in Israel ineligible to receive them from other sources. We can take whatever opportunity God gives us to validate Messianic faith in the face of opposition against it.

My friend Pastor Ché Ahn, who directs an international network of over a thousand churches, risked much by demonstrating Spirit-protocol sensitivity. Ché carries a vision for the salvation of Israel and during his first visit there met several Messianic leaders. He also met secular political leaders, among them a chief assistant to the prime minister. Ché expressed Christian love and blessing to the believers and then to the politicians, including the prime minister's assistant. Grateful for his support, the assistant asked Ché if there was anything he could do in return for him. "Yes," Ché replied at the prompting of the Holy Spirit. "You could extend equal civil rights to Messianic Jews."

According to Ché, the official first denied, then defended, the fact of discrimination against the remnant. Ché's heart, like God's, is big enough to love the lost (the hardened/blinded part of Israel) as well as the saved (the softened/seeing part); the conversation ended warmly and amicably. Nonetheless an important point was made. Ché took a bold but loving stance, risking his political connections. I believe Yeshua is proud of him. (I sure am.)

The Holy Spirit also has a specified protocol for reaching the world with the Gospel, and Paul lays it out for us: "The gospel . . . is the power of God for the salvation of everyone who believes: *first for the Jew, then for the Gentile"* (Romans 1:16, emphasis added). Wherever Jesus, Paul,[18] and the other apostles went, they sought out and spoke to the Jews first, then the Gentiles. This biblical protocol still carries astounding anointing. (Had it been followed, Church history—and therefore world history—might have been different—and better for it.) Accordingly, whenever we take the Gospel to a city on a large-scale basis, we always reach out first to the Jew, then to the Gentile. Time and again, at least as many Gentiles as Jews profess first-time faith in Jesus. Other Jewish evangelistic ministries, some of which do not direct much focus at all to Gentiles, note the same effect.

Can we engage for a moment in what I like to call sanctified speculation? I wonder what would happen if we returned to the biblical order of Gospel outreach. Let's say Jewish and Gentile evangelists co-labored, seeking first, in every missions endeavor, Jews with whom to share the Good News. We could expect a remnant of those Jewish people to embrace Yeshua and, together with newly believing Gentiles, form an indigenous church. Some of these new Jewish and Gentile believers would rise to leadership, bringing to the fore their complementary callings and gift mix. Jew and Gentile together as one in Messiah would prove a tangible, universal and reciprocal witness to the power of God for salvation to all who believe.

Just maybe such a strategy would reach even those many esteemed children of Abraham descended not from Isaac and Jacob but from Ishmael, Esau and the patriarch's other sons—to whom we now turn.

PART 5

The Question of Election

"It is through Isaac that your offspring will be reckoned." . . . Yet, before the twins were born or had done anything good or bad—in order that God's purpose in election might stand: not by works but by him who calls—she was told, "The older will serve the younger." Just as it is written: "Jacob I loved, but Esau I hated." What then shall we say? Is God unjust? Not at all! . . . It does not, therefore, depend on man's desire or effort, but on God's mercy.

ROMANS 9:7–16

CHAPTER ELEVEN

Abraham's Family Feud

At the perimeter of Israel's sun-broiled Negev Desert, I stood on tiptoes and leaned precipitously over a dusty stone ledge, squinting into an obscure, yawning hole in the ground. My two prayer partners and I had climbed a remote sand dune where Abraham's Well, along with other ruins from the ancient biblical town of Beersheva, had presumably been excavated. The Lord had spoken to me about an on-site intercessory prayer assignment at this extraordinary reservoir originally constructed a hundred generations ago by Abraham—and still faithfully pooling rainwater.

The sturdy old well had once sustained the beloved patriarch's thirsty family, servants and flocks. In Abraham's time, however, the arid scrubland on which it stood fell smack in the middle of Philistine territory, and one day servants of the king seized it for themselves. To reclaim his property, Abraham met the Philistine king at the well, where he gave him seven lambs as evidence that he, and not the king's servants, had dug it out. Abraham's sacrifice demonstrated his sincerity. As a result, the two men swore an oath of treaty (see Genesis 21:22–31) and the site became known as *Beersheva* ("Well of the Oath" or "Well of Seven").

153

My assignment in the twenty-first century was not tied so much to a royal ruler with seven extra sheep, as to the covenant of the King of Kings with one aging Abraham—the question of election. To that question, today as much as ever, the world needs an answer.

Redigging Abraham's Well

The Lord had spoken to me about redigging Abraham's well in the Spirit, asking for the patriarch's anointing to flow afresh on his living descendants. Let me explain. The purpose of redigging a well is to restore a pool of needed sustenance. In the natural realm, wells and water were prized essentials of life in the ancient Near East. A good well could last thousands of years and refresh many generations, such as Jacob's well that continued providing water to the Samaritans of Jesus' day. In the supernatural realm it is similar.

The Bible recounts that when Isaac was in need of water, he returned to his father's wells and redug them. The Philistines had maliciously stopped up these wells by filling them with dirt. But Isaac and company, mouths parched, knew redigging would prove simpler than finding a water source and constructing a reservoir from scratch. When dug up and cleaned out, the wells that Isaac had inherited revived his whole household (see Genesis 26:12–18). Similarly, I knew there were prayers to be prayed and prophetic declarations to be made to help spiritually unstop Abraham's well, long ago clogged with intangible but real dirt and debris, rocks and refuse. God wants this well to revive Abraham's whole household—Israel, the Church *and* his Arab children.

I could not have anticipated my experience at the well, where only the occasional bleating of bedouin flocks interrupted a timeless silence. At this concrete point of contact with the memory of our venerated progenitor, I was unexpectedly cut to the core by a strange sense of grief—Abraham's grief—over his unresolvable family feud. Peering into the cavernous well, I found myself gazing at intangible pools of sorrow welling from my ancestral grandfather's soul. The Holy Spirit was tapping me into Abraham's lasting love for his Arabic children, and anguish over their acrimony toward both Jew and Christian. My partners and I asked God to synergize our intercession with the prayers and cries this man of faith must have uttered over the years for the reconciliation of his beloved sons.

The Blessing of Ishmael

What is the real basis of the Arab-Jewish conflict? No satisfactory answer can be found apart from the Bible, where the doleful dispute begins. Therein lie the clues to understanding and unraveling the mess of the Middle East, with its contention and carnage spilling onto every continent. Scattered in the biblical patriarchs' dysfunctional family history (how many of us can relate?), we find seeds of hate and roots of bitterness that we read and hear about in full-blown form in the news today.

The story starts when God makes a promise to Abraham laden with hope for humanity. But it depends on the apparently impossible: an heir. Years pass, until barren Sarah, lacking neither ingenuity nor inexorability, conceives a scheme, if not a son. She directs her husband to deposit his seed with a surrogate, her Egyptian servant Hagar: "Perhaps I can build a family through her" (Genesis 16:2).

Hagar becomes pregnant—and immediately sparks fly. She begins to despise her mistress, who begins to mistreat her. Hagar runs away from home—but not the presence of God. Hagar, a member of Abraham's household honored as a secondary wife (see Genesis 16:3), knows and worships Yahweh. The matriarch of the Arabic peoples is about to become the first woman to whom the Angel of the Lord appears. He sees her plight and pities her in the desert of her distress. But He commands her to go home and submit to Sarah, for she is carrying a special child. Then He prophesies over Hagar:

- "I will so increase your descendants that they will be too numerous to count. . . .

- "You will have a son. You shall name him Ishmael [meaning "God hears"], for the LORD has heard of your misery.
- "He will be a wild donkey of a man;
- "His hand will be against everyone and everyone's hand against him,
- "And he will live in hostility toward all his brothers" (Genesis 16:10–12).

Many years later, still no son by Sarah, Abraham has another talk with God. The patriarch pleads, "If only Ishmael might live under your blessing" (Genesis 17:18). Abraham adores his firstborn son. Not only he, but Sarah, Hagar and consequently Ishmael himself have assumed this boy is the child of promise.

But God has another plan, and His response sets the course of history. He answers his friend's prayer in promising bountiful blessing to Ishmael, for he is Abraham's eldest son. Ishmael will be fruitful and father twelve rulers of a mighty nation. "But," God reiterates emphatically, "my *covenant* I will establish with *Isaac*" (Genesis 17:20–21, emphasis added).

Does Ishmael Get the Land?

To what covenant does God refer? The Abrahamic covenant is Yahweh's *unconditional* promise to make him into a great nation that will bless all peoples on earth. In addition, *as part of the covenant,* God promises Abraham *possession of certain land:* "The LORD made a covenant with Abram and said, 'To your descendants I give this land, from the river of Egypt to the great river, the Euphrates'" (Genesis 15:18; see also 12:7; 13:15–17; 15:7–17).

This covenant, God clarifies, belongs not to Ishmael but to Isaac. Isaac is the son of promise who will inherit "the whole land of Canaan . . . as an everlasting possession" (Genesis 17:8).

Finally, at the age of one hundred, Abraham cradles baby Isaac in his arms. Ishmael is in an understandably tough spot. Suddenly the family spotlight is off him, shining instead on his younger half-brother. In the culture of the day, Isaac has just usurped Ishmael's birthright. I imagine the boy's whole being wracks with pain and rejection. His plight is unprecedented.

His self-worth shattered, Ishmael begins to resent his rival. The Scripture says that he mocks Isaac to such an extent that Sarah perceives her son's inheritance is at risk. The connotation is that Ishmael's taunting and deriding is intended to belittle or diminish (actually, curse) Isaac. From God's perspective, the boy sneers not so much at human favoritism but at His sovereign choice. In effect Ishmael demands of Deity, "What You gave me is not enough; I want it all." It seems the cry still echoes in the Arab world . . . but who among us has not muttered it as well?

Abraham must have grieved over his family feud and mourned deeply when God told him to send both Hagar and Ishmael away for good (see Genesis 21:9–12). Yet it was precisely that: for good. God's seemingly harsh directive would work good for both Isaac *and* Ishmael. (How good could it have been for the older son to live under the constant reminder of the younger's election? How could Ishmael have so grown in stature as to father twelve princes?)

Isaac and Ishmael reunite in the Scriptures at Abraham's death to bury their father. By that time they stand shoulder to shoulder, each the head of a family and nation. Yet Abraham "left *everything* he owned to Isaac" (Genesis 25:5). Normally the law of primogeniture would have delegated at least a double portion of the patriarch's property to Ishmael. Whether Ishmael accepted this disappointing loss graciously or felt further slighted, we do not know.

We do know that to this day, many of his descendants brood over stacks of perceived dishonor at the hands of the Jews—particularly related to land. Our challenge is to love and understand, then empower the Ishmaelites[1] to rise to God's perspective. Israel's inheritance, like Isaac's, is a question of Sovereign election—and the Creator need justify His choice to no one: "Who are you, O man, to talk back to God? 'Shall what is formed say to him who formed it, "Why did You make me like this?"'" (Romans 9:20–21; see also Job 40:2).

Ishmaelites in Bible Prophecy

Consistent with the blessing of Ishmael, we see prophecy already being fulfilled about him in Genesis 25:13–18:

> These are the names of the sons [twelve rulers] of Ishmael, listed in the order of their birth: Nebaioth the firstborn of Ishmael, Kedar, Adbeel, Mibsam, Mishma, Dumah, Massa, Hadad, Tema, Jetur, Naphish and Kedemah. These were the sons of Ishmael, and these are the names of the twelve tribal rulers according to their settlements and camps. . . . And they lived in hostility toward all their brothers.

Ishmael is fruitful and multiplies quickly into twelve rulers—noted for their aggressive hostility. I do not believe God planned for Ishmael's descendants to live at odds with each other, but He did know in advance the choices they would make. These choices may well have been motivated by wounds infected with unforgiveness toward God and His sovereignly elected heirs. In any case, history recounts the violently factious, warring nature of the children of Ishmael. Tribal grudges can go back for generations, based on ubiquitous legends of plunder and murder screaming ceaselessly for revenge. A root of bitterness defiles many; unresolved envy metastasizes to unremitting enmity. God, however, did not plan it that way.

Likewise, the Creator did not condemn Ishmael to become what we today think of as a "wild donkey" of a man. The wild donkey was highly admired in the ancient bedouin culture of the Near East. The Bible describes for us its nature in Job 39:5–8: a fierce and sturdy animal uncontrolled by man, thriving in a wasteland, scorning any but an earthy-raw existence. Theologians Keil and Delitzsch comment on the historical character of the children of Ishmael:

> The figure of a wild [donkey], that wild and untamable animal, roaming at its will in the desert . . . depicts most aptly the bedouin's boundless love of freedom as he rides about in the desert, spear in hand, upon his camel or his horse, hardy, frugal, reveling in the varied beauty of nature, and despising town life in every form.[2]

The biblical depiction of Ishmael may in some respects sound un-flattering but it is only a partial picture. History reflects the choices of Ishmael's descendants (like other nations) made mostly after the flesh, not the Spirit. Therefore the sin-twisted aspects of Ishmael's unique DNA—meant to testify of the Creator for His glory—are predominant. Nonetheless, Abraham's firstborn offspring carry redemptive gifts according to a *Divine Nature Anointing* that will someday spectacularly reflect God's gracious character. The world is yet to behold the blessing of the Ishmaelites according to their redeemed, regenerate nature.

Ishmael's Irrevocable Call

A wild donkey is not a man-pleaser, and someday Ishmael's wild donkey nature will be transformed to reflect the humble servant, burden-bearing character of a gentled donkey seeking to please only the Master. Far from humiliating the Ishmaelites, this high calling will honor them as it did the donkey that Jesus once rode into Jerusalem. It is often said that the way up is down in the Kingdom of God. Ishmael's *Divine Nature Anointing* summons his descendants to greatness through humility, to exaltation through humble service.

Strategically from the beginning, the children of Ishmael have been positioned to serve. Theirs is the territory surrounding Israel both naturally and supernaturally, geographically and spiritually. Like the honored, domesticated donkey in the Gospel accounts, they will uniquely carry the Presence of the Lord to and from Israel, vis-à-vis the more distant Gentile nations. The Ishmaelites will minister in humble but highly honored service to the Lord, and as a result, to the Jews and the nations.

I am convinced that even in our day, as Arabs come to Christ they will be used to bring their Jewish cousins into the Kingdom as well. Those sworn enemies of Israel will someday serve as their best friends—and vice versa.

The Bible elaborates further on Ishmael's character: He will live in enmity toward everyone. True to God's Word, the threads of history not only trace the Ishmaelites' unending bloodlust, but they emerge in our day tied in the knot of global terror. Yet Ishmael's inimical spirit, transformed and sanctified by the blood of Messiah, will someday mediate peace. Such hints of holy revival among the Arabic peoples glare at us from the Scriptures:

> In that day there will be a highway from Egypt to Assyria [modern-day Iraq]. The Assyrians will go to Egypt and the Egyptians to Assyria. The Egyptians and Assyrians will worship together. In that day Israel will be the third, along with Egypt and Assyria, a blessing on the earth.
>
> ISAIAH 19:23–24

As in the natural realm, so it will be in the supernatural. A highway will arise that peaceably bridges all of Abraham's children—all the redeemed peoples who together worship Israel's God. Nations will traverse this highway en route to Zion to visit the mountain of the Lord (see Isaiah 2:3). As God has invested in Arab lands much of the world's wealth in the form of natural oil, I believe He has invested parallel reserves of supernatural oil symbolic of the Holy Spirit. Someday peoples from all over the earth will receive an anointed ministry of hospitality and practical help in preparing themselves for an audience with the King—at loving Arabic hands. An amazing prayer prospect, isn't it?

If you have ever visited a Middle Eastern Arab home, as I have, you know personally the extraordinary hospitality endemic to the Arab culture. Every guest is highly esteemed and receives nothing less than royal treatment. I puzzled at first at this seemingly contradictory quality of hospitality in view of Ishmael's (and the Arabs') penchant for battle. Then I recognized this radical, redemptive gift of hospitality—which technically means "love of strangers or foreigners"[3]—is God-given; it is a *Divine Nature Anointing*. Someday, upon that great prophetic highway, these gracious children of Abraham will roll out a grand red carpet—drenched not with the blood of man, but the Blood of the Lamb. Their passion toward the stranger, boiling for millennia with hate, will melt to divine love, spilling with beauty onto a highway of hospitality.

I believe the Ishmaelites will bring to the Body of Messiah a restored concept of honor and community—biblical values they have extolled through the ages. Certain Arab traditions wrongly written off as primitive or backward by the West will be used to revive virtues associated with the culture of Bible times. Ultimately, the children of Ishmael will reveal to the world how "God hears," in prophetic fulfillment of their forebear's name.

Believing friend, you and I are to help pray and labor this into being.

Israeli writer Avner Boskey foresees a similar future of transformation for the Arabs:

> The [Bible's] prophetic word has shaped much of the destiny of the greater Arab nation and its relationship with the world. Fierce independence, a wild and untamable soul, and arrogant animosity can characterize Arab dealings (at their worst) with the world. But the Arab world at its best manifests freedom of abandoned worship, generosity, graciousness and sacrificial zeal. When Messiah Jesus is allowed to transform their hearts, the descendants of Ishmael will find God bringing sweet out of the bitter, and they will discover the beauty of their Abrahamic connection in a totally new way. Peace and cooperation will supplant wildness and strife, and love between Arab and Jewish cousins will bloom again.[4]

From God's perspective, it is harvest time for Arab Muslim souls, though a stiff price will likely be paid for it. Amid the world's war on terror, expect to see masses of converted Arabs and prepare to undergird them sacrificially. Remember that for the patriarch's sake, they, too, are uniquely beloved.

Abraham's Other Sons

The descendants of Ishmael represent only a portion of the Arabic peoples. Many other nations comprise this vast company the Creator desires to captivate, not with the saber but the Spirit. They too are affected by wounds that will give way to the love of Christ through intercession and evangelism.

After the separation of Hagar and Ishmael, the death of Sarah, and the marriage of Isaac to Rebekah, Abraham takes another wife, named Keturah. By Keturah a rejuvenated Abraham fathers six more sons: Zimran, Jokshan, Medan, Midian, Ishbak and Shuah (see Genesis 25:1–4). He sends them to live in the region east of the Promised Land that Isaac inhabits (see verse 6), toward the area where Ishmael dwells. There in the Arabian Peninsula, the clans intermingle and intermarry.

We can assume that Abraham teaches all his sons to worship Yahweh before he sends them out. His children must choose whether to take with them—and impart to their children—knowledge of the one true God. Sadly, with little exception, they do not follow in the faith of their father, succumbing to the fallen nature instead. Only the Midianites, through Jethro the priest and his daughter Zipporah who becomes Moses' wife, shine as examples of those among Abraham's other sons staying faithful to God. The rest turn to idolatry and enmity against Israel, for which they endure judgment.[5] Their descendants, together with the Ishmaelites, other nations preexisting in Abraham's day, and Lot's descendants (the Moabites and Ammonites) intermingle and usually are collectively known as Arabs.

By New Covenant times, the Arabs dwell from the Euphrates all the way to the Red Sea, shielded from invasion by an unconquerable climate and terrain in which seemingly only they can thrive.[6] At this writing, the Arabic peoples boast possession of 22 states in the Middle East (23, counting an independent Palestinian entity), encompassing close to 5.5 million square miles[7] or 12 percent of the earth's surface. By comparison, this is 650 times the size of Israel.

Esau and Jacob: War in the Womb

The patriarchal tale continues with Isaac's pregnant wife, Rebekah, who finds herself enduring a veritable fetal feud, mopping her brow and puzzling before God: "Why is this happening to me?"

Again, as with Isaac and Ishmael, the war in her womb is a question of election. The Sovereign of the Universe replies, "Two nations are in your womb, and two peoples from within you will be separated; one people will be stronger than the other, and the older will serve the younger" (Genesis 25:23).

When the twins are born, the baby delivered first is named Esau (meaning "hairy"); the second is called Jacob ("heel-grabber"). Now the battle really begins.

In the course of time, Jacob is cooking stew one day when Esau comes home hungry from working outdoors. He prevails upon his brother, "Quick, let me have some of that red stew! I'm famished!" (This is why Esau is also called Edom, meaning "red.")

Jacob seizes the chance to cut a deal and says, "First sell me your birthright."

"Look, I am about to die," Esau mutters. "What good is the birthright to me?"

Jacob answers, "Swear to me first."

The biblical account concludes: "So he swore an oath to him, selling his birthright to Jacob. Then Jacob gave Esau some bread and some lentil stew. He ate and drank, and then got up and left. So *Esau despised his birthright*" (Genesis 25:33–34, emphasis added).

Might Esau have inherited the birthright if he had not despised it? Weaving human free will together with sovereign election, God is not unjust. Esau despises his birthright and thus the One who gave it to him. God says, therefore, "Jacob I loved, but Esau I hated."

Time goes on and Isaac prepares to die. Jacob deceives his father and disguises himself to steal, and this time seal, the birthright blessing. Isaac lays his hands on Jacob and by the Spirit pronounces a powerful prophetic word:

"May God give you of heaven's dew and of earth's richness. . . . May nations serve you and peoples bow down to you. Be lord over your brothers, and may the sons of your mother bow down to you. May those who curse you be cursed and those who bless you be blessed."

GENESIS 27:28–29

Jacob irrevocably inherits Abraham's covenant blessing and Esau is enraged. He implores Isaac to retract the blessing, but this his father cannot do:

> "I have made him [Jacob] lord over you and have made all his relatives [Esau's descendants] his servants. . . . So what can I possibly do for you, my son?"
>
> VERSE 37

Esau weeps at Isaac's feet—over his personal loss, not in godly sorrow—until Isaac prophesies over him, too. But the blessing sounds less than enviable:

> "Your dwelling will be away from the earth's richness, away from the dew of heaven above. You will live by the sword and you will serve your brother. But when you grow restless, you will throw his yoke from off your neck."
>
> VERSES 39–40

Esau is devastated, embittered and bent on revenge. The Scriptures tell us to learn from his example:

> See to it that no one misses the grace of God and that no bitter root grows up to cause trouble and defile many. See that no one . . . is godless like Esau, who for a single meal sold his inheritance rights as the oldest son. Afterward . . . [he] could bring about no change of mind, though he sought the blessing with tears.
>
> HEBREWS 12:15–17

Sons of Esau vs. Sons of Jacob: Womb War II

Jacob must flee Canaan to escape Esau's wrath. Yet in a dream in the desert of his escape, God visits him and sovereignly affirms his inheritance. Jacob's blessing, while obtained by trickery, would have been his anyway:

"I will give you and your descendants the land on which you are lying. Your descendants will be like the dust of the earth, and you will spread out to the west and to the east, to the north and to the south. All peoples on earth will be blessed through you and your offspring. I am with you and will watch over you wherever you go, *and I will bring you back to this land.*"

GENESIS 28:13–15, EMPHASIS ADDED

Many years later, in his struggle with the Angel of the Lord, Jacob is told by God that his name and identity will now be "Israel." At that time, when Jacob surrenders fully to God, He changes Esau's heart to one of love for his long-lost brother. By then, however, Esau has grown into a nation of his own, Edom.

The Bible recounts the Edomites' unceasing enmity against the children of Israel. When God delivers them out of Egypt, Esau's sons refuse them passage through their land (see Numbers 20:21). The Edomite ruler Amalek sets his face like flint against Israel; as a result, God swears He Himself will war against Amalek from generation to generation (see Exodus 17:14). Centuries later, there is reason to think it is a descendant of Amalek who threatens to annihilate the Jews of Persia—but is caught and killed in his own trap.[8] The royal Herods in the New Covenant are Edomites.[9] They continue to oppose the ways of God, especially as embodied in the person of Yeshua, the Perfection of Jacob. For their historically persistent, anti-Israel, anti-God hatred, the Edomites are warned repeatedly of impending judgment. Please read carefully, for the principles behind these words apply today to *us*:

"This is what the Sovereign LORD says: In my burning zeal I have spoken against the rest of the nations, and against all Edom, for with glee and with malice in their hearts they made my land [Israel] their own possession so that they might plunder its pastureland."

EZEKIEL 36:5

"For three sins of Edom, even for four, I will not turn back my wrath. Because he pursued his brother [Israel] with a sword, stifling all compassion, because his anger raged continually and his fury flamed unchecked, I will send fire. . . ."

AMOS 1:11–12

"Edom [will be] a desert waste, because of violence done to the people of Judah, in whose land they shed innocent blood."

JOEL 3:19

In a sense the war of the womb between Jacob and Esau has yet to end. With the inception of the modern Jewish State, their struggle has resumed with a vengeance, this time playing out on Israeli soil. How will the contest be resolved? Jacob will once more undergo a life-changing encounter with the Angel of the Lord. As the God-Man Messiah Jesus manifests Himself to Jacob in the night of his despair, he will emerge humbled and transformed. He will find that God has transformed Esau's repentant heart, too, and the estranged brothers will embrace in conciliatory love as never before. Someday Esau and Jacob will again fall on each other's necks, kiss and weep (see Genesis 33:4).

But a certain duel has complicated the contention, which we next address: Muhammad's Allah versus Yeshua's Yahweh.

CHAPTER TWELVE

Incursion of Islam

Deep in the Arabian desert fourteen hundred years ago, the mystically minded man Muhammad claimed an angel appeared to him. The angel, allegedly Gabriel, dictated revolutionary "truths" that purported to replace the Bible. Muhammad took his revelations to Jews and Christians, but to his dismay they spurned his newfound spirituality. Muhammad's own people, the Arabs, reacted differently. Scarred, perhaps, from millennia-old wounds of rejection, the collective Arab soul yearned to be soothed. Petrified pain may have predisposed them to the drastic—and tragic—deception of Islam.

A detailed study on Islam is beyond the scope of this book. Nonetheless, it is important to see how it has added theological fuel to the fire that burns against the Jewish nation. I share what insights I have gleaned through research and prayer, not to be critical but to provide important facts needed for strategic ministry. Jesus says the truth—not flattery—sets people free. Love rejoices in truth, and I want to see masses of beloved Muslims set free. God is looking for laborers with prophetic clarity to gather an abundant harvest of Arab as well as Jewish souls. Could you be one of them?

A Christian Root of Islam?

Those of us in the West can be quick to condemn the banality of Arab belief, while glossing glibly over the fact of the Church's historical failure to impact Islam. (Keep in mind, however, that not all Arabs are Muslims and most Muslims are not Arabs.) To help put Islam in perspective, recall that it originated and rose to the fore during the Dark Ages. This was a period shrouded in spiritual, and resultant political and cultural, darkness. The Church weakened, evangelism ebbed, the Gospel gained little ground. Christian civilization's bright light was snuffed out.

What gave rise to the Dark Ages? We have noted how, preceding this sordid era, Gentile Christian leaders renounced the Church's Old Covenant heritage, effectively severing its Jewish roots. Edicts were issued ousting Messianic Jews from the fellowship of the faithful. You may hear folks try to blame Israel for the spread of fundamental Islam. But if anyone carries responsibility in the matter, could it be the Church?

In *Foxe's Annals of Martyrs*, historian John Foxe attributes the rise of Islam to the infirm condition of the Church:

> Early in the seventh century a new enemy of Christianity arose. . . . The rapid success of this adventurer [Muhammad] must be classed among the mournful proofs furnished by that age of the decay into which practical Christianity had fallen. . . . It was, unquestionably, the abuses and infirmities of the Christian church that gave Muhammedanism room and leisure to mature its strength.[1]

Could some of these "abuses and infirmities" relate to anti-Semitism? Foxe parallels persecution *by* the Church with persecution *of* the Church:

> We fight against a persecutor, being no less persecutors ourselves. We wrestle against a bloody tyrant, and our hands be as full of blood as his.[2]

Interestingly, after centuries of torment and bloodshed at the hands of the Church, the spread of Islam actually afforded the Jews some reprieve:

> Most Jewish historians . . . are convinced that the Byzantine Church would have attempted to eradicate Judaism totally if the Church itself had not been defeated and its plan for hegemony . . . thwarted by the rising tide of Islam . . . that allowed the Jews to slip between the cracks Islam made in Byzantine Church persecution.[3]

Does Muhammad echo Church fathers who decreed the replacement of Israel? The Quran literally claims to supersede the Bible. It alleges the Jews did not write the Scriptures accurately, but intentionally distorted God's Word to suit their own needs. The Muslim "holy" book purports to correct the Bible, teaching (among other things) that Ishmael is Abraham's rightful covenant heir, not Isaac, and that Jesus is just an unresurrected prophet, not God's Son.[4] Because Jew and Christian alike proved unfaithful to God, He summarily replaced them both with the Muslim.

If the Christian Church lapsed into replacement theology—despite God's gracious warnings—then Islam adopted "replacement-replacement theology" with a vengeance. And so the question must be asked: Could the Body of Christ have opened the door to the devil, so to speak, by ignoring the exhortation of the Scriptures and the Spirit not to be arrogant or ignorant, not to regard Israel as the replaced people of God? Is it possible the Church has reaped for itself the same treatment by Islam that it meted out to the Jews? As we face the Islamic foe afresh in the twenty-first century, it is *critical* that we purge ourselves of any vestige of "theological" anti-Semitism. If we curse Israel, we may expect to be cursed.

Who Is Allah and What Does He Want?

Some claim that because Muslims are monotheists and there is only one true God, *de facto*, it must be He whom they worship. But

Muhammad's Allah does not refer to the Creator of the universe.[5] The nature and attributes of the two differ dramatically. Yahweh is kind; He offers the sacrifice of His own Son, moved by love. Allah is cruel; he demands the sacrifice of Muslim sons, driven by hate. He denies that Jesus is Messiah, showing himself, according to the Bible, to be a liar and spirit of antichrist (see 1 John 2:22–23). Although Arab Christians use the name *Allah* to mean God, to say this proves the Muslim god is the same as Yahweh is to build a superficial case on semantics. Allah's followers simply usurp the only word for *God* in Arabic, claiming he is creator of all.

Allah's identity likely derives from nature folk gods worshiped in the Saudi Arabian peninsula in Muhammad's day.[6] There is evidence suggesting the name was once that of a high-ranking lunar deity; hence the crescent moon symbol of Islam.[7] In any event, the historical underpinnings of the Muslim faith are replete with pagan ritual practices that most Christians would readily acknowledge as demonic. These very real spiritual forces still animate Islam today, entrenching their cruel claws in regions well beyond the shifting sands of the Middle East.

Islam according to the Quran, or fundamental Islam, teaches the Muslim's highest duty is jihad (holy war) and his reward, martyrdom. Simply put, Allah requires submission to him through jihad—willingly, forcibly or by the torturous killing of all those refusing to worship him. Hence Muhammad instigated jihad against Christians from Africa to India and China, and into Spain. Under his orders, Muslim warriors savagely slaughtered masses of believers, overrunning churches and converting them to mosques.[8]

Jihad is not an option; it is a compelling sacrament. For many Muslim Arabs, jihad builds on tribal traditions of warfare going back to biblical times. Fundamental Islam has never relinquished the mandate to conquer the *whole world* and compel its submission to totalitarian governmental religious rule. Tashbih Sayyed is a moderate Muslim and internationally recognized expert on militant Islam. He explains the covert nature of Islam in America, the most powerful non-Muslim nation in the world, as an example:

Most Islamic centers and mosques in the United States are controlled by militant Islamists committed to destroying . . . an America that is not controlled by a militant version of Islam. They are creating fear in Muslims who live in America by teaching that America is controlled by Jews and Zionists . . . determined to destroy them. . . . The lives of Muslims living in America are not governed by the Constitution of America . . . their lives are governed by a fascist Islamist [religious community] that has created itself within the most democratic country in the world.[9]

Moderate Muslims such as Sayyed interpret the Quran more liberally, just as liberal Christians interpret the Bible less strictly. I believe many of them are upright citizens of good will. But as Sayyed attests, the moderates hold little sway in the larger Islamic world. The agenda of radical Islam includes overtaking and forcing them to conform to fundamentalist tenets of the faith as well.

The fastest growing faith in the Western world at this writing, Islam claims a fifth of the world's population.[10] At the same time, many disillusioned Muslims would welcome the opportunity to throw off the Islamic veil. Friends of mine who have ministered in Iraq, Iran and Jordan since Operation Iraqi Freedom attest to much hunger for the Gospel in those lands. God wants us weeping for, and learning how to humbly mediate truth to, Arab and non-Arab Muslims.

The battle for their souls is great.

Ancient Spiritual Strongholds and Terror Today

Islam's tool of terror is not new; it originated fourteen hundred years ago.[11] Muhammad taught his followers that Allah hates those who will not accept his message when they hear it — especially Christians and Jews; therefore, they must not only be savagely punished, they must be *terrified*. Add to this dictate of death the notion that Allah's adherents who fall in battle gain instant entry to a blissful paradise where unending, unimaginable sexual pleasures await them. The result is a seductive toxin of suicidal terror.

The spirit of terror does not operate in isolation. Forces entrenched in the Middle East many thousands of years ago feed into the network of fanatical Islam. This region of the world has been home to some of earth's most "ancient of days." From Satan's attack through the serpent in Eden and the first human murder by Cain nearby, God's spiritual enemies have long staked claim with humankind in this part of the world. That these unclean spirits are rising to the fore in our day with renewed vengeance signals their time is running out; God's Kingdom is advancing and Jesus is returning.

In the book of Daniel we read about the archangel Michael who ministers to the people of Israel. Michael wrestles against the "prince of the Persian kingdom" (Daniel 10:13), a spirit of high-ranking territorial authority set tenaciously against Yahweh. This demonic entity fights against the angel who delivers a message to Daniel about the last days. (Obviously the prince of Persia does not want this information, a perfect and helpful outline of things to come, made available to God's people.)

The biblical land of Persia is the nation of Iran today. Not coincidentally, Persia became the birthplace of revived fundamental Islam in 1979 when Iran's Ayatollah Khomeini formally announced the resumption of Allah's rule. His seemingly delusional declaration carried spiritual authority and power to stoke centuries' old smoldering flames. Soon afterward, covert terror training centers were set up and perfidious propaganda campaigns launched throughout Iran. The country quickly converted into a police state run on ghoulish cruelty. Terror metastasized like a cancer from Iran throughout the Middle East—and beyond. Through ferocious groups like the Iranian *Hizballah* ("Party of God") and Palestinian *Hamas* (*zeal* in Arabic and an acronym for the Islamic Resistance Movement), the prince of Persia spews its venom far and wide.

Other neighboring, dark spiritual vandals haunt the terror-ridden deserts of the Middle East today, such as a spirit of death called Molech. In the Scriptures, Molech foments murder. Thousands of years ago, bewitched parents tossed their young offspring into raging fires in order to appease Molech. In the twenty-first century, Muslim moms and dads proudly dispatch their sons and daughters, strapped to explosives, off on suicide bombing missions. In one form or another, Molech still mulls about, viciously deceiving and destroying human beings created in the image of God who loves and grieves for them.

Why do I take time to talk about these ancient principalities? I believe they still affect the Arabic peoples—and Israel and you and me. Yet, as believers, we have been given authority to war against spiritual strongholds in the power of the Holy Spirit. I want to see Yeshua's army of love raising Him up as the standard, mobilized in prayer and evangelism. I want us to revel in the spoils of war: saved ex-Muslim souls.

Iraq: A Power Portal

Resurrected strongholds of idolatry and destruction reverberate today from Iraq, formerly home to Ur of the Chaldees, Assyria and Babylon. Each of these empires worshiped a powerful lunar god that, again, may be reflected in Islam's crescent moon. Each empire was exceedingly destructive in nature, and Iraq's history has been the most violent in the whole Middle East.

Babylon (meaning, according to folk etymology, "Gateway of the Gods") was grisly ground to a host of anti-God rites and rituals. Numerous portals of spiritual passage were erected in this ancient city, including the Tower of Babel. Though this notorious effort to ascend to heaven was crushed, the Babylonians long indulged in pagan practices wherein they communed and connected with the supernatural. When Saddam Hussein rose to power as a self-declared reincarnate of Babylon's megalomaniacal King Nebuchadnezzar, he drew openly on its spiritual past. At his direction, the city's ruins were excavated and restored—along with the demonic hosts associated with them.

The Scriptures say God Himself (not a military coalition) judges Babylon and its array of demonic gods (see Jeremiah 50:9–10, 18, 24– 25, 31; 51:1–2, 11–12, 40, 53, 55). He is the One who stirs up nations to devastate her—ultimately for her violence against Israel (see Jeremiah 50:11–12, 17–19; 51:24, 35–36, 49). Saddam Hussein was a prime financial as well as ideological sponsor of terror operations against Israel. Yet statues of the defunct leader toppled to the ground in 2003, reminiscent of God's Word to "repay Babylon . . . for all the wrong they have done in Zion" (Jeremiah 51:24). An Arab Christian friend of mine ministered in Iraq a few weeks after U.S.-led coalition troops freed Baghdad. He brought me back an interesting gift, which I consider a token of Yahweh's ultimate victory over Babylon—old Iraqi paper money. On one side of the now worthless bill appears a portrait of Saddam; on the other side, a picture of the Temple Mount. The enemy's intentions could hardly be more clearly expressed.

The Scriptures are replete with prophecies against Babylon, most of which have not yet come to pass. For this reason, I suspect the city may be literally rebuilt and restored—for a last days' judgment of God. According to the prophetic Scriptures, Babylon will pollute the whole world with a system of wickedness. It seems God will allow human depravity to go full circle around the earth before executing His final global judgment.

In the meantime, now is the time to pray and labor that God will use the portal nation of Iraq to invade the world of Islam with the grace of the Gospel. He desires Iraq's military assault in the natural realm to make way for an even greater invasion in the supernatural realm. The Savior wants to spare multitudes of Iraqis, who in turn will penetrate into unreached neighboring nations. It is not likely to prove clean and easy; persecution probably awaits many future Arab saints—and we must prepare to support them steadfastly.

"Satans" Little and Great

As long as Islam rages in the Middle East, its prime target of terror will be Israel. This is because at its core, the evil of terrorism has nothing to do with the smokescreen of a Palestinian state and everything to do with eradicating a Jewish state. Though Palestine was never historically an independent Arab domain, it did fall under Muslim rule for many hundreds of years. According to the Quran, any land that once was Islamic must be recouped for it is holy ground; otherwise, Allah's name is besmirched and his wrath aroused. Israel must, in the Islamic mind, be resubjugated to Allah's rule. Of one thing we can be sure: In and of itself, creating Palestine will not create peace.

In an otherwise wholly Islamic region, Israel is regarded as an unwelcome imposition, even if she is only 1/650 the size of that region. It is Israel's alliance with the West that further galvanizes Muslim rage against a Jewish locale in their otherwise pan-Arab empire. Israel (called "Little Satan") represents an insulting imperial outpost of Western Christian civilization, particularly the United States ("Great Satan"). Israel would be despised merely because she is America's friend, entirely apart from Abraham's family feud. *And the Islamic world would despise America even if we did not stand with Israel.*

What's worse — because there is some truth in it — is that jihad-driven Muslims are bent on America's destruction partly because of our cultural values. They see the United States as the world's principle purveyor of public sewage. Through our visual, printed and electronic media, and our goods peddled abroad, they see moral licentiousness, sexual immorality, self-indulgent wealth and prideful hypocrisy as the chief export of our Judeo-Christian culture. (Could God use even the accusatory finger of Islam to convict us?)

Jihad against Jehovah

In the aftermath of 9/11/01, people in the Western world scrambled to get their hands on whatever they could find about Islam. "Why do they hate us?" one schoolchild asked, and the media echoed his question for months. If we look long and hard into the heart of terror, we discover it really stems from jihad against Jehovah.

Fundamentalist Muslims animated by the evil of jihad are our enemies because they posture themselves as *God's* enemies. They hate us because they hate Yahweh. In its origins and teaching the Quran is so decidedly anti-Christian that I am convinced we are squaring off with the spirit of antichrist. The spirit of antichrist is inextricably related to the spirit of anti-Semitism; one is the flipside of the other. Regardless of what more moderate and sincere Muslims say or think, this spirit entity—Allah—is "anti-the one true God." It is, therefore, inherently and virulently "anti-the Jews" and "anti-the Christians."

Throughout the Muslim world, generations have been raised on barbarously anti-Semitic literature, including viperous Nazi materials, that have long been mainstays in their schools, stores, mass media and political institutions.[12] Whole populations have been indoctrinated since early childhood with draconian lies about the Jews—lies that inflame jihad against Jehovah. Sadly, it continues as of this writing.

Muslims are well aware that true Christians are Israel's staunchest supporters. They seek, therefore, to drive a surreptitious wedge between the Church and the Jews, using media outlets, sermons, seminars and even "Christian" tours to the Holy Land. But the Palestinian presentation is largely unverified—and unverifiable—by the facts of history. Biblical perspectives are offered that amount to updated versions of replacement theology (the "new Christian anti-Semitism"). The well-oiled Islamic propaganda/media machine is an insidious weapon of mass destruction aimed continually at Israel. From it we can expect mostly lies—cunningly devised at the behest of the father of lies.

Inflamed by Islam, issues about Israel will become increasingly complex. The last days' Church will divide more and more over the matter of the Jewish nation. Many believers will fall prey to anti-Semitic (and anti-Christian, however well concealed) propaganda, but many will not. Even "enlightened" democratic countries will align against God's chosen people. Eventually, the Bible says, no nation will stand with them (Zechariah 12:3; 14:2)—only the Body of Christ from among all nations.

Despite everything, Yahweh has the whole matter in hand, and a glorious future ahead.

To God Be the Glory

The coming days and years will be gory—but also bring glory—such as the world has never known. The apostle Paul wraps up for us his revelation of God's plans for Israel with a resplendent doxology—one that can help steer us through difficult and perplexing times. Paul explains that Israel's calling, her election and even her troubles culminate in this: God's wondrous glory! Israel is ultimately all about *Him.* Yahweh has opened the heavens; He has made salvation and blessing available to all, despite humanity's sin. The Spirit catapults the apostle—and us—into sweeping adoration of the Almighty. None but He could mastermind this dazzling display of redemption, this triumph of grace:

> God has bound all men over to disobedience so that he may have mercy on them all. Oh, the depth of the riches of the wisdom and knowledge of God! How unsearchable his judgments, and his paths beyond tracing out! . . . To him be the glory forever! Amen.
>
> ROMANS 11:32–36

Our spirits soar as we peer into the telescopic lens of the ways of the Infinite. We see that before the Creator we stand condemned, Jew and non-Jew alike. All are doomed apart from His intervention—but intervene He does. He sends His Son to this otherwise pathetic planet to redeem, rule and reign over it. God's mercy unveils to the hosts of the universe His sovereign splendor, forever. The picture is bigger than Israel or her conflict with Islam; it is bigger than the Church; the picture is about God. The Jewish people and their story or, more importantly, their role in His story are all about *Him.*

How important then, as we shall see next, to get the story straight.

PART 6

Unraveling the Arab/ Palestinian-Israeli Conflict

Do not conform any longer to the pattern of this world, but be transformed by the renewing of your mind. Then you will be able to test and approve what God's will is—his good, pleasing, and perfect will.

ROMANS 12:2

CHAPTER THIRTEEN

Discerning Truth in Perplexing Times

Afeter his jubilant doxology of supreme praise, the apostle Paul wraps up for us his impassioned revelation on God's heart and mind for Israel in Romans chapters 9 through 11. He has told us of God's inseparable, unconditional love for the Jewish people, their irrevocable calling and election, and His plan for their salvation. We know of the reciprocal relationship of blessing between Gentiles and Jews as one in Messiah. Now, when all is said and done, Paul leaves us with a compelling exhortation: We must not conform our thinking to the world's; we must be transformed by the renewing of our minds in order to discern God's will. The exhortation is found today in Romans 12:2. But originally, as you recall, there were no chapter breaks between the end of Romans 11 and the start of Romans 12. So Paul's instruction by the Holy Spirit is intimately related to Israel.

The connection could scarcely prove more fitting today. You and I are inundated with information about Israel practically daily through the news media. This mounting morass of Mideast intrigue can seem overwhelming. We need to discern the facts, but how truthful, accurate, reliable or even sensible is this barrage of data?

Because tomes have been compiled on the conflict in the Middle East, I shall try to simplify the situation for you. As much as the scope of this book allows,[1] I endeavor to separate fact from fiction. I want you empowered with truth on the issue of Israel—and the larger picture of what God is doing on earth through the Jewish nation. Because whether in war or peace, it's ultimately all about *Him*.

Mind Transformation: The Media

Back in 1982, I visited two different Palestinian refugee camps in the West Bank. From all the news reports, I braced myself for the worst: row upon row of flimsily strung tents surrounded by piles of filth, barefooted women warming measly meals over open fires, angry men cursing and spitting, and crying children with runny noses and distended bellies. What I observed was quite different.

The camps were actually neighborhoods of cinder block and concrete homes, poorly equipped by Western—but not Middle Eastern—standards. The streets were calm. Women strolled about, groceries and other goods balanced on their shoulders. The few men I saw sat and sipped coffee together in the shade of their doorways. Most of the children were in school. Young Israeli soldiers leaned lazily at their posts, puffing cigarettes. Now and then a dog barked, a goat bleated.

I was more than a bit befuddled. The scene, while far less than idyllic, hardly reflected the abject squalor conjured up by newspapers and TV. Admittedly, I had viewed only two of many camps, and neither would ever qualify for anyone's list of residential best picks. Still, the refugees' condition (thankfully) looked nothing like the deplorable imprisonment I had expected.[2]

Two decades later, at this writing, I find that media distortions have only worsened. In 2002, I was in Israel during the infamous Passover massacre at a Netanya hotel, where Palestinian terrorists murdered unsuspecting Jews celebrating the feast. Days later, to curtail the unrelenting slaughter—*not* to retaliate in revenge—the Israeli army advanced its troops into a portion of the Jenin refugee camp. The purpose of the incursion was to weed out and dismantle Jenin's *known* thicket of terror. Each day I watched the newscasts on Israeli TV, read the reports and talked with the locals, including army reservists. Clearly this operation, called Defensive Shield, was war on terror. Just as clearly the war had been started by terrorists and, regrettably, but like any other war, it would not end without tragic suffering.

Defensive Shield was a military operation of limited proportions, and as its name implied, defensive in nature. Soldiers serving in Jenin informed us that Israel undertook extreme measures to curtail casualties in the very difficult setting of house-to-house combat. So, like the Israelis, I was bewildered at charges of wide-scale, holocaust-like genocidal atrocities that echoed via satellite across the globe and landed in the chambers of the United Nations. How did such a distortion, indeed serpentine tale, hatch?

Case in Point: Jenin

The Palestinian Authority (PA) Minister of Local Government, I later learned, had given this summation to reporters: "The Jenin refugee camp is no longer in existence"; it was "totally destroyed."[3] Other PA officials decried to whoever would listen the cold-blooded "massacre" of five hundred innocents. Their bodies, the Palestinians insisted, had been buried under the rubble by Israeli bulldozers.[4] Soon the world was outraged; the UN launched an investigation.

The international media-at-large did not investigate the facts before releasing the story. The London news reported, "We are talking here of massacre, and a cover-up, of genocide" that was "every bit as repellent" as Osama bin Laden's in New York in September 2001.[5] Even Christians felt something had to be done to control the "cruel, power-mongering Zionists."

What was the truth? In sharp contrast to Palestinian allegations, not much publicity was given to the UN's investigation results: *No* evidence of *any* massacre in Jenin.[6] Instead of the refugee camp being "totally destroyed," the only dismantled area was the terror nest itself—which amounted to 10 percent of the camp. Ninety percent of Jenin had been left virtually intact. And as for the ominous death toll of 500, in the end it was found that 52 Palestinians were killed, over half of whom were terrorists.[7] Palestinian News Agency reports about "mass graves" being heaped under rubble and bulldozed to conceal the "Zionist massacre,"[8] were never substantiated. Months later, Israel unearthed Palestinian source documents confirming the trumped-up nature of the charge.[9]

In fact, much of the property damage and death toll in Jenin had been intentionally caused by the Palestinians themselves. They had planted bombs and booby-traps inside homes, buildings[10] and even ambulances to maximize bloodshed, *which could then be blamed on Israel.* In reality, the Israelis had taken extraordinary precautionary measures at great risk to themselves, tediously searching whole neighborhoods house by house (since terrorists operate from homes) in order to avoid unnecessary civilian deaths.

Captured Jenin-based terrorist Thabet Mardawi told CNN that he and other Palestinian fighters had expected Israel to attack with planes and tanks. They were elated when instead the Israelis took care to minimize casualties to noncombatants:

> I couldn't believe it when I saw the soldiers. The Israelis knew that any soldier who went into the camp like that was going to get killed. Shooting at these men as they walked cautiously down the street was like hunting . . . like being given a prize. . . . I'd been waiting for a moment like that for years.[11]

While the UN exonerated Israel of the massacre charge, by the time it released its report few folks were listening. Freshly concocted accusations against the Zionists were capturing media attention instead. In any case, the damage to Israel's reputation had been done. More and more people, including Christians, began to wonder whether the whole world could be wrong about the suspect Jewish State. And, thus, the cycle continues, the well-oiled machine of terror sputtering lies, which, repeated often enough, eventually sound true.

God's Word says to be transformed by the renewing of our minds in order to know and do His will. This requires knowledge of truth—but when it comes to Israel, the one Jesus calls "the father of lies" is traditionally hard at work.

Timeless Weapons of Deceit

"What has been done will be done again; there is nothing new under the sun" (Ecclesiastes 1:9). The biblical truism applies only too well to Israel and her enemies today—as it did yesterday. How has Satan manipulated world weapons of deceit against the Jews? The answer is key to knowing how *not* to fall prey to "the pattern of this world."

In the book of Esther, an egomaniacal Persian official named Haman demands one day that everyone in the palace bow down and worship him. But Mordecai the God-worshiping Jew refuses. At this Haman is outraged. To retaliate he plots the annihilation of all Jews throughout the empire. Haman bases his scheme on a *lie that he reports* to the governing authority.

> "There is a certain people . . . who do not obey the king's laws; it is not in the king's best interest to tolerate them. If it pleases the king, let a decree be issued to destroy them."
>
> ESTHER 3:8–9

For good measure, Haman tosses in the temptation of mammon: "I will put ten thousand talents of silver into the royal treasury for the men who carry out this business" (verse 9). The duped king concedes to Haman's request. The sinister plan is undeserving; there is no mention of sin on the Jews' part, no reference to their rousing God's wrath. On the contrary, it is their dedicated worship of Yahweh that stirs satanic angst and ire. The worship of the one true God inflames His enemies who, through Haman, plan to take it out on His people. While the plan providentially backfires and Haman himself is hanged, the spirit of Haman lives on. The anti-God, anti-Semitic evil forces that once propelled Haman to action still spin lies, weaving webs fueled by propaganda and petrodollars (today's mammon), intent on destroying that same "certain people."

Consider now the book of Ezra. After a lengthy exile in Babylon, the Jewish people have returned to the Promised Land. They plan to rebuild their country and their Temple, and at first things go well. But as soon as the foundation of the Temple—Yahweh's house of homage—is laid, the opposition begins (see Ezra 4:1ff). Again the prospect of worshiping the God of Israel enrages His enemies. When initial efforts to thwart the rebuilding fail, the opposition appeals to the international arena. Once more, cunning deceit mixes with mammon in a complaint registered with the king:

> To King Artaxerxes, from your servants, the men of Trans-Euphrates:
>
> The king should know that the Jews . . . are rebuilding that rebel-lious and wicked city. . . . Furthermore, the king should know that if this city is built and its walls are restored, no more taxes, tribute or duty will be paid, and the royal revenues will suffer. Now since we are under obligation to the palace and it is not proper for us to see the king dishonored, we are sending this message. . . . We inform the king that if this city is built and its walls are restored, you will be left with nothing in Trans-Euphrates.
>
> EZRA 4:11–16

The threat is thoroughly fabricated. But the propaganda cam-paign succeeds, at least temporarily, and the king orders the re-building to stop.

Fast forward with me to the Nazi Holocaust, where lie upon lie built the basis for the most brutal genocidal campaign the world has known. At the beginning of his rise to power, Adolf Hitler publicly noted that people fall victim more easily to a big lie, repeated often, than a little one.[12] Accordingly, he instituted a widespread propaganda campaign—built on lies most of us would regard as outrageous—to set the stage for his future

Jew-free regime. I have listed some of these "Big Lies" below. You may wonder how any thinking person could have believed them. Let me assure you that even today, millions still do. At this writing, each of these preposterous myths still circulates widely in stores, media outlets, government institutions and, perhaps worst of all, in schools throughout the Palestinian and larger Islamic world:[13]

- Jews regularly murder non-Jews to use their blood in religious ceremonies, especially when baking matzah for Passover.[14]
- Jews are a biologically inferior people — part pig or ape — with evil genes that will destroy the human race if they are not destroyed first.
- Jews harbor a pernicious plot to subvert and take over the world, as revealed in their book *The Protocols of the Elders of Zion*. (This egregiously anti-Semitic book, purportedly written by world Zionist leaders, was proved in court to have been forged by the Russian army over a century ago.[15] But the book remains a *best-seller* in the Arab world and was presented at the UN in 2003 by an Egyptian diplomat as "historic truth.")[16]
- Jews caused the Black Plague that decimated Europe in the 1300s,[17] and Jews will cause other life-threatening diseases if they are not killed first.
- Jews are Satan's agents on earth. That is why they "killed Christ."
- Jews control the world's economy and are at fault for every nation's money problems.
- Jews control the media, feeding the world false information to dispute all of the above.

Summarized Josef Goebbels, former Nazi Minister of Propaganda:

All Jews, by virtue of their birth and race, are part of an international conspiracy against us. . . . They started this war [World War II]. . . . The treatment they receive from us is hardly unjust. They have deserved it all.[18]

Do we laugh or cry at this nonsense?

There is nothing new under the sun; what has been done to curse God's people through deceit, false reports and mammon is being done again. Israel's enemies continue to lash at her with the weapon of the twisted tongue; the father of lies still churns them out. How we need to remember the scriptural warnings against ignorance about the Jewish people (see Romans 11:25)! May we be transformed by the renewing of our minds with truth, that we may live according to God's will.

Inventing "News"

I am not suggesting, of course, that Israel is always blameless in battle or sin-free in society. I admit sadly that the opposite is true, as I think most Israelis would. The fact that she is God's chosen people does not give her *carte blanche* to get away with murder. But it does give *us* the responsibility to undergird her in loving prayer and rightly discern truth. To that end, there are more facts you deserve to know.

Israel in the twenty-first century has found herself having to fight a war on two separate fronts: one via the military; the other via the media. Said one European reporter in 2003: "As a journalist I must mention the significant contributions of the mass media to the new antisemitism . . . [that] have given the Israeli-Palestinian conflict some of the most biased coverage in the history of journalism."[19]

Firsthand accounts of what is happening on Palestinian ground are rarely reliable. Palestinian officials hold tight rein over the media, carefully scrutinizing, censoring and even inventing the news. Foreign journalists are not given entry into the PA at all unless their stories pass muster with the government. Once they report news unfavorable to the Palestinian cause, they will not be back.[20] Lives have been threatened[21] and uncooperative foreign reporters so badly beaten as to require hospitalization.[22] Freedom of the press does not exist with Palestinian authorities (or Muslim nations generally). The Independent Committee for Protection of Journalists complains about PA censorship: "Multi-layered security apparatus have muzzled local press critics via arbitrary arrests, threats, physical abuse, and the closure of media outlets . . . to frighten most Palestinian journalists into self-censorship."[23]

The vast majority of Palestinian TV news coverage today is filmed by PA-hired camera operators on whom foreign news agencies have become dependent. Several investigations have revealed that these photographers actually stage "news" events to shoot. In addition, they regularly edit footage of actual events to recast their conflict with Israel in a self-promoting light.[24] These doctored scenes, beamed globally across television stations, web sites and news periodicals, all aim to plant one picture in our minds: the Goliath-like Israeli pitted against brave little David. Thus we view photos of hapless and heartbroken Arab women standing amid rubble that used to be called home; what we are not told is that home served as a terrorist hideout or small munitions plant. A picture can be worth a thousand words, we say. But it is not always *truly* so.

Much of the Western world watched TV with sardonic amusement during Operation Iraqi Freedom in 2003, as Iraq's former minister of information stoutly denied the existence of war in his country. We viewed bombs exploding over Baghdad in the background as he reported: "There are no American troops here." The minister's daily briefings gave us a glimpse of the propaganda war Israel has been up against.

What, then, is the truth about the Arabs' conflict with Israel, and especially the Palestinian plight? How does it fit into the larger picture of what God is doing in this century? To answer those questions and transform our minds according to truth, we must first grasp some compelling historical context.

Historical Context

Historical but little-known facts on the Arab/Palestinian-Israeli conflict could easily fill a book. Time and space allow for me only to summarize them. But I think you will discover that a shocking new grid on the conflict emerges when you consider the neglected, yet well-documented, context from which it arose. You will see that Israel is not so much in a fight for land, but for *life*—and that changes everything.

Up until World War I, the entire Middle East was ruled for centuries by the Turkish Ottoman Empire. No self-governing Arab state was ever on the map; there were merely Arab tribes living under Ottoman rule. The vast majority of them wandered in search of subsistence all over the Middle East.[25]

At the same time, approximately 800,000 Jews also lived in the region, also under Ottoman rule. (A small but continuous, historical Jewish presence has always been maintained in the Holy Land, even after their formal exile.) About 50,000 Jews lived on legally purchased or inherited real estate that would eventually become Israel.

The Ottoman Turks aligned with Germany and lost World War I. As a result the Allies dismantled the Ottoman Empire, creating for the first time in history the countries of Syria, Lebanon, Iran and Iraq for the Arabs, and setting aside Israel (known then as Palestine) for the Jews.

Here we must digress momentarily. An explanation of the term *Palestine* is in order, because the Palestinian people use the name to claim an ancestral tie to Israeli land. The historical fact is that Israel was renamed Palestine by the Romans who invaded and razed it shortly after the time of Christ. The Romans intentionally chose the name as an affront to the Jews in mocking remembrance of their ancient—and extinct—enemy, the Philistine.

The Palestinians of today are not descended from the Philistines of the Bible[26] and never lived as a sovereignly ruled nation. Until the inception of modern Israel, they dwelt as scattered nomadic family tribes, alongside Jewish neighbors, on lands whose boundaries were not drawn into states until after World War I. During the centuries Jews and Arabs sometimes coexisted peaceably, but violence and terror often erupted at the call of Muslim leaders driven by jihad and/or pure hate.[27]

In 1920, the League of Nations (predecessor to the UN) handed Great Britain a Mandate to secure the establishment of a Jewish home in Palestine. The territory reserved for the Jews encompassed not only all of present-day Israel, *but also all of what is today known as Jordan.* The Mandate was scarcely issued when Arab rioting began in order to protest the future existence of a Jewish State. In sneak terror attacks, Arabs fought day and night to destroy nearby Jewish communities, albeit with the sword instead of the bomb. Terror was not conceived by frustrations of life in refugee camps; that tactic is at least as old as Islam.

Ironically, the vast majority of the Arabs decrying the creation of Israel had immigrated to Palestine from surrounding areas only *after* the Zionist pioneers began to reclaim the land in the early twentieth century. With the Jews came new job opportunities and improved medical care, both of which attracted their tribal neighbors.[28] Some of the immigrant Arabs erected makeshift villages. Later, countless others poured in from neighboring countries — not to carry on normal lives, but to undermine establishing the Zionist State.[29]

Wielding terror and oil as tools of intimidation, the Arabs per-suaded Britain in 1922 to grant them a full 78 percent of the land allotted to the Jews. In this futile attempt to appease the Arabs, Britain took most of the land set aside by the international com-munity for the Jewish State, and with it unilaterally created a Pal-estinian Arab state called Transjordan. Transjordan would later be renamed Jordan. But appeasement did not work — which we would do well to remember. The acts we engage in for appeasement today, Britain's Winston Churchill later said, we will have to remedy at far greater cost and remorse tomorrow.[30]

Predictably, Arab rioting and terror persisted until Britain finally turned the political foray over to the newly created UN. Continuing the policy of Arab appeasement, the UN sliced off another sizeable chunk of Israeli soil. It partitioned the remaining 22 percent of the original Mandate for a Jewish homeland into two states: one Jewish and one Palestinian Arab. This Partition Plan of 1947 recognized the Jews' right to sovereign control over a sliver of space amounting to a mere *10 percent of the world community's original Mandate.* The same plan offered the Arabs who lived within Mandate territory another Palestinian state in addition to Jordan, consisting of Judea, Samaria and Gaza. The Jews accepted the plan; the Arabs rejected it. This time, however, the motive was clear; they wanted it *all*—a pan-Arab Islamic empire spanning the entire Middle East, leaving no place on earth for a Jewish nation.

The world wondered, How will Israel survive?

Rebirth of Israel

Try to picture the scene: On the prophetic watershed date, May 14, 1948, and pursuant to the UN Partition Plan, Jews in Israel prepare at last to declare their state. The air is electric. After two thousand years of exile, the sons and daughters of Jacob have come home, and high-pitched excitement circles the globe.

That morning, Israel's founder and first prime minister, David Ben-Gurion, pores over maps showing the array of Arab armies and fragile Jewish defense forces poised for battle. The Jews are outnumbered one hundred to one.[31] "I feel like a mourner at a wedding," he writes in his diary.[32]

In a few hours Ben-Gurion will deliver Israel's Declaration of Independence. He scribbles down notes for his speech on the only writing material at hand—sheets of rough toilet paper.[33]

At exactly 4:00 P.M., he steps to the podium in an overcrowded hall in Tel Aviv before a hushed group of Zionist leaders. This is the moment for which millions of Jews have lived and died. Ben-Gurion begins reading the Declaration, recounting biblical Jewish history. Then, with prophetic clarity he decrees:

> By virtue of the natural and historic right of the Jewish people . . . we hereby proclaim the establishment of the Jewish state in Palestine, to be called the State of Israel . . . for the fulfillment of the dream of generations—the redemption of Israel.

At once, cheers and tears resound. Golda Meir, one of the statespeople present, loses control and cannot stop crying. Her sobs, she says, are for the many who should have been there, but are no more.[34]

The nation's chief rabbi pronounces, "The dawn of redemption has broken."

Euphoria erupts in Jerusalem and Tel Aviv, where traffic stops as streets swell with dancing and singing. But the party is soon interrupted. Sirens wail to warn of Egyptian bombers overhead. The Egyptians are quickly joined by the armies of Syria, Jordan, Lebanon and Iraq, as well as irregulars from other Arab nations. All have a common goal: to annihilate the Jewish State in Allah's name. The War of Independence has begun.

Happy birthday, Israel.

Refugees: Fact vs. Fiction

The survival of the Jewish nation proved nothing short of miraculous.

Aided by the armies of heaven, Israel defended her borders and held her ground. But by the time a cease-fire went into effect, those areas the UN had allocated for a separate Arab Palestinian state were illegally annexed and occupied—*not* by Israel, but by Jordan and Egypt. Now, the Arabs' publicly stated goal in the war had been to liberate Palestine. But neither Jordan nor Egypt ever gave the territories (Judea, Samaria and Gaza) they "liberated" back to the Palestinians. Why not? The reason is that the pan-Arab plan, had they won the war, was to divide up Israel among themselves, leaving nothing for sovereign Palestinian, let alone Jewish, rule. Palestinians in Israel were not regarded as a people group in need of their own country.[35]

As is often the case with war, the aftermath of Israel's fight for independence (a war she did not start) left large numbers of refugees in the Middle East. It is a well-documented fact that more Jewish refugees left Arab countries (approximately 800,000) than Arab refugees left Israel. But unlike the "volunteer" Arab refugees (see chapter 14), the Jews were forcibly expelled by Arab governments empty-handed. These oil-wealthy nations have stoutly refused to compensate them for their homes and properties left behind, valued today at billions of dollars.[36] Israel, meanwhile, has in effect compensated Palestinian refugees many times over via funds poured into the camps and PA.

In the meantime, no Arab country other than Jordan has been willing to grant citizenship to their Palestinian kin, though many sought and even begged for it. Why not? Liberation of the Palestinians has never been the goal as much as liquidation—of Israel. The Arabs reasoned that if they literally held "their" ground—in proxy through the Palestinians—they would have a better chance of eventually overtaking the Jewish State. Thus the Palestinians became hapless pawns of their own people.

Former Israeli Prime Minister Benjamin Netanyahu summed up the situation well:

> The consistent refusal of Arab leaders to solve this [refugee] problem is particularly tragic because it would have been so easy to do. After all, since World War II there have been well over fifty million refugees from *many* countries, and almost all have been successfully resettled. . . . That the fifty million Arabs in 1948 could not absorb 650,000 Arab refugees—and have not finished the job even after half a century, and even after the fantastic multiplication of their oil wealth—is an indication of [how] the Arabs have manipulated the refugee issue to create reasons for world censure of Israel.[37]

As you can see, the root of the Palestinian plight is well hidden beneath the surface tension exposed to public view. Deep-seated issues that will not go away unless faced forthrightly are being obscured and distorted. I do not minimize the genuine suffering, frustration and injustice that pervades Palestinian life. But, fundamentally, these conditions are not the *cause* of Arab enmity toward Israel; they are the *result* of it. The distinction is monumental. Arab hatred of Israel created the refugee situation. And Arab hatred of Israel perpetuates Palestinian privation. That the world faults *Israel*—and would threaten her survival—for an Arab-generated Arab problem is another instance of a big lie, repeated long enough, taking on a bizarre life of its own—and scapegoating the Jews.

Perhaps you think: That was then, this is now. Not so; the reason I spend so much time on history is that it is repeating itself before our eyes, on our watch. We still hear the lies, we still misjudge God's people.

How will you respond? Are you convinced God still blesses those who bless Israel and curses those who curse her? Do you want your heart and mind set on His? Then I encourage you not to conform to the world's pattern but discern truth—however His enemies try to hide it. Love the Palestinians and love the Israelis, adding to your love both knowledge and the fear of the Lord, the beginning of wisdom (Psalm 111:10). For God is testing your heart.

CHAPTER FOURTEEN

Agenda to Annihilate

I own a crinkly, brown-edged copy of a Jewish newspaper dated May 18, 1948. My parents were newlyweds when it arrived in the mail, and they never could bring themselves to throw it away. The paper now serves as an original (and personally sentimental) documentation of Israel's revived statehood. Beneath its headline, "World Salutes Israel," appears an astounding invitation—extended to Arabs living in the land. It is incorporated into the country's Declaration of Independence proclamation:

> In the midst of wanton aggression, we yet call upon the Arab inhabitants of the State of Israel to preserve the ways of peace and play their part in the development of the State, on the basis of full and equal citizenship and due representation in all its bodies and institutions. . . . We extend our hand in peace and neighborliness to all the neighboring states and their peoples, and invite them to cooperate with the independent Jewish nation for the common good of all.[1]

The invitation to stay was repeated over and again in the weeks leading up to the War of Independence. Newspaper articles, radio announcements, policy statements, meetings with Arab leaders—even leaflets airdropped over Arab villages by the Israelis—pleaded with them to remain and live in peace. Said one Palestinian Christian priest, "[The Arabs] fled in spite of the fact that the Jewish authorities guaranteed their safety and rights as citizens of Israel."[2]

British Mandate authorities described Israel's attempts to keep the Arabs at home: "Every effort is being made by the Jews to persuade the Arab populace to stay and carry on with their normal lives . . . and to be assured that their lives and interests will be safe."[3]

Only 160,000 Arabs were willing to stay and trust the Jews. Today they and their children enjoy democratic rights of Israeli citizenship, including a standard of living much higher than that of their brethren anyplace else in the Middle East. Approximately 650,000 Palestinians fled instead (though they allege various and different numbers—always a few times higher).

In isolated instances, Jewish soldiers did forcibly, even cruelly, evacuate relatively small numbers of Arabs. Some Israelis were wrongly bent on revenge for the preceding decades of terror. Such actions are inexcusable. At the same time, of the relatively small minority of Palestinians expelled at gunpoint, many of their tales have proved unverifiable or outrageously embellished.[4] The stories, enhanced by legendary anecdotes that tend either to romanticize Arab tribal-village life or represent it as a bustling, thriving society,[5] rarely resemble historical fact.

Voluntary Refugees

The overwhelming majority of Arabs who fled their homes and set up camp did so for one reason only: *Their Arab leaders told them to.* As a result most Palestinians became *voluntary* refugees. Why the mass evacuation? Arab political and religious leaders directed them to go and make way for approaching armies that would quickly destroy the Jewish State.[6] Israel, they boasted, would within days be "driven into the [Mediterranean] sea."

The Higher Arab Executive gave Palestinians a choice: quit and run, or accept Jewish protection and be regarded as a renegade in the Arab world that would imminently take over. The Arab National Committee in Jerusalem ordered its constituency out of their homes, adding, "any opposition to this order . . . is an obstacle to the holy war . . . and will hamper the operations of the fighters in these districts."[7]

Similarly, the Arab Legion and Arab Liberation Army directed whole-scale evacuations of various villages. Leaders like Iraqi prime minister Nuri Said warned:

> We will smash the country with our guns and obliterate every place the Jews seek shelter. The Arabs should conduct their wives and children to safe areas until the fighting has died down.[8]

Arab leaders planted and propagated rumors (that is, lies) of Israeli terror operations under way for those who foolishly stayed behind. Panic resulted; a mass Arab-initiated Palestinian exodus was successfully achieved.[9] Shortly after the war—which to their humiliation they did not win—Arab government leaders freely admitted to having created the refugee problem.[10] Former prime minister of Syria in 1948–49, Haled al Azm, voiced the consensus:

> Since 1948 we have been demanding the return of the refugees to their homes. But we ourselves are the ones who encouraged them to leave. Only a few months separated our call to them to leave and our appeal to the United Nations to resolve on their return.[11]

Palestinian leader Mahmoud Abbas, aka Abu Mazen, freely confessed:

> The Arab armies entered Palestine to protect the Palestinians from the Zionist tyranny, but instead they abandoned them, forced them to emigrate and to leave their homeland, and threw them into prisons similar to the ghettos in which the Jews used to live.[12]

Contrast such historical accounts with the words of one contemporary, internationally known Palestinian *Christian* spokesman who blames the refugee situation on the Jews for "forcibly subjugating another nation through superior military might, political maneuvering and economic manipulation."[13] True facts are important because those responsible for an unnecessary problem and curse created from ill will ought to resolve it.

The Right to Return or the Deed to Destroy?

When neighboring Arab countries persistently refused to take the refugees in, Israel began offering, as early as 1949, to negotiate for the refugees' return and full repatriation. The Arabs, however, were unwilling even to negotiate a plan for the Palestinians' return. Why? To negotiate with Israel, they insisted, would first require an implicit recognition of her existence, and this they vowed never to do.[14] Further, by refusing to negotiate for the refugees' return, the war against Zionism could still be waged in the political arena. In 1957 an Arab summit in Syria regarding the Palestinian refugees reached this conclusion:

> Any [political] discussion aimed at a solution of the Palestinian problem which will not be based on ensuring the refugees' right to annihilate Israel will be regarded as a desecration to the Arab people and an act of treason.[15]

In 1949 the United Nations established a relief fund (United Nations Relief and Works Agency, or UNRWA) to provide for the refugees' basic needs. At this writing, cumulative Arab financial support toward the refugee problem has amounted to about two percent of UNRWA's budget, while the United States and Israel foot much of the bill.[16] Former UNRWA director Ralph Galloway astutely noted in 1958:

> The Arab States do not want to solve the refugee problem. They want to keep it as an open sore, as an affront to the United Nations and as a weapon against Israel. Arab leaders don't give a damn whether the refugees live or die.[17]

Transferring blame onto the Jews for the Arab-generated Palestinian plight quickly became a powerful propaganda tool. Frustrations of life in refugee outposts bred upon already existing bitterness, hate and violence. After years, then decades, without the deliverance promised by their Arab brethren, Palestinian tempers skyrocketed. The Arab nations ensured, however, that Palestinian rage would be directed not against them but against Israel.

Succeeding decades have effected little change in the Arab position, regardless of the existence of signed statements about a Palestinian polity. I refer to the "Arab position" because the Palestinians have always strategized and operated in connection with the larger Arab world. Together they have kept locked in limbo, out of the twentieth century's 135 million refugees worldwide, only their 650,000 kinsmen — and, unlike any other refugee group, their kinsmen's children and children's children.[18] Of the refugees and their neighboring states' position in the twenty-first century, Arab American journalist Joseph Farah offers these remarks:

> Those poor unfortunates could be settled in a week by the rich Arab oil states that control 99.9 percent of the Middle East landmass, but they are kept as virtual prisoners, filled with misplaced hatred for Jews and armed as suicide martyrs by the Arab power brokers.[19]

> What are the real roots of this [Arab/Palestinian-Israeli] conflict? . . . That Palestinians want a homeland and Muslims want control over sites they consider holy? . . . These two demands are nothing more than strategic deceptions, propaganda ploys. They are nothing more than phony excuses and rationalizations for the terrorism and murdering of Jews. The real goal of those making these demands is the destruction of the State of Israel.[20]

In 1964, when Yasser Arafat took over the Palestine Liberation Organization, its stated purpose was to liberate all of Palestine. His meaning, however, is often misunderstood. The PLO was not created to liberate the West Bank (that is, Judea and Samaria) and Gaza; this is not the "Palestine" to which it refers. Since 1964 the aim has been to liberate a Palestine that includes, according to official definition, every square inch of land between the Mediterranean

Sea and the Jordan River: that is, Israel. This would be achieved through a contrived right to return.

Bear in mind that the distance between Palestinian territories and the "homeland" is often only 10 to 25 miles. When Palestinians—both Muslims and Christians—insist on a "right of return," they really demand title deed to destroy Israel by flooding it with millions of militant refugees. The goal of eradicating the Jewish State would be achieved simply by repopulating it with Arabs. Israel's concession to such a proposition would be suicidal—which is exactly what her enemies want.

Is there no place on earth the Jewish nation can live?

What I write is not to disparage the Arab people Jesus loves and died for, especially, as we will see later, those who truly worship and follow Him. I do not intend to minimize the honest reality of Palestinian suffering. But reality viewed out of perspective turns into distorted and dangerous misperception. God may call us to account for it.

What the West Does Not Understand

Much of the world wants to believe that after decades of suffering and negotiations toward peace, the Palestinian people must surely be willing to compromise on the objective of obliterating the Jewish State. But Western standards of logic and justice differ dramatically from those of the Muslim East, where traditionally little value is placed on honesty, goodwill and fair compromise. The world's postmodern, humanistic and relativistic mindset finds itself up against—and in denial of—Islamic absolutes. Let us not be naive; history shows that ideology, not occupation, is the primary cause of today's terror. Until Yahweh dramatically intervenes (and I believe He will), we ought not to expect things to change very much for very long. Neither should we expect—let alone force—Israel to behave as if they have.

Shortly after the PLO published its agenda of annihilation, Israel fought for her life in the Six Day War of 1967. Amazingly—and I believe miraculously—she acquired Gaza from Egypt and the West Bank (which includes East Jerusalem) from Jordan. In 1973, Egypt and Syria launched another unprovoked attack on Israel, the Yom Kippur War. After what can only be described as God's gracious intervention, Israel again prevailed. As a result of these mounting Arab defeats the PLO announced its new "Phased Plan" the following year. The Phased Plan has represented Palestinian/Arab strategy ever since.

The Phased Plan refers to the slightly revised goal to "liberate" the Jewish State not all at once but in steps. Phase One is the establishment of an independent combatant national authority as a state consisting of Gaza and the West Bank. To help accomplish Phase One, the terrorist is touted worldwide as a "freedom fighter" morally equivalent to the "Zionist entity." Once liberated, Gaza and the West Bank will serve as a launching pad for Phase Two, the provoking of all-out war, in which the Arab nations plan to wipe Israel off the map.[21] At this writing and as peace talks sputter along, Palestinians still blatantly broadcast their plot from behind the scenes.[22] Not quite so covertly, their government logos and web sites show Palestine encompassing all of Israel, with Israel nonexistent.[23]

Pretense of Peace and Intent of Intifada

At Camp David in 2000, the United States made an effort to resume the failed Oslo peace plan. At that time Israel offered the Palestinians sovereignty to approximately 95 percent of the disputed territories, including much-coveted East Jerusalem. There was virtually nothing left to offer. But the Palestinians said no, and, without a single counterproposal, walked out on the deal.[24] According to U.S. Middle East envoy Dennis Ross, their main objection was the insertion of one critical clause in the agreement: "This is the end of the conflict."[25] That should have been no surprise. The Palestinians—actually the whole Arab Muslim world engaged in holy war against Israel—cannot "end the conflict" with anything less than ending Israel. Declared Arafat:

Peace for us means the destruction of Israel. We are preparing for an all-out war, a war which will last for generations. . . . We have become the most dangerous enemy that Israel has. . . . We shall not rest until the day when we return to our home, and until we destroy Israel.[26]

In the Arab world there is a false peacemaking concept based on a precedent set by Muhammad in dealing with his enemies of the Qurayish tribe. The Hudaibiya Agreement established the right within Islam, called *hudna*, to fake peace when you are weak so you can wait for better timing to conquer your enemy.[27] An Arab saying goes like this: When your enemy is strong, kiss his hand and pray that it will be broken one day.[28] Even while the Oslo Accords were technically in effect, Arafat admitted, "I do not consider the [Oslo] agreement any more than the agreement which was signed by our prophet Muhammad and the Qurayish."[29]

King David said, "With their mouths they bless, but in their hearts they curse" (Psalm 62:4). David's son Solomon said there is nothing new under the sun. They speak to us today.

When Arab Muslims talk about settling their conflict with Israel once another Palestinian state is created, it is most likely just that — *talk.* Former prime minister Ehud Barak, Israel's representative at Camp David, understands the reality behind the rhetoric:

What they want is a Palestinian state in all of [Israel]. . . . They are products of a culture in which to tell a lie . . . creates no dissonance. They don't suffer from the problem of telling lies that exists in Judeo-Christian culture. Truth is seen as an irrelevant category. There is only that which serves your purpose and that which doesn't. They see themselves as emissaries of a national movement for which everything is permissible.[30]

Little wonder that when peace talks collapsed, the second Intifada (Uprising) began. Faisal Husseini, a "moderate" Palestinian leader, gave an interview comparing the whole peace process to the proverbial "Trojan horse."[31] From the Arab perspective, it had been designed to fool the Israelis into letting the Palestinians arm themselves inside the Jewish State *in order to destroy it:*

If you are asking me as a pan-Arab nationalist what are the Palestinian borders according to the higher strategy, I will immediately reply, from the [Jordan] river to the [Mediterranean] sea.[32]

Accordingly, at a UN Human Rights Commission in Geneva in 2003, official Palestinian observer Nabil Ramlawi "slipped," and called *explicitly* for the elimination of Israel.[33] This ongoing pan-Arab agenda to annihilate is seen in the unrelenting terror Israel has endured. Since the turn of the twentieth century to this writing, Israel—a country the size of New Jersey—has suffered more than eighteen *thousand* terrorist incidents.[34] Behold the hard facts: In the ten years prior to Oslo in 1993, a total of 211 Israelis were killed by Palestinian terror, while in the ten years since the peace agreement, that number has surpassed 1,110, an increase of more than 425 percent.[35] In addition, Israeli security forces have thwarted more than *double* that number of planned attacks. Do such numbers reflect genuine intent to live harmoniously, or even tolerantly, side by side?

What do you suppose the average Palestinian would say?

The Not-So-Silent Palestinian Majority

The goal of obliterating Israel is not an obstreperous ideal espoused by the fanatical fringe. Replace the leadership, we like to think, and normalcy will result. But that is not what the Palestinians themselves say. Polls taken in 2002 and 2003 report that a full 80 percent of them, as well as their leaders, view their conflict with Israel as a battle over the existence of the Jewish State.[36] A full 70 percent of Palestinians approve of terrorists killing women and children if the targets are Jews. Even during their short-lived *hudna* in 2003, 75 percent still wanted to keep up the Intifada terror![37] A separate poll taken of PA residents by the Jerusalem Media and Communication Centre, a Palestinian organization, reported that 51 percent insisted a future Palestinian state occupy *all* of Israel proper.[38]

What affects popular Palestinian ideology and feeds the fighting? Foremost, their faith. To illustrate, local sermons, aired every Friday on state-run TV, rail words of "inspiration" by Islamic clerics:

Allah willing, this unjust state will be erased — Israel will be erased. . . .
Blessings to whoever put a belt of explosives on his body or on his
sons' and plunged into the midst of the Jews crying, "Allahu akbar"
[Allah is great]. There is no God but Allah and Muhammed is His
messenger.

SHEIK IBRAHIM MADI, GAZA[39]

O Allah, annihilate the Jews. . . . O Allah, raise the flag of jihad. . . .

SHEIKH IBRAHIM MADHI,
IJLIN MOSQUE, GAZA CITY[40]

Fundamentalist Islamic ideology pervades secular thought; there
is virtually no separation. According to the Arab Psychiatrists Association, murder is good for mental health:

The psychological structure [of a suicide terrorist] is that of an individual who loves life. . . . When the martyr dies a martyr's death,
he attains the height of bliss. . . . As a professional psychiatrist, I
say that the height of bliss comes with the end of the countdown . . .
and then you press the button to blow yourself up.

DR. ADEL SADEQ, CHAIRMAN OF THE ARAB
PSYCHIATRISTS ASSOCIATION AND HEAD
OF DEPARTMENT OF PSYCHIATRY AT
EIN SHAMS UNIVERSITY IN CAIRO[41]

The Palestinian ideology is supported by every fundamental Islamic state in the world. Neighboring Arab media regularly decry
the existence of Israel and Jews. In 2003 the Saudi government's
daily newspaper warned: Beware of Jews on the hunt for fresh
Muslim or Christian blood needed for baking kosher pastries. The
paper actually provides a presumed recipe for the pastries and
kosher, human bloodletting slaughter.[42]

Senseless hatred against the Jewish nation permeates the Middle
East. At this writing, for example, Egyptian jurists are planning an
enormous lawsuit against Israel and all Jews of the world. Headed
by the dean of the Faculty of Law at the University of Al-Zaqaziq
in Egypt, the suit seeks to recover the current monetary value,

including 5,758 years' interest, of all the gold and goods allegedly stolen by the Israelites the night of their exodus from Egypt.[43] In the meantime, in Syria, Lebanon and Iran, state-supported terror training bases route arms-laden, jihad-driven "warriors" into the Jewish State as reinforcements for brethren Palestinian terrorists.

Arab oil underwrites the Palestinian cause. Arab billionaires send huge sums to Palestinian families sacrificing loved ones to jihad.[44] The money is both bribe and reward. Astronomical amounts are exported and expended for the purchase of terror technology. Still other monies flowing in from Israel and the UN—intended for the building of a Palestinian infrastructure—are waylaid for weapons. *More than enough finances have flooded the Palestinian Authority with which to eliminate squalor, establish decent government services and businesses, and build good schools and hospitals.* But that has never been the real goal; their agenda is to annihilate Israel.

It is said that if the Arabs put their weapons down today, there would be no more violence. If the Jews put their weapons down today, there would be no more Israel. The issue is not a "cycle of violence"; it is the survival of the Jewish people on their miniscule historical homeland.

Where, you may ask, is the Palestinian church in all this?

The Church of Palestine

Genuinely God-loving, Bible-believing Christians can be found scattered among the Palestinian people. I have met a few and have tremendous admiration for each one. They endure much persecution at the hands of their Islamic kinsmen-according-to-the-flesh, and I urge you to pray passionately for them. May God open doors through which Jewish and Gentile believers can bless and minister to them in love. He wants us standing solidly with those true brothers and sisters in the household of faith. Sadly, however, such genuine lovers and followers of Jesus Christ do not represent the majority of Palestinians who identify themselves as Christians. To my knowledge, the vast majority are nominal in their faith.

Political-nationalist aspirations often seem more important to them than regenerate relationship with Jesus, faithfulness to His Word and spiritual fruit-bearing.

Palestinian Christians are confronted with a painful dilemma: Should they side with Palestinian nationalism or with a biblical view supportive of the Jewish State? Many have resolved the issue by downplaying or denying God's present restoration of Israel. They interpret the Scriptures symbolically or allegorically, rather than literally, so that any right to the land the Jews may have once had is now superseded by the New Covenant Church. At the core of their reasoning is a hermeneutic of the Bible similar to that of the replacement proponents of the early Church. A Christian leader affiliated with Bethlehem Bible College expresses the local consensus:

> [The] concept of a promised land is expired to give way to the new concept of the kingdom of God, which resides in every believer's heart.[45]

They usually deny it, but in reality most Arab Christians are unabashed advocates of replacement theology. They are convinced that the Old Covenant promises, especially those about land, are now mystically fulfilled in Jesus Christ and the "internal" Kingdom of God.[46] Because of their anti-Israel sentiment, many Arab Christians find it difficult to read the Old Covenant; when they do, they use it very selectively.[47] The problem is, they often simply do not see the hate in their hearts toward the Jews.

To those of us in the Western church, Palestinian Christians typically say something like this: "I am not against the Jewish people and I am not anti-Semitic. There is something unique about the Jews. I do not believe in replacement theology. But the Bible does not justify the existence of the State of Israel. Don't you want to hear the side of the story from your Christian brothers?" What follows is often a sad diatribe of anti-Semitism combined with liberation theology, buttressed by heavily slanted historical and present-day accounts.

Palestinian Liberation Theology

Palestinian Christian Bible colleges and ecumenical organizations, supported by the Western church, have developed a unique application of the Scriptures based on liberation theology.[48] Liberation theology regards justice for the oppressed as the foremost theme of the Bible. "Proof" of oppression (by Israel, not the Arab nations) is backed by heaps of anecdotal material. Rare, isolated cases of unjustifiable aggression on Israel's part are offered as evidence of widespread, unrelenting suppression. Many of these stories in essence rewrite both history and the Bible. They teach the following "facts," for example:

- There is no longer a Jewish people because the Jews are no longer the direct descendants of Isaac.
- Israel started the 1948 War of Independence because it insisted on existing.
- Israel's modern-day survival is not miraculous and is not in God's will.
- Israel is responsible for the refugee situation because it expelled all its Arabs.
- The Jews stole their land from the Arabs, or took it by brutal force, or still greedily grasp at it.
- The New Covenant mentions no specific plan for the Jewish people.[49]
- Jesus was a Palestinian, His Jewish identity merely a misconception of Western Christianity.[50] "Real Christianity exists only in Palestine."[51]
- Christian Zionism, according to a Palestinian Christian conference held in Bethlehem in 2003, "is not connected to [true] Christianity in any way."[52]

Such misstatements repackaged in replacement theology go on and on. Like many Palestinian Christian leaders, one prominent Palestinian Lutheran pastor concedes the Jewish people have a right to exist, but *not* as a sovereign nation in the Promised Land:

> As Palestinians, we have nothing against Jews for being Jews. But we do have something against them insofar as they are an alien occupation force in . . . our land [Israel proper].[53]

Sadly, these Christian leaders are turning many sympathetic believers in the West against Israel. Their intriguing books and stirring speeches tug at our heartstrings, misrepresenting the Jewish nation as tyrannically oppressive and themselves as pitiably victimized. More and more, we believe them: After all, they're *Christians*, we say to ourselves. Christian or not, they are to varying degrees mistaken or deceived, yet certainly much in need of compassion and help. We must recognize their hardships and not dismiss their difficulties. But we must lovingly, for their sake, minister to them in truth. God wants us humbly helping to set them free from traps of anti-Semitism that historically ensnared the Western church. *He wants them recognizing and repenting of the Jew hatred and cursing in their hearts so they in turn can be blessed, not cursed. He wants to use them to bring not just other Arabs but also Israel to a saving knowledge of their Messiah.*

Sunday Sermons on the Savior?

The typical Palestinian Christian disposition toward the Jewish State does little to quell the local conflict. Christian pulpits spew scathing sermons against the Jews throughout the Middle East,[54] mirroring the broader Palestinian Muslim perspective.[55] Here is what some Palestinian/Arab Christian leaders teach their flocks.

> Palestine is from the [Mediterranean] sea to the [Jordan] river. . . . They [the Jews] have no right to live or settle in it. . . . We encourage our youth to participate in the resistance, to carry out martyrdom attacks [terrorism] and participate in removing the occupation. . . .

Martyrdom [terrorist] operations are an excellent and a good way to resist the Zionists.

ARCHIMANDRITE THEODOSIOS HANNA,
GREEK ORTHODOX PATRIARCHATE[56]

Had we lived in the days when the church was a church . . . a Crusader war crueler than the Crusader wars of the past would have been waged against Israel. I, the Christian Palestinian, say in all rage and daring to the Christians of the world: You are loathsome! You are contemptible! . . . We are facing the filthy Christians of the West. . . . Our Jesus is not their Jesus. . . . Our God is not their God.

FATHER MANUEL MUSALAM, DIRECTOR,
LATIN CHURCH, GAZA[57]

This religion [Judaism] is the enemy of God, the enemy of people, and the enemy of Christianity. . . . As Jesus once said to the Jews, "You are the sons of Satan, and you do the will of your father Satan."

GEORGE SALIBA, ASSYRIAN ORTHODOX CHURCH
OF MT. LEBANON AND TRIPOLI, BISHOP[58]

The existence of Israel is an historic sin. . . . Israel managed to drug the leaders of those Christian countries . . . because of their surly nature. Israel planted among them the spirit of hatred and rage. . . . If only God would intervene to defend the world from these enemies of peace [Israel and Western Christians].

MARCUS AZIZ KHALIL, EGYPTIAN COPTIC PRIEST[59]

Can we legitimately accept what we hear from these people as a Christian perspective? Jesus said, "Anyone who claims to be in the light but hates his brother is still in the darkness . . . and walks around in the darkness; he does not know where he is going, because the darkness has blinded him" (1 John 2:9–11). In the self-cursing diatribes of these religious leaders, I hear an awful lot of hate, darkness and blindness—as well as a pressing need for the true Gospel to reach a very pained people.

Is There a Solution?

Israel wants *desperately* to make peace with her Arab neighbors and Palestinian population.[60] But how can she, surrounded by millions of militants steadfastly bent on her destruction? As the saying goes, even paranoid people can have enemies.

By now you may wonder, If the plot to exterminate the Jewish nation is so clear, why doesn't the whole world see it? There are many reasons, but I believe four main ones. First, Arab states carry considerable political clout. The Arab League boasts a membership of 22 nations (23 counting Palestine), and they are aligned with 46 Muslim countries.[61] These nations are all well represented in international governing bodies, aided by Arab oil and the perfidious spread of Islam. Second, as we near the end of this present age, underlying currents of anti-Semitism and anti-Christ are also gaining momentum. With increasing globalization, values of multicultural relativism and humanism impinge more and more on biblical values, clouding discernment even in the Church. Third, God is sovereignly allowing the nations to play out a prophetic scene that will culminate in their blessing and cursing, judgment and redemption. Lastly, with Israel serving as a point of division to separate sheep from goats, Jesus is purifying His Bride for His glorious presence. In that refining process she helps prepare the way for His return.

The Israelis say there are two possible solutions to their conflict with the Arabs: the realistic and the miraculous. The realistic solution, they quip, involves divine intervention; the miraculous, a voluntary agreement between the parties themselves.[62] To God's will for a just peace and the realistic hope for a miracle, we now turn.

CHAPTER FIFTEEN

Just Peace in the Land

My Israeli friend Yossi tells a story about an Israeli Arab whom I will call Rifat Ghabim.[1] When Rifat took a municipal construction job, he spoke no Hebrew. Sitting down to eat lunch one day on the same grassy knoll as a Jewish worker who spoke no Arabic, he found himself the object of a fumbling effort to make conversation.

"*Be'teavon,*" said the Jew, using the Hebrew expression for *bon appétit.* Rifat thought the Jew was asking his name so he replied, last name first, "Ghabim, Rifat." The next day at lunch the same thing happened.

"*Be'teavon,*" said the Jewish worker.

"Ghabim, Rifat," replied the Arab.

Rifat decided he had better find out the exact meaning of *be'teavon,* and learned, rather sheepishly, it was simply a wish that he enjoy his meal. The Jew, meanwhile, thought that he had memorized the appropriate reply in Arabic, and so when they next sat down together, Rifat greeted him with "*Be'teavon,*" to which the Jew answered proudly, "Ghabim, Rifat."[2]

The anecdote is not so much about Hebrew and Arabic as it is about two people groups incapable of communicating without a common language. How, then, is just peace to be had in the land?

Unsanctified Mercy

I assume that you, like me, deplore the fact of human suffering. We cringe at sights of Palestinian squalor and suppression. We watch and hear with horror about Jews being blown to bits in buses, buffet restaurants and Bat Mitzvahs from terror attacks. Not only have thousands of innocent Israeli civilians been murdered over the years, but thousands more remain disfigured, in wheelchairs, in constant pain until the day they die. Children are without limbs, without eyes or with cracked skulls on life support indefinitely. Teenagers are so emotionally scarred they have to be institutionalized. We want the brutality and bloodshed to end; enough is enough! On a raw emotional level, some of us are losing patience with Israel, demanding mercy on behalf of the perceived Palestinian victim. Just give them the land and get it over with, we say. Eventually more land may be handed over. But would this be right, fair and in accordance with God's will? Or would it be *unsanctified mercy?*

There are times when mercy, as *we* understand it, is not appropriate in God's economy. I am not saying Israel is without fault. Neither am I saying the Palestinian people do not need mercy; they do desperately. These folks (especially the true Christians) lay claim to a genuinely tragic plight. But the overwhelming Muslim majority would not live peaceably side by side with Israel in a Palestinian state. Instead they intend to wipe her off the map, using the acquisition of land as an attack-launching pad. With Islam's theological and historical precedent of faking peace through a temporary truce, Israel is in a fight for her life. And as the Jewish nation of Israel goes, so go the Jewish people of the nations.

God loves mercy. He is compassionate, taking no delight in the sufferings of humanity. I think He particularly grieves over pain caused by any cruelty on the part of His covenant people. But He has established prophetic principles that define His response to suffering. We would be wise not to try overriding them in unsanctified mercy.

Does God want to bless unrepentant Palestinians who treat Him and His covenant people and land with hatred? I am convinced He does. He is shredding the veil of Islam with the sword of the

Spirit, His goodness affording opportunity to repent. The ultimate solution to jihad against the Jews (and Jehovah) rests in the salvation of both peoples.

God wants to open heretofore closed doors for the salvation of the Arabs as well as the Jews. He may accomplish this through any number of possible scenarios that alter the political-military landscape of the Middle East. One possibility is the establishment of a sovereign Palestine undergirded by the West, though I personally see this as less than ideal. At the other extreme is the possibility of dismantling the PA altogether and transferring its population to the already existing Palestinian state of Jordan. And with God being God, He may well rearrange things in a manner no human genius could ever conceive of.

In any case, the Hebrew prophets leave no doubt that in the last days—which increasingly seem to be our days—He will judge the Arab nations that refuse to set their sabers down against Israel. His judgment is likely to achieve what C. S. Lewis calls a severe mercy. God's sovereignly merciful but sometimes painful judgments are designed to draw His enemies to Himself. Who knows but that He may judge the powers of Islam and liberate millions of Muslims in a sweeping display of sanctified mercy?

The Bible leaves room for a scenario of divine military intervention in which God could even expand the boundaries of the Jewish State through, perhaps, cataclysmic regional war. The timing, if it occurs, is not clear and nothing to look toward cheerfully. In any case, God is commissioning His spiritual battalions (you and me) to be ready to fight—not against flesh and blood, but against powers and principalities of wickedness in high places—for the *spiritual* liberation of not just Palestine, but Israel and the whole Middle East.

That's mercy.

The Prince of Peace

In 2002 I participated in a remarkable nationwide conference of Israeli Jewish and Arab believers. The timing of this gathering was uncanny, overlapping with the outbreak of war. As the Israeli army advanced into the PA to dismantle terrorist nests in Operation Defensive Shield, the conference (a sort of "Operation Divine Shalom") kicked into gear just a few miles away. Praising and worshiping Yeshua together as one body, thousands of Arabs and Jews found forgiveness for one another, releasing a power surge of love and reconciliation that would affect congregations throughout the country. I witnessed a miraculous melting of ancient hatreds as tears emptied reservoirs of resentment. Defensive shields indeed gave way to divine shalom.

Similar gatherings are taking place in Israel and in different cities with sizeable Messianic Jewish and Christian Arab populations. Behind the scenes, God is healing the children of Isaac and Ishmael, Jacob and Esau, and *all* the descendants of our common forebear, Shem. Lasting peace between us will not be brokered by a United States, a United Nations or a united coalition. It will not come about through the antics of the Antichrist. It will come at the hand, through the heart, of the Prince of Peace.

A just peace for the land of Israel is about much more than land. It is about the Lord of the land and His love for Jew and Arab alike. There is a subtle trap in which we Zionists, as well as Christian Arabs, can all focus far more on the land issue than the Lord issue. Should promises about soil be more important to us than promises about souls? When Yeshua came to earth, most of God's people were so fixed on the political scene they missed the day of His visitation. May He keep us from succumbing to the same temptation.

While God does not want us idolizing Israel's land, He does want us giving it proper respect. The land, like all the earth, belongs to its Creator (see Leviticus 25:23; Psalm 24:1). We worship Him alone, not His creation. Still, part of our worship involves honoring His covenants and commands even when the choices are tough—like those described below.

Covenants and Commands

Like every other nation, Israel is not without sin, and in the Bible Israel's sin was reason for her to lose habitation, temporarily, of her land. Could we Jews lose our land again on account of our disobedience to God's commands, and is this reason to support another Palestinian state?

God's promise of the literal land of Israel is part and parcel of His unconditional covenant with the literal children of Abraham, Isaac and Jacob (see Genesis 12:1–3; 15:7–21; 13:15–17; 17:7–8, 19; 26:3; 28:13; 48:4; 50:24). He reaffirms this promise of perpetual steward-ownership of the land throughout the Scriptures. In one of these gripping reaffirmations, He vividly shows Moses how the Jews' future disobedience to the law will result in their exile (see Deuteronomy 30). But He then tells of their return and physical restoration to the land. The passage illustrates that steward-ownership of the land is not necessarily always the same as its physical inhabitation. While Israel retains, so to speak, title deed to the Promised Land forever, her full inhabiting of it seems conditional—to some extent—on her obedience to God's commands (see Deuteronomy 28:58–64; 30:1–5; Joshua 23:16). Generally speaking, to the degree Israel is at peace with Him, she enjoys peace in the land. But the same is true of the Arabs. Physical possession of their lands is also a condition of the *Arabs'* obedience:

> This is what the LORD says: "As for all my wicked neighbors who seize the inheritance I gave my people Israel, I will uproot them from their lands and I will uproot the house of Judah from among them. But after I uproot them, I will again have compassion and will bring each of them back to his own inheritance and his own country [as seems to have occurred in the last century]. And if they learn well the ways of my people and swear by my name, saying, 'As surely as the LORD lives'—even as they once taught my people to swear by Baal—then they will be established among my people. But if any nation does not listen, *I will completely uproot and destroy it,*" declares the Lord.

JEREMIAH 12:14–17, EMPHASIS ADDED

Yahweh is to be worshiped in both Jewish and Arabic lands, lest grave consequences befall them both. Never in Israel's history has she been perfectly obedient. Never in her history has she inhabited all the Promised Land, either. She inhabits varying degrees of it, as she does today. But note: Never in the Scriptures, once God entrusts Israel with His land, does He direct her to relinquish it voluntarily. When her land is involuntarily relinquished, He says He "will completely uproot and destroy" those "wicked neighbors" whose hands "seized" it.

Exile Again?

God judged Israel's disobedience twice with dispersion (though in each case a cluster of Jews remained in the land). The first exile, in 586 B.C. (see 2 Kings 17:6; 25:21), was followed by a return described in the books of Ezra and Nehemiah. The second dispersion occurred in A.D. 70. Its regathering takes place today, each time another wide-eyed Jewish immigrant steps off a plane or boat to settle in his or her beloved covenant country. The Scriptures prophesy both regatherings, but the second and present is different from the first in several respects. For at least eight important reasons, we can conclude from the Bible that God does *not* intend to exile the Jewish people again, despite their sin (see Amos 9:15).

1. The Scriptures indicate that the Jews' last days' regathering and physical restoration to the land would take place while most of them are still in spiritual unbelief or sin (see Ezekiel 36:24–28; 37:12–13). This is how events have played out, with Israel remaining a largely secular state.
2. This present physical restoration to the land is a necessary step toward the nation's corporate repentance and spiritual restoration to the Lord (see Ezekiel 20:35; 36:24–28; 37:12–13). The Bible does not prophesy a third regathering for this purpose.
3. The second and present restoration is to occur from the four corners of the earth, gathering Jewish people from throughout the nations (see Isaiah 11:10–12; Jeremiah 16:15; 23:3; Ezekiel 36:24; 39:27–28), whereas Israel's first exile was limited to

Assyria and Babylon. Again, this matches the phenomenon of Zionism in our day.

4. Israel's sin does not justify her enemies' overtaking her inheritance. When those who wrest land from her claim, "We are not guilty, for they [Israel] sinned against the Lord," He answers, "You who pillage my inheritance" will surely reap "the vengeance of the LORD" (see Jeremiah 50:7, 11–15).

5. The Gentile Christian Church has now been called and commissioned to intercede on Israel's behalf. God wants to stay, as it were, His execution of judgment through the ministry of intercessory reconciliation (see, for instance, Genesis 18:23–33; Jeremiah 5:1; Ezekiel 22:30).

6. Israel's present re-gathering and survival against all reasonable odds, though under secular Zionist leadership, has proven so miraculous as to demonstrate that God is behind it.

7. Since the Word of God is to be interpreted literally, we cannot say with integrity that God's prophetic promises about the land are all fulfilled spiritually in Christ. Too many of these promises make little or no sense apart from a literal interpretation and application. Just as Old Covenant prophecies about Yeshua's first coming were fulfilled literally, likewise, prophecies about His second coming will be fulfilled literally. We should expect Messiah to return to earth in the Jewish capital of a Jewish nation (see Matthew 23:37–39; Zechariah 14:3–4); therefore, that nation must exist as a literal Jewish geopolitical entity.

If God does not intend to exile Israel again, but she fails to fully obey His commands, might He mandate the loss of a portion of her land? We must remember that Yahweh is supremely concerned with the motives of men's hearts.

Is the loss of land for the sake of plundering God's people? Is it to exalt the entity Allah? To appease terrorists bent on Israel's annihilation? Or to achieve genuine and sincere peace that promises to spare human life and alleviate unjust suffering? To see whether or not our hearts align with God's, look with me at some key biblical principles—starting with an important principle of law that Israel is *not* guilty of breaking.

Justice for the Foreigner

A popular pro-Palestinian argument being made by Christians, including many evangelicals, goes like this: Israel has failed to treat the foreigner or alien (that is, Palestinian) according to the law of Torah. The Jews have grasped at the gift of God's land instead of meekly waiting to inherit it. They should follow the tenets of justice written in the same Book on which they base their covenant land claims. If not, they have no right to retain the land.

These same Bible believers seem to find little relevance for Old Covenant law in any other context. Their perspective condemns Israel to subjugate herself to the law—without offering the redemptive grace of salvation by faith in Messiah. Notwithstanding the highly selective nature of this appeal to Torah, its provisions pertaining to the treatment of foreigners are certainly relevant to the present situation. But the law's proper interpretation brings us to an opposite conclusion.

The Old Covenant requires that the Israelites not mistreat or oppress a foreigner or alien in the land (see Exodus 22:21; 23:9). The Jews are to extend compassion, protection, civil rights, justice, even love to the stranger among them. Yahweh says that if Israel does "not oppress the alien, the fatherless or the widow . . . then I will let you live in this place, in the land I gave your forefathers for ever and ever" (Jeremiah 7:6–7).

Notice, however, the law also presupposes that the foreigner or alien *has first submitted to the God of Israel and the covering of His people.* Bible dictionaries explain the relationship:

> A *ger* was a foreigner who put himself under the protection of Israel and of Israel's God, who submitted to the many requirements of the law of Israel, and who was thereby given certain privileges not accorded to other strangers.[3]

Foreigners eligible for protection and blessing under the laws of Torah were required to obey many of its same provisions as their host Jewish nation. They were, for example, to observe the Sabbath and Day of Atonement (see Exodus 20:10; 23:12; Leviticus 16:29; Deuteronomy 5:14) and could be stoned for reviling or blaspheming God's name (see Leviticus 24:16; Numbers 15:30). As a result, law-abiding foreigners were treated almost the same as full-fledged citizens. Equal status with native-born Israelites could be obtained by circumcision, which then placed the foreigner in covenant relationship with God.

A foreigner *not* submitted to the ways of the Lord, however, was *not* to be tolerated. Especially repugnant to Yahweh was the idolatrous foreigner who polluted His land with the worship of false gods (such as Allah): "Do not make a covenant with them or with their gods. Do not let them live in your land, or they will cause you to sin against me, because the worship of their gods will certainly be a snare to you" (Exodus 23:32–33).

Naturally, the foreigner who despised the people of God, and whose aim was their annihilation, could not claim protection under the law. Such a person was not considered a foreigner, but an *enemy*.

Has modern-day Israel treated the foreigner according to biblical principles? An abiding Jewish presence has remained there ever since the conquest of Jericho. In the past thousand years, additional lands were obtained legitimately by purchase; they were *not* stolen. Then, by legal resolution of the UN, God granted the Jews sovereign statehood. They did not, for the most part, imperialistically grasp at His gift; they waited for it for two thousand years. Israel invited the Arabs to stay and live peaceably as full-fledged citizens. But most refused, running into self-imposed exile, refugees determined to terrorize Israel out of existence with the backing of Arab brethren. As a result the Jews were forced to fight a series of wars in self-defense, thereby securing additional land—which the world community had originally designated theirs,[4] and in any case, never legally belonged to a sovereign Arab polity. This additional land Israel has repeatedly demonstrated the willingness to return—for true peace.

So much for the law of the foreigner. We turn next to biblical principles relating to the enemy.

Warning to the Nations

The little one-chapter book of Obadiah practically shouts with prophetic directive today as Muslim-influenced nations of the world take their stand vis-à-vis Israel. Obadiah writes originally to Edom (Esau's descendants), denouncing its persistent anti-Israel, anti-God posture of heart. But his predictions of retribution according to divine principles are timeless and universal. He warns that God will treat us according to how we have treated Israel—in this case, cursing those who curse her.

The Lord speaks strongly through the prophet, addressing all—including Christians—who endorse measures leading to violence against Israel: "Because of the violence against your brother Jacob, you will be covered with shame; you will be destroyed forever" (Obadiah 1:10).

Ignoring Israel's exploitation by other nations is the same, in God's eyes, as *active aggression* against her: "On the day you stood aloof while strangers carried off his wealth and foreigners entered his gates and cast lots for Jerusalem, you were like one of them" (Obadiah 1:11).

The Living Bible says even more pointedly: "For you deserted Israel in his time of need. You stood aloof, refusing to lift a finger to help him when invaders carried off his wealth and divided Jerusalem among them. *You were as one of his enemies*" (emphasis added).

Obadiah uses a Hebrew phrase for *stood aloof* that speaks to the heart of nations today. The word for *stand* implies the positioning of oneself figuratively, as in taking a stand for a certain cause. So to stand aloof refers to a position of intentional abstention from positive action or a stance of distancing oneself. Is it possible that *we* have been guilty in the matter? Isn't this what happens when we sigh, "This Mideast mess is just too complicated," and then move on to something more "manageable" or "compelling"? God wants our hearts and helping hands close to, not distant from, the Jewish people.

If we do not get involved, *we ourselves* may be counted as Israel's enemies. Consider how Israeli foreign minister Abba Eban, *á la* Obadiah, described the nation's quandary at the inception of the Six-Day War in 1967: "As we looked around us we saw the world divided between those who were seeking our destruction and those who would do nothing to prevent it."[5]

Obadiah goes on to admonish those who delight in Israel's defeat. The next time you see Palestinians sneer at Israeli suffering after another terror assault—and then appealing to Christians for support—remember the prophet's words:

> "You should not look down on your brother [Israel] in the day of his misfortune, nor rejoice over the people of Judah in the day of their destruction, nor boast so much in the day of their trouble. You should not march through the gates of my people in the day of their disaster, nor look down on them in their calamity in the day of their disaster, nor seize their wealth in the day of their disaster. You should not wait at the crossroads to cut down their fugitives, nor hand over their survivors in the day of their trouble."
>
> OBADIAH 1:12–14, LB

Next, Obadiah issues a clarion call to our generation:

> "The Lord's vengeance will soon fall upon all Gentile nations. *As you have done to Israel, so will it be done to you.* Your acts will boomerang upon your heads."
>
> VERSE 15, LB, EMPHASIS ADDED

Obadiah applies the Abrahamic promise of blessing and cursing to all nations through all time. What would you like to boomerang on your head? How about your church? Your country? Send it to the Jews, and you will get it back.

The Bible and the West Bank

God once gave the prophet Ezekiel a message to deliver to "the mountains of Israel," which He also called the "ancient heights." The message is in response to Israel's enemies seeking to overtake these high places. These mountains and ancient heights are located in Judea and Samaria—the heartland of Israel—otherwise known as the West Bank or Palestine. Ezekiel's admonition applies astonishingly to the situation of our day.

God denounces those staking claim to Judea and Samaria and terrorizing the country from every side. Then He chastises all other nations that have joined in the enemy's slander and occupation of His land:

> "'The enemy said of you, "Aha! The ancient heights have become our possession."' Therefore prophesy and say, 'This is what the Sovereign LORD says: Because they ravaged and hounded [terrorized] you from every side so that you became the possession of the rest of the nations and the object of people's malicious talk and slander [propaganda] . . . I have spoken against the rest of the nations, and against all Edom [descendants of Esau and Arabic peoples], for with glee and with malice in their hearts they made my land their own possession so that they might plunder its pastureland.'"
>
> EZEKIEL 36:2–5

God's wrath is aroused and He "swears with uplifted hand" that these nations will suffer scorn. As for the mountains and heights of Israel, He promises they will be returned to the Jewish people with blessing and favor (see verses 7–12). God will even build settlements there: "I will settle people on you as in the past" (verse 11).

The prophetic principle forebodes judgment against those who aid or abet Israel's enemy seeking to usurp her hotly contested ancient heights. God's road map would steer us clear away from the mountains. Whatever the need (if any) for another Palestinian entity, we cannot ignore what God says to nations that divide Israel's land.

In checking the motives of our hearts, consider yet another word of gracious caution. The prophet Joel speaks in the context of the last days' judgment, but his words reflect that irrevocable principle of blessing and cursing God's people:

> "I will enter into judgment against them concerning my inheritance, my people Israel, for they scattered my people among the nations and *divided up my land.*"
>
> JOEL 3:2, EMPHASIS ADDED

Is it possible to create another Palestinian state without violating Scripture? If we lend even a hand to the endeavor, I suggest it be with nothing less than prayerful and godly fear and trembling, for surely we will answer to Him.

I encourage you, in the days ahead, as Israel stands precariously in the bull's-eye spot of the world's spiritual dartboard, to recall God's loving warnings from the prophets of old. Not just for you, or for your country, or for Israel, but for the sake of countless misguided Arab souls in need of sanctified mercy, will you ask, What would Jesus do—and then do it?

Offenses Must Come

Jesus tells us that offenses and sins must come in this world. But "woe," He says, to the one through whom they come (see Matthew 18:7). Such a person is not unlike Pilate, who in the supposed course of justice, condemns the Innocent One to death. Pilate seeks to appease those people opposed to God and, though he tries, he can never quite wash his hands of the matter. Similarly, Judas betrays the One born for betrayal and destined for death; nonetheless, this disciple through whom it all happens is doomed.

Contrast Judas and Pilate with David in the Old Covenant. The valiant, young prince is pursued relentlessly by a crazed King Saul determined to kill him. Given the opportunity, David refuses to harm God's anointed, knowing He will judge Saul in His own time and way. When He does, the shepherd-warrior weeps over Saul's demise. David is a man after God's own heart.

Are our heart motives, like David's, aligned with God's? It may be that He will permit Israel's land to be divided up; as I have said, several scenarios are possible. But woe to the nations and peoples who lend a hand to *improperly* slicing up Israel's sliver of real estate! And woe to those who refuse to lift a finger to help her!

The Bride of Christ will not harm God's anointed. She simply will not be the one through whom offenses, even if they are inevitable, come. Neither will she stand idly by; she will be laboring in practical ways for peace in sanctified mercy, her heart aligned with the Master's. She will be praying for the peace, not preying for the piece, of the Jewish nation.

Jerusalem: Pray for the Peace or Prey for the Piece

In Psalm 122:6 God gives us a prayer request, plain and simple: "Pray for the peace of Jerusalem: 'May those who love you be secure.'" Notice that your own security is tied to your love and prayers for Jerusalem. The peace of Jerusalem—or lack thereof—relates to your personal well-being; what takes place in the holy city ripples in the Spirit across the earth. Love and pray for His shalom in Jerusalem.

I am often asked by Gentile believers how best to pray for the peace of Jerusalem. My answer is always the same: Pray for the Prince of Peace to be welcomed into the hearts of those who live in the holy city and Holy Land. Make this your priority in prayer, then go on to the issues of the day. Because whether we pray or not, there is a *prey* for the *piece* of Jerusalem.

The Prince of Peace wants to be welcomed into Jerusalem and take up residence *now* in human temples. God wants to transform flesh-and-blood bodies, fashioned from the dust of the earth, into living temples by the indwelling presence of the Holy Spirit. The more living temples built in Jerusalem through saved souls, the more of the presence of the Prince of Peace. Since only the Prince of Peace will bring lasting peace to Jerusalem, the most effective way to pray for genuine peace in Jerusalem is to pray for the personal salvation of those who live there.

Once our priorities are right, fixed on God's covenantal love, we will hear more clearly from Him in praying for specific issues according to His strategy. Jerusalem is destined to become the focal point of Kingdom conflict on earth, empires and entities preying for their piece of God's select city. As He leads, I suggest the following matters are all high on His agenda:

- Blessing and strengthening of those in true spiritual authority
- Outpouring of grace leading to repentance for unsaved Jews and Arabs
- Revival and maturity in the Israeli body of Messiah
- Blessing and wisdom for government authorities and others in spheres of leadership
- God's sending and sustaining of laborers into Israeli harvest fields, opening doors for Messianic Jewish *aliyah*
- Sending of resources to the Messianic community in Jerusalem and the rest of Israel by believers in the nations
- Jerusalem's (Israel's) protection from enemy attack, physical and spiritual
- Jerusalem's (Israel's) enemies to be delivered from darkness into light
- Material prosperity despite Israel's economic woes due to war
- Your particular nation's blessing of Jerusalem and Israel
- The nations' recognition of Jerusalem as Israel's eternal capital city
- Protection from the spirit of antichrist
- The fulfillment of Jerusalem's redemptive purpose on earth as the City of the Great King, a city of peace that blesses the nations
- The gift of intercessory tears to be shed on her behalf until these things come to pass

God's goal for Jerusalem is to "make her the praise"—not the problem— "of the earth" (see Isaiah 62:7). What will it take on our part to get from here to there—the place of answered prayer for Jerusalem's peace that transforms her to the earth's praise? It will take the kind of prayer life that makes our lives a prayer: "You who call on the LORD, give yourselves no rest, and give him no rest till he establishes Jerusalem and makes her the praise of the earth" (verses 6–7).

The great news is, God will—through the sacrament of service.

PART 7

Living Sacrifices

Therefore, I urge you, brothers, in view of God's mercy, to offer your bodies as living sacrifices, holy and pleasing to God—this is your spiritual act of worship.

ROMANS 12:1

CHAPTER SIXTEEN

Israel on a Last Days' Altar

Krrr-*ish!* It is the sound of shattering glass traditionally smashed underfoot by the bridegroom at every Jewish wedding. One breath later, the crowd claps and cheers, *"Mazel tov!"* (congratulations) and nuptial festivities begin. Many people attach some covenantal or at least convivial symbolism to this uniquely Jewish custom. The shattered glass, however, is actually meant to remind the happy celebrants of something very sober—the destruction of Israel's Holy Temple. During even the most joyous moments of Jewish life, the nation's hope to rebuild its house of worship is recalled.

As we will see later, the Jews will indeed rebuild their Temple, and they will aim to construct it on its original, Bible-designated site. Presently holding shrines of Islam, the Temple Mount is going to become an international target of control and controversy. And so it must be, for the Temple Mount is an altar, a place of sacrifice. An altar on which the world would eventually sacrifice Israel.

Modern Anti-Zionism Equals Anti-Semitism

The Arab/Palestinian-Israeli conflict has re-ignited smoldering fires of anti-Semitism across the globe. Through the guise of mounting anti-Israel sentiment called anti-Zionism, flames of old-fashioned

Jew-hatred are being satanically stoked—and not just at Israel, but the sons and daughters of Jacob worldwide.

Please do not misunderstand me. I do not suggest that any and all criticism of Israel is tantamount to anti-Semitism or opposition against God. Like every other nation, Israel sins and acts wrongly at times, and her friends ought not deny it. At times, we may need to express our loving disapproval of those whom we care about most deeply—for their benefit. The issue is the disposition of heart motive behind our reproof. And that disposition is precisely what is most troubling.

In 2002 former U.S. ambassador to the United Nations Jeane Kirkpatrick spoke of her "very deep shock" over the anti-Semitism that pervades the UN. Concerned about the potential for another Holocaust worse than the first, Kirkpatrick described the international community's treatment of Israel as "nearly unbelievably insulting and outrageous."[1] Kirkpatrick pointed out that in the history of the UN and its agencies, *more than one thousand resolutions have condemned Israel*—but *not one* resolution has ever passed specifically condemning Arab terror against the Jewish State.[2] Author-activist Mike Evans states: "The United Nations has become, quite literally, a forum for the expression of antisemitism."[3]

At the watershed UN Conference on Racism in Durban in 2001, the international community reached a turning point vis-à-vis Israel. The conference gave a call for the virtual dismantling of the Jewish State.[4] Israel (not Iraq, Iran, Afghanistan, Sudan or any totalitarian regime) was accused of apartheid, racist crimes against humanity, ethnic cleansing and acts of genocide. A policy of complete isolation of Israel, including sanctions, embargoes and severing diplomatic ties, was recommended. Other conference recommendations included equating Zionism with racism and, at the request of the World Council of Churches, repealing the UN's condemnation of anti-Semitism.[5] Jewish delegates were sought out, spat upon, shoved and asked to leave public sessions.

In 2003 the UN Human Rights Commission passed a resolution affirming Palestinian armed struggle as a legitimate means of resistance for self-determination. The resolution was carefully crafted so as to implicitly condone terror — *if* the target happens to be Israel.[6] Notes one European commentator:

> Being anti-Israel has become somehow "legitimate" today [which in turn] gives a new "legitimacy" to the old antisemitism.[7]

Attacking Jews All Over the World

Lest these sound like isolated incidents, here are just a few of the many other ways the Western world is taking aim at Israel. Across Islam-influenced Europe, synagogues are burned and vandalized; Jewish graves are desecrated; Jews are beaten; respected news magazines and journals feature not only Israel-bashing articles but Jew-vilifying political cartoons practically indistinguishable from those of the Nazis; kosher meat production is banned; public billboards promote "death to the Jews"; Israeli businesses are mass-boycotted; and Jewish shops are vandalized.[8]

At this writing, anti-Jewish episodes are escalating in non-European Western nations as well, such as Canada, Australia and the United States. In 2003 a respected Jewish international monitoring agency concluded that anti-Semitism had reached its highest level since the Holocaust.[9]

In retribution for Israel's defensive stand against another terrorist state in the world (namely, Palestine), hundreds of professional academics in Europe and the Americas called for boycotts and dismissals, starting in 2002, of all Israeli scholars and their research. The president of Harvard University noted that academic anti-Semitism was escalating to heights he never thought possible. He was appalled at the extent to which long-respected intellectual communities were propagating anti-Jewish/anti-Zionist/anti-Israel political and social views.[10]

The rising tide of academic bigotry has affected even Christian colleges and seminaries, where classes on the Arab/Palestinian-Israeli conflict tend to be decidedly anti-Israel. In 2003 I was guest lecturer in one such class at a reputable Christian college. I was shocked and grieved at the impassioned anti-Semitic rhetoric I encountered in this *Christian* institution. In the students' minds, Israel bore the blame not only for the Palestinian plight but much of the world's war with terror. For my staunch support of the Jewish State, one student intimated I could not be a believer in Jesus.

Indeed, this is not a war against Israel; this is a war against each and every individual—Israeli or not, religious or not, Zionist or not, right- or left-wing—who is Jewish. For the first time in a century, many Jews no longer feel, as they once did, that they will necessarily find refuge in their own state. At this writing, construction of a security wall around Israel's shrinking borders is under way. Will it prove any more life-sparing than the many pre-Holocaust ghetto walls forcibly erected around twentieth-century European Jews? I shudder to think of the parallel—and the enemy's even larger-scale attempt to abort God's promised restoration of Israel by transforming the tiny nation into a giant ghetto built from desperation, "conveniently" gathered at death's door. "There's no haven for Jews. Not within Israel, and not without," wrote a sympathetic Canadian journalist in 2002.[11]

Global anti-Semitism is dreadfully consistent with Bible prophecy, as we will see in a moment. Does that mean we can shrug our shoulders or, worse yet, feel some secret delight because this prophetically inevitable phenomenon signals the Lord's return? God forbid that any child of His ever gain satisfaction over the hatred of His people for any reason! God grieves over the suffering of Israel, and if we know and love Him, we will too. Though we yearn for the Lord's return, He wants His Body of believers lovingly supporting (praying for, strategically aiding and abetting) the Jewish people up until then—even if they must—together with Israel—serve as a metaphorical last days' altar.

Last Days' Principles

A detailed discussion on eschatology is well beyond the scope of this book. Rather than predict for you a timeline of future events, the details of which remain debatable, I believe the Lord has called me to a different task. My purpose throughout this book has been to share with you key biblical principles, from a Messianic Jewish perspective, reflecting the heart and character of God. As you understand these principles, and stay submitted to the Master, He will equip you to respond in the grace and power of the Holy Spirit, however the precise details play out.

Be assured, God will provide the clarity of prophetic knowledge you need—when you need it. Sometimes He withholds information intentionally in order to test us. He wants to expose our hearts, showing us how we are disposed to respond when the heat is on and there is no "personal word" from Him. He takes note of our choices and determines destinies based in part on them. He dispenses mantles of authority and anointing in response to our attitudes and actions. Remember, God uses the Jewish nation to sift souls. One principle is that Israel is a testing ground.

God does not test us to torment us. His tests are designed to refine us for Kingdom purposes and conform us to the image of His Son. He wants us shining as beacons of light to a perplexed world in the throes of Kingdom conflict intensifying like labor pains, birthing the dawn of the Messianic Age. Expect Israel to remain the epicenter of this conflict. Both good and evil will heighten simultaneously, reverberating largely around her.

Signpost Events

An obvious principle is that God reveals His ways through His Word, which, concerning the future, includes certain signpost events. Signposts are meant to encourage and empower us. They let us know where we are and tell us whether or not we are on the right track. They come into sharper focus the closer we get to them. They point to our destination, enabling us to plan along the way.

Messianic Israeli leader Keith Asher Intrater suggests a simple signpost chronology of eschatological events concerning Israel. This flexible chronology is based on Joel 2–3 but also lines up well with other end times Scriptures. As you can see, the signpost categories overlap as they flow into the future:

1. Call to God's people to intercede and repent (Joel 2:12–17)
2. Restoration of the land of Israel (Joel 2:18–27)
3. Worldwide spiritual revival (Joel 2:28–32)
4. Battle of Armageddon (Joel 3:1–17)
5. Peace and prosperity after the war (Joel 3:18–21)[12]

Where are we now? Globally, the twenty-first century church has experienced an unprecedented groundswell of intercession and repentance, which continues to grow. Israel's restoration, together with worldwide spiritual revival, is under way. Next to come—perhaps preceded by short-term peace—is likely to be larger-scale warfare in the Middle East, culminating, in days or decades, in the final battle at Armageddon.

Regardless of the scenario, our prayers for and ministry to the hearts of humankind must not cease. *God does not want us thinking or behaving like fatalists!* He wants our intercession to keep ascending to the throne on behalf of world governors and leaders. I believe He wants us beseeching Him for peace in His Holy Land, that His goodness might bring Israelis and Arabs to repentance. I do not think we should be anything less than excited and optimistic about the future—as long as we are willing to lay down our lives to follow Jesus into it.

Arab Alignment

God takes no delight in the suffering or death of humanity. So I feel no joy in telling you that despite what I have just said, war is ahead for Israel. Lulls in the fighting—some significant—should be prayed for and expected. But the Scriptures seem to suggest that aggression against the Jewish State continues on and off until Yeshua's return. The Arab-Israeli wars of 1948, 1956, 1967, 1973 and 1982, plus the Intifadas of the 1980s and twenty-first century, bear lamentable witness to the Word.

I believe Israel's enemies today stand in a somewhat parallel position with the Amorites of old. God could have wiped out the Amorites long before He did but He gave them time to repent, waiting until their sin "reached its full measure" (Genesis 15:16). Only then did He execute judgment against them through Israel's conquest of the land. In principle, God is waiting, preferring repentance to unleashing His wrath. But when the time is ripe, He will vanquish Israel's foes not unlike the Amorites of old.

Psalm 83 describes a besetting Arab alignment against a beleaguered Jewish State. It is particularly relevant to us because, as of this writing, such an alignment has not yet historically taken place. Verses 5–8 tell how every nation in the neighborhood (except Egypt) unites against Israel: Edom and the Ishmaelites (southern Jordan and Saudi Arabia); Moab (central Jordan) and the Hagrites (Syria and Arabia); Gebal (southern Jordan); Ammon (central Jordan) and Amalek (Sinai desert); Philistia (Gaza Strip area); Tyre (southern Lebanon) and Assyria (Syria/Iraq). Verse 4 sounds their bellicose battle cry: "Come . . . let us destroy them as a nation, that the name of Israel be remembered no more."

Indeed, since the moment she became a nation, Israel's enemies have rallied under this iniquitous refrain. By day, they chant it from their mosques and schools. By night, they and their children dream wistfully of a world without Jews.

How does God's prophetic psalmist respond to these nations assailing Israel? He prays for God to exalt Himself—for those nations' good: "May they ever be ashamed and dismayed. . . . Let them know that you, whose name is the LORD—that you alone are the Most High over all the earth" (Psalm 83:17–18).

Psalm 83 reflects an important principle for us: Yahweh's overriding and supreme goal in times of testing and judgment is to glorify Himself. He will ultimately use the Arab/Palestinian-Israeli conflict to do it. He wants both blood-drenched peoples to know that He alone is Most High—not Allah, not Judaism without Jesus, not global secular humanism, not anything.

Psalm 83 may prophesy a unified Arab operation undertaken in the future against Israel. Such an attack could occur utilizing weapons of mass destruction in the Middle East. If that is the case, the Scriptures hint at a providentially profound victory that may result in a sizeable expansion of Israel's borders. The purpose? To "let them know that you, whose name is the LORD—that you alone are the Most High over all the earth."

Such a war may either precede or be part of the one foretold by the prophet Ezekiel.

Armies from the North

Ezekiel describes a battle of cataclysmic proportions in chapters 38 and 39. Armies from the north known as Gog and Magog spearhead a coalition directed at Israel's destruction. But God initiates this attack. He Himself will "put hooks in [their] jaws" (38:4) and reel them in toward the "land of unwalled villages," a "peaceful and unsuspecting people" (38:11). This passage shows that a significant—but not lasting—period of peace is ahead.

Since Ezekiel refers to armies from the north, this fearsome confederation (Gog/Magog, Gomer and Beth-Togarmah) could well be composed of Russia and certain Islamic, former Soviet republics located to the north of Israel. Other Muslim and Turkic nations will join them: Persia (Iran); Cush (Sudan/Ethiopia); Put (Libya); and Meshech/ Tubal (Turkey); with support from Sheba (Yemen) and Dedan (Saudi Arabia).

Yahweh plans to pulverize this coalition that invades Israel at a time when she is apparently enjoying relative, albeit temporary, peace. *Perhaps this peace is related to believers' intercessory prayer and pro-action.* In any case, He so stuns the world in His defense of Israel that His demonstrated Glory draws all to Himself:

"And so I will show my greatness and my holiness, and I will make myself known in the sight of many nations. Then they will know that I am the LORD."

EZEKIEL 38:23

"I will display my glory among the nations, and all the nations will see the punishment I inflict and the hand I lay upon them. From that day forward the house of Israel will know that I am the LORD their God."

ᴇᴢᴇᴋɪᴇʟ 39:21–22

The Nations vs. Jerusalem

The prophet Zechariah foretells another sobering scenario. He describes a day in which God's wrath is poured out on an alignment of nations invading Jerusalem. Zechariah's words reflect once more that fundamental principle: "I will bless those who bless you, and whoever curses you I will curse" (Genesis 12:3). Remember that to curse means to make little—as in making Israel even littler by taking away her land. Read the Scripture below carefully; could it be the judgment spoken of here relates, either directly or indirectly, to the nations' present-day efforts to divide Jerusalem?

Behold, I will make Jerusalem a cup of trembling unto all the people round about, when they shall be in the siege both against Judah [representing the rest of Israel's land] and against Jerusalem. And in that day will I make Jerusalem a burdensome stone for all people: all that burden themselves with it shall be cut in pieces, though all the people of the earth be gathered together against it.

ᴢᴇᴄʜᴀʀɪᴀʜ 12:2–3, ᴋᴊᴠ

And it shall come to pass in that day, that I will seek to destroy all the nations that come against Jerusalem.

ᴢᴇᴄʜᴀʀɪᴀʜ 12:9, ᴋᴊᴠ

I will gather all the nations to Jerusalem to fight against it. . . . The LORD will go out and fight against those nations, as he fights in the day of battle.

ᴢᴇᴄʜᴀʀɪᴀʜ 14:2–3

Yahweh destroys all the nations coming against Jerusalem, even though Israel has not yet turned corporately to embrace Messiah and is stained with sin. Then He magnificently graces the Jewish people:

"And I will pour out on the house of David and the inhabitants of Jerusalem a spirit of grace and supplication. They will look on me, the one they have pierced, and they will mourn for him as one mourns for an only child, and grieve bitterly for him as one grieves for a firstborn son. . . . On that day a fountain will be opened to the house of David and the inhabitants of Jerusalem, to cleanse them from sin and impurity."

ZECHARIAH 12:10–13:1

Spectacular revival follows on the heels of God's deliverance. But take note: This future, culminating event, whenever it is destined to occur, reveals principles as to how the Spirit is *already* working with Israel. As the nations assail her, Yahweh is *already* releasing, if not pouring out, a spirit of grace and supplication. The more the world comes against the Jewish nation, the more we are to pray and labor that "they will look on [Yeshua], the one they have pierced," and "grieve bitterly for him as one grieves for a firstborn son." And the more we can expect to hear that they are.

Before that final fulfillment, however, a certain figure called the Antichrist comes to the fore.

Jacob's Trouble with the Antichrist

Not long ago the subject of the Antichrist, or anti-Messiah, was relegated mostly to the realm of doomsday prophets and rapture-intent radicals. But times have changed. From seminaries to secular news magazines, more and more attention is being given to this diabolical "man of perdition" or "lawlessness" (2 Thessalonians 2:3). The Bible says he will make war on the people of God—Christians and Jews—as never before. Yet we will overcome him by the blood of the Lamb and word of our testimony. Then King Jesus will descend in vengeance, vanquishing the imposter altogether.

This odious character, the Scriptures forewarn, will be a master deceiver. Now, to be forewarned is to be forearmed. Because the spirit of antichrist is inextricably bound up with anti-Semitism, we are forewarned about the increase of both. Anti-Semitism will be fed first to an unsuspecting world, which, when swallowed, will render anti-Christianity quite palatable.

Do you plan to be raptured out of the nasty plot before this pernicious personality rises to the fore? If so, I urge you to read on anyway. For the Bible teaches us another principle: The spirit of antichrist, released long ago on earth (see 1 John 2:18, 22; 4:3; 2 John 7), is already laying its last days' groundwork, especially concerning Israel. Besides, if you're reading this book, I'm guessing you have not been raptured. God might just speak to you about how He wants to use you today, tomorrow—and the days after that.

When the time is right (remember, God is calling the shots), the man of false peace will emerge. We will not need to guess who he is. Hailed by war-weary nations, he will be handed global powers of unprecedented proportions. This man of perdition will even keep some semblance of a Mideast peace plan that works—for a while.

If you have been to Israel recently, you know that billboards, banners and even secular songs proclaim, "We want *Mashiach* [Messiah] now!" Many religious Jews expect the soon coming of Israel's messianic redeemer. But they believe he will be a *human being*, definitely not God. This harbinger of salvation is expected to possess supernatural power that will enable him to instill peace; indeed, he will be heralded as messiah precisely because of this demonic anointing to mediate peace on earth.

According to biblical Jewish belief, the time for Messiah is at hand. The Hebrew Scriptures suggest that God has ordained seven thousand years for our planet's existence. Just as He created a seven-day week as a complete measure of time, He has determined a type of seven-day life span for the earth. As the seventh day of the week is a Sabbath, so, too, the seventh "day" of earth's existence will be a Sabbath. This Sabbath will amount to a one-thousand-year-long "day" of rest and peace, or true shalom. The New Covenant speaks of this parallel between a day and a millennium: "With the

Lord a day is like a thousand years, and a thousand years are like a day" (2 Peter 3:8).

The Hebrew calendar, based on the creation of the world in Genesis, presently puts us near the year 6000 (at this writing, 5764 to be exact). Many Jews anticipate the beginning of the Messianic Age in approximately the year 6000—the start of the seventh day—which could now actually be *any* day.

By this reasoning, and in His grand design, God will have given humanity six days, or six thousand years, to rule the earth. (Not coincidentally, the number six in the Bible stands for humanity, whereas the number seven represents completion.) The climax of the collective human effort will literally bring the world to the brink of destruction under the rule of Antichrist. Then *Christ* will enter the scene as Judge, Savior and King.

In the meantime, as surely as Messiah Yeshua is destined to rescue, then rule and reign from Jerusalem, anti-Messiah's target will also be Jerusalem. As surely as Yeshua will be extolled in glory on the Temple Mount, anti-Messiah will usurp control of this power point on earth. He will demand to be worshiped as God in a rebuilt third Temple. (Recall that Israel's first Temple was built by King Solomon; construction of her second Temple was authorized by King Cyrus and its expansion continued on through King Herod's time.)

Apparently this pretender to the throne will be so self-deluded as to think he actually stands a chance against the Creator. His true colors revealed, anti-Messiah will quickly lose Jewish support. Earth's worst tribulation and persecution against God's people follows. Then Yahweh's wrath and severest judgments are released on earth (which I do *not* believe His redeemed ones will experience). The Old Covenant refers to this entire period as the "time of Jacob's trouble" (see, for example, Jeremiah 30:7, NKJV).

Keep these matters in mind as the perfidious international struggle continues over this small parcel of real estate—Jerusalem's Temple Mount—and as the Jewish people seek to rebuild a Temple there.

Rebuilding the Temple

The Temple held an important place in the hearts of Israel's earliest Zionist pioneers. Today it is central in the minds of Jewish zealots busily gathering the ritualistic paraphernalia (including special animals and people) necessary to resume Temple worship and sacrifice according to the biblical pattern. I often meet Christians who are interested in, even fascinated by, the future third Temple. "How should we pray and contribute to this exciting project?" they ask.

As we talk, I usually discover their enthusiasm stems from their belief that the Temple heralds the second coming of Christ. By supporting the project, they say, believers can hasten the day of His return. Maybe so. But first, I tell them, there are other factors to consider.

The Jewish people engaged in rebuilding the Temple are reconstructing not just a building but a whole system designed to substitute the blood of bulls, goats and sheep for His once-for-all atonement. Resumed animal sacrifice will render the Cross and Crucified One more irrelevant in their eyes than ever. At the same time, these zealots anticipate that the Temple, once up and running, will hasten the coming of *their* messiah — a *man*, definitely *not* Jesus, who establishes world peace. The project is mentioned in the Scriptures only in connection with its desecration (see Daniel 9:25–27; Matthew 24:15; 2 Thessalonians 2:3–4; Revelation 13:14–15); it seems laden with spiritual undertones of Antichrist.

The Antichrist will lead Israel and the nations down a path deceptively designed for their destruction (see verses above). During the Great Tribulation, this imposter will brazenly desecrate the Temple's innermost sanctum. Because he is so keenly set on this site, the man of lawlessness may even play a pivotal role in garnering support for the Temple's construction. I differ, therefore, from some Christian teachers in that I am not convinced Yeshua will ever occupy a house defiled by the Antichrist, the embodiment of humanity's sin-stained attempt to attain righteousness with God.

The Scriptures tell us a glorious *fourth* Temple will also be built in Jerusalem, wherein the one true Messiah will be worshiped in holy splendor (see Ezekiel 40–48).[13] This Temple will be enormous in size, many times larger than the entire, present-day Temple Mount (see Ezekiel 42:15–20).[14] Unlike the second or third Temples, over this sacred structure the *Shekhinah* will magnificently and definitively descend and dwell.[15] Sacrifices will again be made from its sanctified altar — but *not* as atonement for sin and *not* in substitution for the blood of Yeshua (see Ezekiel 40:39, 42; 43:18–27; 45:15–19, 23–24; 46:4–7, 13–15). Instead, these Messiah-centered offerings will take place in memorial commemoration of His once-for-all redemption.

From this Holy Temple the biblical feasts will again be celebrated, the law of the Lord go forth and rivers of life flow through the land. The Bible identifies this breathtaking palace of praise as the Millennium Temple. It is the one I personally yearn to behold as part of the culminating manifestation of God's glory on earth.

In the meantime, if we find ourselves overly magnetized to the matter of the Jews' rebuilding the Temple, we may want to ask ourselves a question: Is it possible we value Israel more as a prophetic timepiece than the object of God's passionate love? As I've said, my perspective may differ from others, but the principle is this: If our hearts beat with heaven, there is still other Temple-building in Israel to be excited about before He returns — living temples whose bodies the Spirit desires to indwell, prophetically unleashing life from the dead.

. . . And death for life.

Why do I speak of death for life? The closer we come to the Lord's return, the more ferocious the fight against God's people. The devil knows that if he could ever annihilate the Jewish nation, he could prevent his own apocalyptic demise. In the end, I believe he will try to convince the world to crucify Israel, in a sense, on a type of last days' altar.

If Israel is made an altar of sacrifice, where does God want you in that day?

CHAPTER SEVENTEEN

The Sacrament of Sacrifice

I love stories about heroes of the faith. Not only Bible accounts, but biographical tales of tried and true saints through history who have stood valiantly for God at great personal cost. Their courage convicts and inspires me. I am convicted because I want to be so rapturously and steadfastly in love with Yeshua that nothing, no matter how grueling, will quell that love. I am inspired because deep down, I know all true believers are called, to one degree or another, to the sacrament of suffering for the Kingdom's sake. "*All* that will live godly in Christ Jesus shall suffer persecution" (2 Timothy 3:12, KJV, emphasis added).

The story of the Reverend Richard Wurmbrand, a Romanian Jewish believer imprisoned by Nazis, then Communists, is known the world over.[1] For fourteen years, Reverend Wurmbrand endured excruciating, repulsively inhuman tortures on account of his loyalty to Yeshua. During that time he also experienced unspeakable joy in the Savior's abiding, intimate presence. After his miraculous release, Reverend Wurmbrand founded a ministry that continues to reach out and support the persecuted Church.

I met Reverend Wurmbrand when he was in his eighties. His face was weathered with crevices and grooves that bore witness to pain, and he limped from his lashings of long ago. But Reverend Wurmbrand's sparkling eyes and serene smile made him glow with glory. Every word he spoke rippled supernatural love and otherworldly shalom into the atmosphere. The aged Jewish saint had offered his body a living sacrifice as his spiritual act of worship. That his offering had been holy and pleasing to God was strikingly evident.

I asked Reverend Wurmbrand if he felt that such extraordinary depth of spirit and Messiah-likeness could be attained only through suffering. I will never forget his reply. I would have liked it so much more if Reverend Wurmbrand had simply said no. But instead he fixed his eyes on mine with deep fatherly compassion and, after a brief silence, assured me that opportunities to die to self to live for Yeshua, and so share in His sufferings, were not limited to dank Romanian prisons. "Each day," he said, "wherever you are and whatever your circumstances, you can choose to offer your body as a living sacrifice—or not."

Living Sacrifices

Sacrificial service and Christian maturity are inextricably linked with Israel. God's call to offer our bodies as living sacrifices flows *directly* from and concludes His keynote message to the Church about the Jewish people. Recall with me once more the order of the Scriptures, in which revelation knowledge of divine love in Romans 8 leads us straight to the topic of Israel in Romans 9 through 11. Our hearts ignited for His Jewish people, God guides us along to Romans 12, where He tells us how, in light of all He has just said, we are to live.

The first word of the first verse of Romans 12 is *therefore*. You have probably heard it said that when we see the word *therefore* in the Scriptures we need to ask what it is *there for*. In this instance, *therefore* is there to explain what God wants from us. Our response to the impassioned information He has just imparted ought to be one of worship by offering ourselves in sacrificial service.

Mark Nanos interprets this passage as a call for Christian sacrifice, specifically in reciprocal exchange for Israel's sacrifice on
behalf of believers:

> They [the Romans] are . . . benefiting from the "stumbling" on the
> part of Israel, whom they are so quick to condemn for not believing
> what they now believe. Certainly, this is cause for humility where
> arrogance had once been tempting, *laying the groundwork for the commit-
> ment Paul urges from 12:1 onward* toward God . . . and the "stumbling"
> of Israel . . . in the tradition of the suffering of Christ Jesus.[2]
>
> EMPHASIS ADDED

In view of the mercy demonstrated toward Gentiles and evidenced through the Jewish people, Paul pleads, "offer your bodies
as living sacrifices" as "your spiritual act of worship." Sovereign
symmetry calls us to offer ourselves as living sacrifices in reasonable worship. As this present age draws to a close, saying yes to
the call will not be easy.

Some, therefore, will be willing—but some will not.

The Amplified Bible describes it this way:

> I appeal to you therefore, brethren, and beg of you in view of [all]
> the mercies of God, to make a decisive dedication of your bod-
> ies—presenting all your members and faculties—as a living sacrifice,
> holy (devoted, consecrated) and well pleasing to God, which is your
> reasonable (rational, intelligent) service and spiritual worship.
>
> ROMANS 12:1, AMPLIFIED

Wouldn't it have been nice if God had said to offer up our songs
or conferences or church services? Surely this sort of "worship"
would be more consistent with our concept of "reasonable." But
the Almighty said to offer up our bodies—as Yeshua did.

> Be *imitators* of God, therefore . . . just as Christ loved us and *gave
> himself up* for us as a fragrant offering and sacrifice to God.
>
> EPHESIANS 5:1–2, EMPHASIS ADDED

"If anyone would come after me, he must deny himself and take up his cross and follow me. For whoever wants to save his life will lose it, but whoever loses his life for me and for the gospel will save it."

MARK 8:34–35

The Choice

Israel is destined to summon forth sacrifice, a testing ground that exposes the intents of our hearts. It has always been so, even for the One we follow, Yeshua crucified and resurrected—who said that greater love has no one than to lay down his life for his friends.

In God's hand and plan, Israel will prove a last days' great divide—a point of division among humankind. The Church will not be exempt. Lies will arise about the Jewish people obscured in a worldly reasonableness that will persuade and pervert many. Slowly and subtly, as in the past, devilish deceptions about Israel/Zionism/the Jews will sway many Christians. In fact, it is already beginning to happen.

Basilea Schlink wrote many decades ago that future Christians who support anti-Semitism may suddenly find themselves on the wrong side, just as many German believers failed to recognize Nazism and its theology as the enemy of God. She forewarns with inspired clarity:

As God's plan of salvation nears its final consummation . . . and hatred flares up against Him more than ever, there will be a bringing together of those who belong together because they fear the living God and give Him glory—Jews and Christians. . . . But if all the time we have been opposing God's people or else condoning the attacks made on them by powers hostile to God, woe betide us later when the whole world is caught up in a rebellion against God! Then, even without noticing it, we shall suddenly find ourselves on the side of the antichristian kingdom, whose prime target will be the Jews. . . . [For] our relationship with them is indicative of our true relationship to the Lord Jesus, showing whether it is a relationship of love. If we love Jesus, we shall love the people whom He loves and always will love and who will yet be the centre and blessing of all nations.[3]

In the end, only the Bride of Christ—those loving Him, obeying Him and denying themselves for Him—will stand in unity with Israel. Will you?

Are you waiting to get a personal word from God? My friend, you may never hear it. You see, this is about *your* choice, based on *your* heart and the Word that is already in you.

Are you holding out until a major stand *must* be taken? Are you waiting until your Jewish neighbor shows up unexpectedly one day on your doorstep, in need of a hiding place?

In case you have not realized it, the test has already begun. You are already taking a stand each time you choose how to process the evening news, or how to pray, or how to study the Scriptures, or how to speak within your personal sphere of influence, or how to get informed, or how to relate to Jews . . . or how to respond to this book. As Israeli ambassador Don Gillerman pointedly told the United Nations in 2003, "God is watching."[4]

Standing for God and sharing the burden of His heart demands sacrifice of self. Yet the sacrifice is divinely surprising, for its end result yields great blessing. Those who bless Israel are blessed; they have blessed God who blesses bountifully of Himself in return. To make a choice for His chosen people is to choose *Him.*

Jesus cautions that in the last days, because of the increase of wickedness—some of which will revolve around Israel—the love of many will grow cold. Unprecedented dimensions of heaven—and hell—will flood the nations. Riptides of revival will meet with reprisal. In the glorious last days' harvest, many will be persecuted for righteousness' sake. Jesus wants us prepared to consider it pure joy when we face such trials, for the testing of our faith molds us into maturity and wholeness (see James 1:2–4); in other words, Messiah-likeness. At such times His presence abides with us in the sweetest of communion. He wants us rejoicing when we participate in His suffering so, as He promised, we can be lavishly blessed when His glory is revealed (see 1 Peter 4:13).

The Remnant in Revelation

Will you be part of God's joining His New and Old Covenant people in a shared, last days' destiny? He is preparing the way for Yeshua's return by preparing hearts. He is looking for those prepared to love unconditionally (suffer long) and bless (kneel to enrich), not as a means to an end but for Love's own sake: to bless the Blesser. Those who know Him intimately resonate to the divine heartbeat. They share His longing for Israel, His "firstborn son" who has suffered much on behalf of the Gentiles. He will take the hands of Gentile believers (including Arabs) with prepared hearts and interlock them with Israel's. He will have many of you strategically holding hands with Messianic Jews. You will be setting the stage for the greatest revival on earth.

The book of Revelation, with its mystifying and pulsating prophetic symbolism, also reports some plain down-to-earth, soon-coming events. One of these involves "the 144,000." Appearing twice in the book's apocalyptic account (chapters 7 and 14) is a company of revived Messianic firebrands known collectively as the 144,000. Coming from "all the tribes of Israel," 12,000 per tribe, they are distinct from another, larger group, the "great multitude" (see 7:4–9). The great multitude comes from every nation, tribe, people and language; they are not necessarily Israelis, but all believers who have come out of the Great Tribulation.

The 144,000, described as a pure and blameless subgroup of the great multitude, are "standing on Mount Zion" (14:1), "follow the Lamb wherever he goes" and are "offered as firstfruits to God and the Lamb" (14:4). Apparently they are gathered from within the Jewish State—and quite possibly martyred.

A sacrament of suffering awaits us. We have an opportunity to worship in sacrifice to the Worthy One, just as His courageous followers have done throughout history. As in the past God is looking for those who will take up a cross for Israel, not in imperialistic conquest, but as the instrument of death to *self* . . . like the ten Boom family.

Corrie ten Boom's Blessing

The beloved and unforgettable Corrie ten Boom, together with her family, took up the cross of self-sacrifice for the Jews of Holland during the Holocaust. Like Ruth in the Bible, the ten Booms were extravagantly blessed. But not as you or I would expect.

When the Nazis overtook Holland, Jews came knocking, one by one, on the ten Booms' front door. "In this household," Corrie's father would say, "God's people are always welcome."[5] The ten Booms loved the Jewish people, ultimately, for one reason: They loved God. Their home quickly became a hiding place for Dutch Jews with nowhere else to go—until, one horrifying day, German soldiers knocked at the door.

What was this family's reward for their blessing of Israel, their kneeling to enrich the Jewish people? Imprisonment and concentration camp (Ravensbrük), where they all, except Corrie, died as martyrs. Did the ten Booms know what they were getting into? Indeed. Losing their lives for the Jews, Corrie's father said from the start, would be "the greatest honor that could come to my family."[6]

Corrie was miraculously released from Ravensbrük one day before her scheduled execution, the result of a "clerical error." In years to come millions would hear her story: His story of love. They would meet a woman who lived extraordinarily beyond a place of blessing; they would meet the Blesser Himself.

The Jewish nation ultimately summons us to the cross—and the cross summons God's Son to us. Do you really desire more of the Blesser? Is God your goal? In blessing Israel, this goal you will attain. (And to Messianic Jewish believers, could it be that *our* greatest blessing—and fulfillment of the call to serve as a light to the nations—involves laying down our lives for the nations?)

Abigail's Anointing

In 2003, in view of God's mercy toward Israel, a lovely teenage girl named Abigail Litle imitated Yeshua, gave herself up and offered her body as a living sacrifice. God honored—and I believe He treasures—her offering.

Abigail was murdered in a terrorist bombing of an Israeli bus she was riding with her friends in Haifa. While terror is no stranger to the Jewish State, Abigail was unique. She was martyred as an American-born, evangelical Christian living in Israel with her missionary parents. After her seemingly senseless death, extraordinary, spiritually groundbreaking things happened.

Nearly a thousand Israeli Jews, including the mayor of Haifa, came to Abigail's funeral to stand alongside her grieving family. The funeral, which spoke explicitly of eternal life in Messiah Jesus, was aired on Israeli TV and reported by the national press. *The International Jerusalem Post* featured a poignant, full-length story about Abigail, her family and their faith.[7] Amazingly, the journalist—who is not a believer—provided an explanation of the saving atonement and grace of Yeshua the Messiah so her readers would understand the story. For years Messianic Jews had tried to get the Gospel explicitly published in the Israeli media, to virtually no avail. But the blood of the martyrs is the seed of the Church.

Israeli Messianic leader Barry Segal, who attended Abigail's funeral, served in the Israeli army and is well acquainted with the heartache of bloodshed. Of her living sacrifice, he wrote:

> I think that this event was the breaking of ground for a new season of God's outpouring of grace in relations between Israel's Jewish community, Messianic Jews and Christians. . . . Never have I seen out of tragedy so much love and such a testimony as when Abigail was buried as a seed into the ground. She was truly a "bridge over troubled waters."[8]

A member of the Israeli Knesset (Parliament) who was present at the funeral said that Abigail's coffin, draped by both the U.S. and Israeli flags, represented a sign from God that Christians and Jews have entered a new era of partnership after two thousand years. "This speaks far more deeply," he added, "than all the friendship/unity meetings we could possibly organize."[9]

The Mantle of Martyrdom

Dietrich Bonhoeffer wrote, "When Christ calls a man, He bids him come and die."[10]

Blessing the Jewish nation and people in our day may come at a cost. For some the cost may be great; perhaps like Abigail Litle or Corrie ten Boom's loved ones, it will mean martyrdom. But then the reward will be exceedingly great as well. As missionary-martyr Jim Elliot said, "He is no fool who gives what he cannot keep to gain what he cannot lose."

I have learned that the more a sacrifice costs, the more blessing it tends to release. The more I give myself to Messiah, the more He gives Himself to me. I discover that whatever was to my profit is loss for the sake of His presence. I am told to consider everything as rubbish compared to the surpassing greatness of knowing Yeshua my Lord. I am told to share in the fellowship of His sufferings, becoming like Him in His death—that I may know Him in the power of His resurrection.

My Messiah is coming for a pure and spotless Bride whose love for Him is stronger than death. She will gladly lay down her life for the One who offered Himself up for her. She will not run from the cross; in adoring love she will embrace the altar of atonement that binds her heart to His. She will gaze at the holy blood of her Beloved, and see in it the ultimate power of the universe. She, too, will take up her cross to follow Him. This will be her most powerful act of worship and intimate identification with the Infinite One.

We in the West have experienced little serious persecution for our faith. But that is not the case in much of the world. Daily there are cases of cruelty against Christians and reports of martyrdom. Christian Zionist Don Finto urges the Church to heed Jesus' words in preparation for His second coming:

As the time of Messiah's return draws near, the warfare will only escalate. Evil and righteousness are maturing together until the harvest, just as Jesus told His listeners (see Matt. 13:30). . . . Believers may go through great tribulation, but they will never experience God's wrath. . . . In times of great persecution, many die for their faith. For others, the Lord stays the hand of torturers and executioners.[11]

Yeshua endured the cross for the joy set before Him. So, too, do His people. When their crosses are borne for loving Israel, they can expect lavish and extravagant joy. God says, "Rejoice with Jerusalem and be glad for her, all you who love her; rejoice greatly with her, all you who mourn over her" (Isaiah 66:10).

Unspeakable delights await you as you weep into heaven's tear bottle over Zion. As you pour yourself out for God's prodigal nation, prepare to toss your head back in exultant laughter, dance in holy delirium and revel with your King on and on, and on and on. Because it's all about *Him,* now and forever.

Notes

Chapter 1: God, Israel and You

1. *The NIV Study Bible: New International Version* (Grand Rapids: Zondervan, 1985), see note for Matthew 25:31–46; *The First Scofield Study Bible, King James Version* (Grand Rapids: World Publishing, 1986), see note for Matthew 25:32. The NIV note (correctly, in my opinion) does not limit the interpretation of "these brothers of mine" to only the Jewish people.

2. John F. Walvoord, *The Prophecy Knowledge Handbook* (Wheaton, Ill.: Victor Books, 1990), 398; Dan Gruber, *The Church and the Jews: The Biblical Relationship* (Hagerstown, Md.: Serenity Books, 1997), 199–200.

3. Very preliminary research suggests the Temple Mount may also have been the location of the Garden of Eden.

Chapter 2: Blessing for Blessing

1. In the New Covenant Greek, *bless* conveys a slightly different meaning, stressing the result (happiness and prosperity) more than the process. The two meanings in Hebrew and Greek are not inconsistent, the latter assuming and elaborating on the former, as in Jesus' Sermon on the Mount.

2. James Strong, *The Exhaustive Concordance of the Bible* (Nashville: Abingdon, 1977), see *bless* in Main Concordance, see *barakh* in Hebrew and Chaldee Dictionary; Francis Brown, S. R. Driver and Charles A. Briggs, *A Hebrew and English Lexicon of the Old Testament* (Oxford: Clarendon Press, 1980), see *barakh*.

3. Allen P. Ross, *Creation and Blessing: A Guide to the Study and Exposition of the Book of Genesis* (Grand Rapids: Baker, 1988), 263.

4. *Merriam-Webster's Collegiate Dictionary*, 10th ed. (Springfield, Mass.: Merriam-Webster, 1994).

5. Andrew Murray, *Humility* (Springdale, Pa.: Whittaker House, 1982), 28.

6. Ibid., 93.

7. See Genesis 18:22–32; 1 Corinthians 7:14.

8. Arnold G. Fruchtenbaum, *Israelology: The Missing Link in Systematic Theology* (Tustin, Calif.: Ariel Ministries Press, 1993), 343.

9. Ibid., citing J. Dwight Pentecost, *Things to Come: A Study in Biblical Eschatology* (Findlay, Ohio: Dunham Publishing Company, 1958).

Chapter 3: Accursed: Who, Why, When

1. Some interpreters of the ancient Scriptures deviate from the literal-grammatical-historical approach. For a more complete study, see Richard N. Longenecker, *Biblical Exegesis in the Apostolic Period* (Grand Rapids: Eerdmans, 1975).

2. See Roy B. Zuck, *Basic Bible Interpretation: A Practical Guide to Discovering Biblical Truth* (Wheaton, Ill.: Victor Books, 1991), 27–55.

3. Ernest F. Kevan, "The Principles of Interpretation," in *Revelation and the Bible*, ed. Carl F. H. Henry (Grand Rapids: Baker, 1958), 291.

4. As summarized in Hal Lindsey, *The Road to Holocaust* (New York: Bantam, 1990), 58–59: "In essence, he [Origen] ignored the example of the apostolic fathers (who were virtually all literalists), leap-frogged right over the lessons of the post-Reformation, and plunged head-long into the allegorical method of interpretation that gave us the Dark Ages."

5. As another example of allegory, consider that two hundred years later Augustine, whose influence still affects the church, had this to say about the book of Genesis: The four rivers flowing from the Garden of Eden were four cardinal virtues; Adam and Eve's fig leaves represented hypocrisy; and Noah's drunken stupor depicted Messiah's crucifixion. Zuck, 39–40.

6. This approach runs counter to the notion that the New Covenant must always be our grid for interpreting the Old. See, for example, Walter C. Kaiser Jr., "The Land of Israel and the Future Return," in *Israel: The Land and the People*, ed. H. Wayne House (Grand Rapids: Kregel, 1998), 219–20.

7. Though allegorical influence remains, the literal (or, more technically, literal-grammatical-historical) method has been the basis of orthodox Christianity's approach to Bible interpretation since the Protestant Reformation. It is generally the approach of Protestant evangelicalism. See J. Dwight Pentecost, *Things to Come*.

8. Strong, *Concordance*, see *curse* in Main Concordance, see *alah, arar, qalal* in Hebrew and Chaldee Dictionary. See also, Ross, *Creation and Blessing*, 264.

9. G. B. Funderburk, "Curse," in *The Zondervan Pictorial Encyclopedia of the Bible*, ed. Merrill C. Tenney, vol. 1 (Grand Rapids: Zondervan, 1976), 1046.

10. Ross, 263–64; Walter C. Kaiser Jr., *Mission in the Old Testament: Israel as a Light to the Nations* (Grand Rapids: Baker, 2000), 19.

11. The promise is reaffirmed to Abraham, after God's initial pronouncement, at different times in the patriarch's life.

12. From the Library of Congress web site: "American Memory: Historical Collections for the National Digital Library." <http://lcweb2.loc.gov/cgi-bin>.

13. Iain H. Murray, *The Puritan Hope: Revival and the Interpretation of Prophecy* (Edinburgh: Banner of Truth Trust, 1991), 41–48.

14. Claude Duvernoy, *The Prince and the Prophet*, trans. Jack Joffe (Jerusalem: Christian Action for Israel, n.d.), 7–13.

15. John McTernan and Bill Koenig, *Israel: The Blessing or the Curse* (Oklahoma City: Hearthstone Publishing, 2002), 103–4, 212–18.

Chapter 4: Through the Lens of Love

1. R. E. O. White, "Love," in *Baker Encyclopedia of the Bible*, ed. Walter A. Elwell, vol. 2 (Grand Rapids: Baker, 1989), 1357.

2. A. W. Tozer, *The Knowledge of the Holy* (San Francisco: Harper & Row, 1961), 97.

3. I do not mention the New Covenant words for *love* here, as we are discussing the love of God for the Jewish people as He reveals it in the Hebrew Scriptures.

4. *Zondervan Pictorial Encyclopedia*, vol. 3, 989.

5. Strong, *Concordance*.

6. Francis Brown, *The New Brown-Driver-Briggs-Gesenius Hebrew and English Lexicon* (Boston: Houghton Mifflin, 1983), 888. *Keenah* is not translated as "love," but it describes key qualities of God's love.

7. J. H. Laenen, *Jewish Mysticism: An Introduction* (Louisville: John Knox, 2001), 255–58; Bruce K. Waltke and M. O'Connor, *An Introduction to Biblical Hebrew Syntax* (Winona Lake, Ind.: Eisenbrauns, 1990), 45; Ellen Frankel and Betsy Platkin Teutsch, *The Encyclopedia of Jewish Symbols* (Northvale, N.J.: Jason Aronson, 1995), 4–5.

8. Frank I. Seekins, *Hebrew Word Pictures* (Phoenix: Living Word Pictures, 1994), 14–19, 28–29; Edward Horowitz, *How the Hebrew Language Grew* (New York: Ktav Publishing House, 1960), 14, 312–13; Frankel and Teutsch, 5.

9. J. I. Packer, *Knowing God* (Downers Grove, Ill.: InterVarsity Press, 1973), 112, quoting James Orr, *Hasting's Dictionary of the Bible*, vol. 3.

Chapter 5: Love Calls

1. The grammatically correct usage of *ahav* (*love* as a verb) here is *ahava* (*love* as a noun).

Chapter 6: The Purpose of Service

1. As referenced in Rabbi Shalom Schwartz, "To Live As Jews," Aish.com, December 30, 2002, <http://www.aish.com/jewishissues/israeldiary/To_Live_As_Jews.asp>.

2. Yiddish is a variant of combined Hebrew, German and Slavic, spoken by the Jews of Eastern Europe.

3. *Ivri* is Hebrew for a Hebrew person; a different word is used to refer to the Hebrew language.

4. Bill Bjoraker, *Hebrew Nuggets: Truth That Impacts You, Mined from the Riches of Our Hebrew Heritage* (Pasadena: Operation Ezekiel, 1997), 7; *Zondervan Pictorial Encyclopedia*, vol. 3, 66. I owe many of the linguistic concepts expressed here and elsewhere in this chapter to Bjoraker's research.

5. Any reference to an individual personally unknown to the author is purely coincidental.

6. Isadore Epstein, ed., "Sanhedrin 99b," in *The Babylonian Talmud* (London: The Soncino Press, 1935), 675.

7. There is a historical explanation for the use of the word *Jew*, stemming from Judah. Judah's tribal land inheritance was located in the southern part of Israel. Close to 1000 B.C., the nation divided into two kingdoms, one in the north and one in the south. At that time, the whole southern kingdom became known as "Judah," much as "Washington" is used to refer to the entire United States.

8. Bjoraker, *Hebrew Nuggets.*

9. Kaiser, 56–57.

10. As quoted in Evangelical Sisterhood of Mary, *Changing the Future by Confronting the Past: Talks and Testimonies — Jerusalem 2001 Convention* (Darmstadt, Germany: Evangelical Sisterhood of Mary, 2001), 203–4. Used by permission.

11. For a more thorough discussion on this issue see, for example: Chaim Potok, *Wanderings: Chaim Potok's History of the Jews* (New York: Fawcett, 1990); Max I. Dimont, *The Indestructible Jews* (New York: Signet, 1973); Fr. Edward Flannery, *The Anguish of the Jews: Twenty-Three Centuries of Antisemitism* (New York: Paulist Press, 1985); Michael L. Brown, *Our Hands Are Stained with Blood* (Shippensburg, Pa.: Destiny Image, 1992).

Chapter 7: An Irrevocable Calling

1. John Piper, *The Justification of God: An Exegetical and Theological Study of Romans 9:1–23* (Grand Rapids: Baker, 1993), 24, 33.

2. David H. Stern, *Complete Jewish Bible* (Clarksville, Md., and Jerusalem: Jewish New Testament Publications, 1998).

3. *Zondervan Pictorial Encyclopedia*, vol. 2, 540.

4. Merrill F. Unger, *Unger's Bible Dictionary* (Chicago: Moody Press, 1966), 367.

5. George Buttrick, gen. ed., *The Interpreter's Dictionary of the Bible*, vol. 2 (Nashville: Abingdon Press, 1981), 270–71.

6. See James D. G. Dunn, "Romans 9–16," in *Word Biblical Commentary*, vol. 38B, gen. ed. David A. Hubbard and Glenn W. Barker (Dallas: Word, 1988), 533–34.

7. Merrill C. Tenney, ed., *The Zondervan Pictorial Bible Dictionary* (Grand Rapids: Zondervan, 1967), 315.

8. Perhaps this quality of God's presence refers to an aspect of the glory for which all humanity was created, but it was exchanged and lost due to sin (see Romans 1:23; 3:23).

9. C. E. B. Cranfield, *The International Critical Commentary on the Epistle to the Romans*, vol. 2 (Edinburgh: T & T Clark, 1979), 446–47.

10. Dietrich Bonhoeffer, *The Cost of Discipleship* (New York: Simon & Schuster, Inc., 1995), 45.

11. See, for example, J. M. Myers, *Grace and Torah* (Philadelphia: Fortress Press, 1975), 33; and Ariel Berkowitz and D'vorah Berkowitz, *Torah Rediscovered: Challenging Centuries of Misinterpretation and Neglect* (Littleton, Colo.: First Fruits of Zion, 1996), xv.

12. See George Eldon Ladd, *The Gospel of the Kingdom* (Grand Rapids: Eerdmans, 1990).

13. See note 14 in Piper, 37–38.

14. Abraham Cohen, *Everyman's Talmud: The Major Teachings of the Rabbinic Sages* (New York: Schocken, 1949), 63; Daniel C. Juster, *The Irrevocable Calling* (Gaithersburg, Md.: Tikkun Ministries, 1996), 21.

15. Reuven Doron, *One New Man* (Cedar Rapids, Iowa: Embrace, 1993), 81.

Chapter 8: Rejected Roots, Broken Branches

1. Marvin R. Wilson, *Our Father Abraham: Jewish Roots of the Christian Faith* (Grand Rapids: Eerdmans; Dayton, Ohio: Center for Judaic-Christian Studies, 1989), 88–89, 94.

2. James Carroll, *Constantine's Sword: The Church and the Jews* (Boston: Houghton Mifflin, 2001), 144–48 (excerpts).

3. Quoted in Malcolm Hay, *The Roots of Christian Antisemitism* (New York: Liberty Press, 1981), 27, cited by Brown, *Our Hands Are Stained with Blood*, 11.

4. Clarence H. Wagner Jr., "Where Was Love and Mercy? The History of Christian Antisemitism." <http://www.israelmybeloved.com/history_prophecy/antisemitism/where_love_part1.htm>.

5. William Nicholls, *Christian Antisemitism: A History of Hate* (Northvale, N.J.: Jason Aronson Publishers, 1995), 90, as cited in Ken Spiro, "Crash Course in Jewish History, Part 41: From Paul to Constantine," April 7, 2003, <http://www.aish.com>.

6. James M. Hutchens, "Israel: Superseded or Replaced?" *Jerusalem Connection* (September 2002): 2.

7. Martin Luther, *The Jews and Their Lies* (1543), as quoted in *Medieval Sourcebook*, <http://www.fordham.edu/halsall/source/luther-jews.html>. Contemporary Lutheran denominations have renounced Luther's diatribes against the Jewish people.

8. Quote attributed to Raul Hilberg.

9. Hal Lindsey, *The Road to Holocaust* (New York: Bantam, 1990), 24.

10. Patricia Golan, "Communal Spirit," *The International Jerusalem Post* (February 14, 2003):19, quoting Rudolf Pesch.

11. Flannery, *The Anguish of the Jews*, 1, cited in Brown, *Our Hands Are Stained with Blood*, xii.

12. Jim W. Goll, *Exodus Cry* (Ventura, Calif.: Regal Books, 2001), 76.

13. Daniel Juster, acknowledging Peter Hocken, John Dillon and Catholic University research for *Toward Jerusalem Council II*, in "Anti-Messianic Judaism: A Brief Summary," <http://www.baruchhashem.com/resources/antimessjud.html>. *Toward Jerusalem Council II* represents an excellent collaborative work of Christian and Messianic Jewish leaders seeking to repeal these decrees.

14. Elwood McQuaid, *The Zion Connection* (Eugene, Ore.: Harvest House Publishers, 1996), 42.

15. F. F. Bruce, "The Epistle of Paul to the Romans," in *The Tyndale New Testament Commentaries*, ed. R. V. G. Tasker (Grand Rapids: Eerdmans, 1963), 217–18.

16. Gerald McDermott, "The Land: Evangelicals and Israel," *Books & Culture: A Christian Review* (March–April, 2003): 9, citing Paul Charles Merkley, *The Politics of Christian Zionism 1891–1948* (London: Frank Cass, 1998).

17. World Council of Churches, <http://www.wcc-coe.org/wcc/what/international/palestine/eap.html>.

18. World Council of Churches, Office of Communication Press Update, August 8, 2001, <http://www.wcc-coe.org/wcc/news/press/01/25pu.html>.

19. Teresa Watanabe, "Christians Split Over Conflict in the Mideast," *Los Angeles Times*, May 5, 2002.

20. McDermott, "The Land," 40–41; see also Colin Chapman, *Whose Promised Land? The Continuing Crisis Over Israel and Palestine* (Grand Rapids: Baker, 2002), 189. Chapman notes that the creation of Israel did not solve the problem of anti-Semitism as the Jews had hoped. His book lays groundwork "justification" for terminating the sovereign Jewish State—and, thereby, the Jewish people.

21. Moshe Aumann, "An Israeli Response," in *Changing the Future by Confronting the Past* (Evangelical Sisterhood of Mary: Darmstadt, Germany, 2001), 28.

Chapter 9: The Jews and the Gospel

1. The Christian Scholars Group on Christian-Jewish Relations, "A Sacred Obligation: Rethinking Christian Faith in Relation to Judaism and the Jewish People," September 1, 2002, <http://www.bc.edu/research/cjl/meta-elements/partners/CSG/Sacred_Obligation.html>.

2. Walter Bauer, *A Greek-English Lexicon of the New Testament and Other Early Christian Literature*, 2d ed. (Chicago: University of Chicago Press, 1979), 672; Strong, *Exhaustive Concordance*; W. E. Vine, *A Comprehensive Dictionary of the Original*

Greek Words with their Precise Meanings for English Readers (Iowa Falls: Riverside Book and Bible House, n. d.), 477.

3. Mark D. Nanos, *The Mystery of Romans: The Jewish Context of Paul's Letter* (Minneapolis: Fortress Press, 1996), 265–66.

4. Michael L. Brown, *Answering Jewish Objections to Jesus*, 3 vols. (Grand Rapids: Baker, 2000–3) is an excellent guide.

Chapter 10: Revival of the Remnant

1. This unprecedented revival is documented in Sandra Teplinsky, *Out of the Darkness: The Untold Story of Jewish Revival in the Former Soviet Union* (Jacksonville, Fla.: Hear O Israel Ministries Publishing, 1998).

2. This figure is derived from a December 2002 estimate of the International Alliance of Messianic Congregations and Synagogues, calculating roughly 1.5 to 2 million Jews who express belief in Jesus, based on a 1991 survey by the Council of Jewish Federations in the United States. Patrick Johnstone and Jason Mandryk, *Operation World: 21st Century Edition* (Pasadena: US Center for World Mission; Bulstrode, Gerrards Cross, England: WEC International Research Office, 2001), 362, sets the number of congregational-affiliated Jewish believers at 332,000. Bear in mind, however, that most Jewish believers worldwide do not affiliate with congregations for various reasons, including fear of reprisal or discrimination.

3. Johnstone and Mandryk, 362.

4. Maarit Eronen, "Caught in Israel's Crossfire," *Charisma* (September 2002): 60. Johnstone and Mandryk, 362, reports similar numbers.

5. Eronen, 58.

6. Michael Freund, "Israel's Best Defense," *Jerusalem Post*, August 29, 2002.

7. Am Echad Resources, "Storm the Heavens," February 18, 2003, <http://www.aish.com/spirituality /prayer/Storm_the_Heavens.asp>.

8. Haim Shapiro, "Russian Olim Swell Ranks of Messianic Jews," *Jerusalem Post*, October 1, 1999, 32.

9. Ibid., citing Kai Kjaer-Hansen and Bodil Skjott, *Facts and Myths About the Messianic Congregations in Israel* (Jerusalem: United Christian Council and Caspari Center for Biblical and Jewish Studies, 1999).

10. Ibid., 60, note 6, quoting Avi Mizrachi of Congregation *Adonai Roi*, director of *Dugit* Ministry in Tel Aviv and former head of the Israeli National Evangelism Committee.

11. Quote attributed to Messianic pastor David Lazarus of Jaffa, Israel, in 2002.

12. Ari and Shira Sorko-Ram, untitled letter, *Maoz Israel Report* (Israel: Maoz Ministries), November 2002.

13. Not all Pharisees rejected Jesus; many followed Him.

14. See, for example, Jonathan Miles, "Firebombs Bolster Prayers Among Messianic Believers," *Christianity Today* 34, no. 6 (June 6, 1999): 34.

15. Disproportionate power rests with the ultra-Orthodox *Haredim* for reasons that are historical and politically complex, based on Israel's multiple-party system of government.

16. Pending in the Israeli Knesset as of this writing, the "Gafni-Lapid" bill's most salient provision states, "Anyone who attempts to persuade a person to change his religion by approaching him directly, will be liable to one year imprisonment; and if the person is a minor, he will be liable to two years imprisonment."

17. See, for example, "Facts You May Not Know," Maoz Ministries, <http://www.istandwithisrael.com>. Rare exceptions exist in which Christian organizations circumvent the law to aid the Messianic community.

18. When Paul speaks in the synagogue in Corinth, "We now turn to the Gentiles" (Acts 13:46), he is not announcing a policy shift of now going solely to Gentiles. He means that in that particular city, he now turns to the Gentiles. This is clear because after ministering in Corinth, he resumes the pattern of preaching first to the Jew, then to the Gentile. See Acts 17:1–4, 10, 17; 18:4, 19; 19:8, 10; 20:21.

Chapter 11: Abraham's Family Feud

1. No group exists today by the name "Ishmaelites," but I use it here to refer to Ishmael's various Arabic children.

2. C. F. Keil and F. Delitzsch, "Genesis," in *The Pentatuch*, trans. James Martin, vol. 1 of *Commentary on the Old Testament* (Grand Rapids: Eerdmans, 1983), 220, as cited in H. Lindsey, *The Everlasting Hatred: The Roots of Jihad* (Murietta, Calif.: Oracle House Publishing, 2002), 58.

3. *Zondervan Pictorial Bible Dictionary*, 362.

4. Avner Boskey, *A Perspective on Islam* (Nashville: Final Frontier Ministries, 2001), 16.

5. Jeremiah 25:18–26 speaks judgment against people groups believed to comprise the descendants of Abraham's other sons.

6. Josephus, *Antiquities*, i. 12, 4, as cited in Lindsey, *The Everlasting Hatred*, 89.

7. David Allen Lewis, *The Last War* (Green Forest, Ariz.: New Leaf Press, 2001), 19.

8. Haman may have been descended from the Amalekites.

9. D. Guthrie, ed., *The New Bible Commentary Revised* (Grand Rapids: Eerdmans, 1981), 742.

Chapter 12: Incursion of Islam

1. John Foxe, *Foxe's Annals of Martyrs* (Burlington, Ontario: Inspirational Promotions, n.d.), 247–48. See also, John Foxe, *The Acts and Monuments of John*

Foxe, vol. 4, 4th ed. (London: Religious Tract Society, n.d.), 18–23. In agreement, see Paul Marshall, Roberta Green and Lela Gilbert, *Islam at the Crossroads: Understanding Its Beliefs, History and Conflicts* (Grand Rapids: Baker, 2002), 49; Anis A. Shorrosh, *Islam Revealed: A Christian Arab's View of Islam* (Nashville: Thomas Nelson, 1988), 182–83.

2. Foxe, *Acts and Monuments*, 19.

3. Rabbi Berel Wein, *Echoes of Glory: The Story of the Jews in the Classical Era* (New York: Mesorah Publications, 1995), 299, as cited in Ken Spiro, "Crash Course in Jewish History, Part 42: The Rise of Islam," September 14, 2003, <http://www.aish.com>.

4. David K. Shipler, *Arab and Jew: Wounded Spirits in a Promised Land* (New York: Time Books, 1986), 162–64, citing Quran, Sura 2:59, 83, 121–22; Sura 3:60; Sura 4:48; Sura 58:15–16; Sura 9:29–30; Boskey, 7, citing Quran, Sura 2:89, 105, 213; Sura 9:30; Sura 4:171; Sura 5:72–75; Sura 19:88–93; Sura 5:116–18; Sura 2:113, 120, 159; Sura 4:46; Sura 5:41; Sura 57:27; Sura 8:39; Sura 9:5; Sura 29:47; Sura 47:4. See also Sura 4:157; Sura 5:17, 75; Sura 9:30.

5. See, for example, Ergun Mehmet Caner and Emir Fethi Caner, *Unveiling Islam* (Grand Rapids: Kregel, 2002), 105–7.

6. Robert Morey, *The Islamic Invasion* (Eugene, Or.: Harvest House Publishers, 1992), 211–18.

7. George Otis Jr., *The Last of the Giants: Lifting the Veil on Islam and the End Times* (Tarrytown, N.Y.: Chosen Books, 1991), 64.

8. Foxe, *Annals of Martyrs*, 248–67.

9. Melissa Radler, "A Different Face of Islam," *International Jerusalem Post*, July 18, 2003.

10. David B. Barrett and Todd M. Johnston, "International Bulletin of Missionary Research," January 2003, cited in World Evangelism Research Center, "Status of Global Missions, 2003." <http://gem-werc.org/>.

11. Quran, Sura 8:12–17, 60.

12. Joseph Farah, "Gaza's Preschool of Hate," World Net Daily, June 26, 2002, <http://www.worldnetdaily.com/news/article.asp?ARTICLE_ID=28085>. Andrea Levin, "Palestinian Textbooks Teach Anti-Israel Hate," Committee for Accuracy in Middle East Reporting in America, June 1, 1999, <http://www.world.std.com/~camera/docs/oncamera/oc99incite.html>. John Perazzo, "Palestinian Schools: Breeding Grounds for Hate," FreeRepublic.com, April 10, 2002, <http://www.freerepublic.com/focus/news/663607/posts>. Mitchell G. Bard, "Arab/Muslim Attitudes Toward Israel," Jewish Virtual Library, Myths and Facts Online: The Refugees, 2002, <http://www.us-israel.org/jsource/myths/mf25.html>. Middle East Media Research Institute, Arab AntiSemitism Documentation, Special Reports No. 9, September 13, 2002, No. 93, May 1, 2002, No. 98, June 7, 2000, No. 241, July 13, 2001, No. 375, May 3, 2002, No. 421, September 19, 2002, <http://www.memri.org/bin/articles.cgi?Page=subject &Area=antisemitism&ID>. Intelligence and Terrorism Information Center at the

Center for Special Studies: "Information Bulletins," September 2002, October 2002, January 2003, <http://www.intelligence.org.il/eng/>. David A. Harris, "Saudi Schools Keep Sowing Seeds of Hate," *Forward*, March 7, 2003; Caroline Arnold and Herma Silverstein, *Anti-Semitism: A Modern Perspective* (New York: Julian Messner, 1985), 143–48; John Hagee, *Attack on America* (Nashville: Thomas Nelson, 2001), 27–28; Shipler, 255–59; Joan Peters, *From Time Immemorial: The Origins of the Arab-Jewish Conflict Over Palestine* (New York: Harper & Row, 1984), 73, 78–79.

Chapter 13: Discerning Truth in Perplexing Times

1. This book does not offer a complete and thorough treatise on the Arab/Palestinian-Israeli conflict. My goal is to summarize the conflict and disclose key facts and perspectives not typically reported through the mainline media due to anti-Israel bias.

2. Two years later, Joan Peters's best-selling and superbly researched book, *From Time Immemorial: The Origins of the Arab-Jewish Conflict Over Palestine* (New York: Harper & Row, 1984), 394, 398–99, 401, reported that most men in Palestinian camps were gainfully employed in Israel, while obtaining rent-free residence, frequently in an urban setting far superior to their pre-Israel or other possible habitat.

3. Yehuda Kraut, "Palestinian Spokesmen, Jenin Lies and Media Indifference," *Committee for Accuracy in Middle East Reporting in America Media Report* 12, no. 1 (winter 2003): 22, quoting Saeb Ereket interview with Jim Clancy of CNN, April 10, 2002, repeated with Wolf Blitzer, April 17, 2002.

4. Kraut, "Jenin Lies," 31–32, quoting CNN's Bill Hemmer interview with Saeb Erekat, April 14, 2002, and FOX News' Greta Van Susteren interview with Abdel Rahman, April 14, 2002.

5. As quoted by "Dishonest Reporting Award for 2002," HonestReporting.com, April 14, 2003, <http://www.honestreporting.com/articles/critiques/Dishonest_Reporting_Award_for_2002>, citing *London Evening Standard* and *The Guardian*.

6. United Nations General Assembly Report of the Secretary-General Prepared Pursuant to the General Assembly Resolution ES-10/10, July 31, 2002.

7. Kraut, "Jenin Lies," 32, quoting the *Washington Post*, May 1, 2002: 33; AP, "U.N. Report: Jenin Not Massacre," August 1, 2002, <http://foxnews.com/story/0,2933,59276,00.html>.

8. Kraut, "Jenin Lies," 21–22, 31–35.

9. Joel Leyden, "Palestinian Sources Confirm No Massacre in Jenin," *Jerusalem Post Internet*, July 14, 2003, <http://www.jpost.com/servlet/Satellite?pagenmae=JPost/A/JPArticle/ShowFull&cid=1058>.

10. Kraut, "Jenin Lies," 34, citing Qatari television channel *Al Jazeera* interview with Palestinian guerilla fighter from Jenin; Egyptian government newspaper *Al-Ahram Weekly* quoting "Omar," an Islamic jihad bomb maker in Jenin.

11. Jerome Marcus, "Jenin's War Criminals," *Wall Street Journal*, April 30, 2002.

12. As quoted in Brown, *Our Hands Are Stained with Blood*, 60.

13. See chapter 12, note 12.

14. Potok, 405–6, 426, 429–30; Peters, 36–37; R. Po-chia Hsia, *The Myth of Ritual Murder: Jews and Magic in Reformation Germany* (New Haven, Conn.: Yale University Press, 1988); Haim Hillel Ben-Sasson and Yehuda Slutsky, "Blood Libel," in *Encyclopedia Judaica*, vol. 4 (Jerusalem: Keter, 1974), cols. 1120–31, with the literature cited there, as cited in Brown, *Our Hands Are Stained with Blood*, note 5, 195.

15. Herman Bernstein, *The Truth About the Protocols of Zion: A Complete Exposure* (New York: Ktav Publishing House, 1935), 36ff.; John Shelton Curtiss, *An Appraisal of the Protocols of Zion* (New York: Columbia University Press, 1942); Mark Vishniak, "Antisemitism in Tsarist Russia: A Study in Government Fostered Antisemitism," in *Essays on Antisemitism*, ed. Koppel S. Pinson, (New York: Council on Jewish Relations, 1946), 121–44, as cited in Salo W. Baron, *The Russian Jew Under Tsars and Soviets* (New York: Macmillan, 1976), 61, 311, 359, note 13. *The Protocols* is posted on various Arab web sites and represented as a factual account. See, for example: <http://www.radioislam.net/ islam/english/toread/pr-zion.htm>.

16. "Egyptian Diplomat at the UN Human Rights Commission Defends 'Historical Truth' of 'Protocols,'" March 25, 2003, Simon Wiesenthal Press Information, <http//:www. wiesenthal.com/social/press/pr_item.cfm?ItemId=7378>.

17. Flannery, 109–11; Potok, 424–26.

18. Josef Goebbels, "Die Juden Schuld!" *Das Eherne Herz* (Munich: Zentralverlag der NSDP, 1943): 85–91, as cited in <http://www.calvin.edu/academic/cas/gpa/goeb1.htm>.

19. Fiamma Nirenstein, "How I Became an 'Unconscious Fascist,'" *Jewish World Review*, July 15, 2003, <http://www.jewishworldreview.com/0703/nirenstein_2003_07_10.php3>.

20. Dan Diker, "The Influence of Palestinian Organizations on Foreign News Reporting," *Jerusalem Issue Brief* 2, no. 23, March 27, 2003, <http://www.cjpa.org/brief/brief2-23.htm>.

21. "AP Protests Threats to Freelance Cameraman Who Filmed Palestinian Rally," September 12, 2001, <http://arabterrorism.tripod.com/terrorism3.html>.

22. Judy Lash Balint, "Palestinian Harassment of Journalists," WorldNetDaily.com and *Emunah Magazine*, as cited in *Jerusalem Diaries*, February 25, 2001, <http://www. jerusalemdiaries.com/article/20>.

23. Diker, "Palestinian Organizations." <http://www.cjpa.org/brief/brief2-23htm>.

24. Amnon Lord, "Who Killed Muhammed Al Dura? Blood Libel — Model 2000," *Jerusalem Letter/Viewpoints*, 482, July 15, 2002, <http://www.jcpa.org/jl/vp482.htm>.

25. Peters, 392.

26. The Palestinians, a Semitic people, are not even remotely related to the Philistines, who were Japhethites.

27. Peters, 392.

28. Ibid., 223, 396; Shimon Apisdorf, *Judaism in a Nutshell: Israel* (Pikesville, Md.: Leviathan Press, 2003), 62–64.

29. Benjamin Netanyahu, *A Durable Peace: Israel and Its Place Among the Nations* (New York: Warner Books, 2000), 84.

30. Peters, 412.

31. *The Peace Encyclopedia: Palestine,* 2002, <http://www.yahoodi.com/peace/palestine.html>.

32. Charly Wegman, "Friday May 14, 1948: Israel Becomes a Nation," *Agence France-Presse,* 1998, <http://archive.nandotimes. com.nt/special/israel34.html>.

33. Ibid.

34. Golda Meir, *My Life* (London: Futura Publications, 1989), 186.

35. British Mandate authorities, expecting the Jews to lose the war, had predicted Syria, Jordan and Egypt would simply stake out their separate portions of Israel. Efraim Karsh, "What Occupation?" *Commentary* (July–August, 2002), as reprinted in <http://www.aish.com/jewishissues/middleeast/What_Occupation$.asp>.

36. "Refugees Forever? Issues in the Palestinian-Israeli Conflict," *International Jerusalem Post,* February 21, 2003, special supplement.

37. Netanyahu, 155.

Chapter 14: Agenda to Annihilate

1. *The New Palestine* 38, no. 18 (May 18, 1948): 1.

2. Monsignor George Hakim, Greek Catholic Bishop of Galilee, *New York Herald Tribune,* June 30, 1949.

3. British Superintendent of Police Memo, Haifa, April 26, 1948, as quoted in Samuel Katz, *Battleground: Fact and Fantasy in Palestine* (New York: Bantam Books, 1973), 19; *London Economist,* October 2, 1948, as cited in Marie Syrkin, "The Palestinian Refugees," in Irving Howe and Carl Gershman, *Israel, the Arabs and the Middle East* (New York: Bantam Books, 1972), 163; Terence Prittie, *Israel: Miracle in the Desert* (Baltimore: Penguin Books, 1971), 119–20; General John Glubb Pasha, *London Daily Mail,* August 12, 1948.

4. See, for example, Peters, 395.

5. Shipler, 52–60.

6. Peters, 12–13, citing Habib Issa, ed., *Al-Hoda,* Arabic daily, June 8, 1951; see *Economist* (London), May 15, 1948, and October 2, 1948.

7. As reported in *Middle Eastern Studies,* January 1986, cited in Bard, Myths and Facts Online, 2003, <http://www.us-israel.org/jsource/myths/mf14.html>.

8. Myron Kaufman, *The Coming Destruction of Israel* (New York: American Library, 1970), 26–27, cited in Bard, Myths and Facts Online, 2003; Iraqi prime

minister Nimr el-Hawari, *Sir Am Nakbah* (Nazareth, Israel: 1952), as cited in "Refugees Forever?" *International Jerusalem Post*, February 21, 2003, special supplement.

9. Syrkin, 159–67.

10. Arab admissions besides those in the main text include the following:

"It must not be forgotten that the Arab Higher Committee encouraged the refugees' flight from their homes in Jaffa, Haifa and Jerusalem, and that certain leaders . . . make political capital out of their miserable situation." — Near East Arabic Radio Broadcasting Station, April 3, 1949

"The Arab States encouraged the Palestine Arabs to leave their homes temporarily in order to be out of the way of the Arab invasion armies." — *Filastin*, February 19, 1949

"The Secretary-General of the Arab League, Azzam Pasha, assured the Arab peoples . . . it would be a simple matter to throw Jews into the Mediterranean. . . . Brotherly advice was given to the Arabs of Palestine to leave their land, homes and property . . . lest the guns of the invading Arab armies mow them down." —Habib Issa, Al Hoda, June 8, 1951

"The tragedy of the Palestinians was that most of their leaders had paralyzed them with false and unsubstantiated promises that they were not alone; that 80 million Arabs and 400 million Muslims would instantly and miraculously come to their rescue." —King Abdullah of Jordan

11. Haled al Azm, *The Memoirs of Haled al Azm*, part 1, (Beirut, 1973), 386–87, as cited in Bard, Myths and Facts Online, 2002.

12. Reported in *Falastin a-Thaura*, March, 1973, as cited by Bard, Myths and Facts Online, 2002.

13. Alex Awad, *Through the Eyes of the Victims: The Story of the Arab-Israeli Conflict* (Bethlehem, Israel: Bethlehem Bible College, 2001), 88.

14. Terence Prittie, "Middle East Refugees," in *The Palestinians: People, History, Politics*, ed. Michael Curtis, Joseph Neyer, Chaim Waxman and Allen Pollack (New Brunswick, N.J.: Transaction Books, 1975), 66–67.

15. *Beirut al Massa*, July 15, 1957.

16. Bard, Myths and Facts Online, 2003; "Refugees Forever? Issues in the Palestinian-Israeli Conflict," *The International Jerusalem Post*.

17. As cited by Prittie, "Middle East Refugees," 71.

18. Daniel Pipes, "The Refugee Curse," *International Jerusalem Post*, September 5, 2003, 13.

19. Joseph Farah, WorldNetDaily.com, as cited in *Jewish Voice Today* 36, no. 3, (July–August 2002): 11.

20. Joseph Farah, in a speech given in Grantham, Pennsylvania, July 3, 2003.

21. "Political Plan of the PLO Council," June 8, 1974.

22. See, for example, Yoel Marcus, "Truth Serum on the Tip of a Missile," Haaretz.com, June 17, 2003, <http://www.haaretz.com/hasen/pages/ ShArt.jhtml ?itemNo=304476>.

23. Ephraim Shore, "15 Things I Don't Understand About the Mideast Peace Process," September 14, 2003, <www.aish.com/jewishissues/middleeast>.

24. Benny Morris, "Camp David and After: An Exchange (Interview with Ehud Barak)," *New York Review of Books* 49, no. 10, June 13, 2002, <http: //www.nybooks.com/articles/15501>.

25. Ambassador Dennis Ross, U.S. Mideast envoy under the Clinton administration, in a Fox News interview, reported by David Kupelian, "The Real Reason Arafat Rejected a Palestinian State," *Whistleblower* 12, no. 3 (March 2003): 7.

26. Yasser Arafat, as quoted in *El Mundo*, Caracas, Venezuela, February 11, 1980, cited in Leonard J. Davis, *Near East Reports' Myths and Facts* (Washington, D.C.: Near East Research, 1985), 201–2.

27. HonestReporting.com, June 23, 2003, <http://www.honestreporting.com/ articles/critiques/Rooting_Out_Hamas$asp>; The Peace Encyclopedia, 2003, <http://www. yahoodi.com/cgi/peace/peace.htm>.

28. Kupelian, 8–9; Daniel Pipes, "Lessons from the Prophet Muhammed in Diplomacy," *Middle East Quarterly*, September 1999, <http://www.meforum.org/ article/480>.

29. Speech by Arafat in Johannesburg, May 10, 1994 (while Oslo was in effect), as cited in *Middle East Quarterly*, September 1999, <www.meforum.org/ article480>.

30. As quoted in Benny Morris, "Camp David," <http://www.nybooks.com/ articles/15501>.

31. As quoted in David Remmick, "In a Dark Time," *New Yorker* (August 18, 2001): 51; Ambassador Jeane Kirkpatrick, introduction to *The Case Against Arafat: The Campaign by Yasser Arafat and the Palestinian Authority to Destroy Israel*, by Morton Klein (New York, 2002), 5, as cited in David Horowitz, *Why Israel is the Victim in the Middle East* (Los Angeles: Center for the Study of Popular Culture, 2003), 18.

32. As quoted in Remmick, 51; Horowitz, *Why Israel Is the Victim*, 18. Libyan President Qaddafi succinctly states the pan-Arab position: "The battle with Israel must be such that, after it, Israel will not exist." Maryaan Jaffe, "Impending War on Iraq Leads to Antisemitism Around the World," Israel Hasbara Comitee, March, 2003, <http://www.infoisrael.net>.

33. Herb Keinon, "Palestinian Observer to UN Human Rights Commission Calls for 'Elimination' of Israel," *Jerusalem Post Internet*, March 31, 2003, <http://www.jpost.com/ servlet/Satellite?pagename=JPost/A/JPArticle/ShowFull&cid=1049>.

34. Israeli Defense Forces, "Monthly Analysis of All Terrorist Incidents Since September 2000," July 1, 2003, <http://www.idf.il/daily_statistics/english/4.gif>. These figures reflect unprovoked terror incidents against Israeli soldiers.

35. Michael Freund, "Oslo-September 1993: The Victims," *Jerusalem Post,* September 10, 2003.

36. Rabbi Shalom Schwartz, "To Live as Jews," December 30, 2002, <http://www. aish.com/jewishissues/ israeldiary/ To_Live_As_Jews.asp>. Poll of June 2003 by Pew Research Center for the People and the Press, a Washington, D.C., independent polling center.

37. Jerusalem Media & Communication Centre, *Public Opinion Poll No. 48,* April 2003, <http://mail.jmcc.org/>.

38. As cited in Daniel Pipes, "What To Do About Palestinian Aspirations," *Jerusalem Post Internet,* February 18, 2003, <http://www.jpost.com/servlet/ Satellite?pagename=JPost/A/JPArticle/ShowFull&cid=1045>.

39. "Friday Sermon on PA TV," MEMRI Special Dispatch No. 228, June 12, 2001, <http://www.memri.org/bin/artiucles.cgi?Page=archives&Area=sd&I D=SP22801>.

40. "Friday Sermon on Palestinian Authority TV," MEMRI Special Dispatch No. 370, April 17, 2002, <http://www.memri.org/bin/articles.cgi?Page=archives &Area=sd&ID=SP37002>.

41. "Chairman of the Arab Psychiatrists Association Offers Diagnosis," Middle East Media Research Institite Special Dispatch No. 373, April 30, 2002, <http: //www.memri.org/bin/articles.cgi?Page=archives&Area=sd&ID=SP37302>.

42. "Saudi Government Daily," Middle East Media Research Institute Special Dispatch No. 354, March 13, 2002, <http://www.memri.org/bin/articles.cgi? Page=archhives&Area=sd&ID=SP35402>.

43. "Egyptian Jurists to Sue 'The Jews' for Compensation for 'Trillions' of Tons of Gold Allegedly Stolen During Exodus From Egypt," MEMRI Special Dispatch No. 556, August 22, 2003, citing *Al-Ahram Al-Arabi* (Egypt), August 9, 2003, <www.memri.org>.

44. *Jerusalem Post Internet* Staff, "Saddam: A Free Palestine from the Jordan River to the Mediterranean Sea," March 23, 2003; and Khaled Abu Toameh, "In Ramallah, Palestinians Rejoice at Saddam's 'Victories,'" *Jerusalem Post Internet,* March 24, 2003, <http://www.jpost.com/servlet/Satellite?pagename=JPost/A/ JPArticle/ShowFull&cid=1048>.

45. Awad, 86.

46. Lisa Loden, "Knowing Where We Start," in *The Bible and the Land: An Encounter,* ed. Lisa Loden, Peter Walker and Michael Wood (Jerusalem: Musalaha, 2000), 21–23; Colin Chapman, "Getting to the Point," ibid., 147–59; Canon Naim Ateek, "Putting Christ at the Center," ibid., 56–57, 60.

47. Loden, 21.

48. See, for example, Rana Elfar, "Dealing with the Scriptural Past," ibid., 95–98; Naim Stifan Ateek and Rosemary Radford Ruether, *Justice and Only Justice: A Palestinian Theology of Liberation* (Maryknoll, N.Y.: Orbis Books, 1990); "PA Conference Denounces Christian Zionists," Arutz Sheva IsraelNationalNews.com,

July 4, 2003, quoting the Palestinian daily *al-Hayat al-Jadida*, July 2, 2003, <http://israelnationalnews.com>.

49. See, for example, Awad, 14, 24–26, 54, 86–88, 96; and Joseph Farah, "The Truth About Christians in 'Palestine,'" February 28, 2003, <http://www.World NetDaily.com>.

50. As stated by Suhail Akel in *International Relations Magazine*, no. 22 (Argentina: University of LaPlata, 2002), as cited in "Wiesenthal Center Protests Antisemitic Statements by the Palestinian Authority Representative in Argentina," Simon Wiesenthal Institute, April 2, 2003, <http://www.wiesenthal.com/social/press/pr_item.cfm?ItemId=7426>.

51. Bishop Alex, Head of the Roman Orthodox Bishopric of Gaza, *Al-Quds* (PA), April 24, 2002, as translated in "Arab Christian Clergymen Against Western Christians, Jews, and Israel," MEMRI Inquiry and Analysis Series No. 93, May 1, 2002, <http://www.memri.org/bin/opener.cgi?Page=archives&ID=IA9302>.

52. "PA Conference," <http://israelnationalnews.com>.

53. Mitri Raheb, *I Am a Palestinian Christian* (Minneapolis: Augsburg Fortress Publishers, 1995), 103.

54. As cited in "Trouble in the Holy Land: Arab Christian Clergymen Call Jews 'Satanic,'" WorldNetDaily.com, May 1, 2002, <http://www.worldnetdaily.com/news/article.asp?ARTICLE_ID=27454>.

55. "Shorrosh: Islam is on the Decline," *Messianic Times* (summer 2002): 7, quoting Christian Arab and Muslim evangelist Dr. Anis Shorrosh.

56. Excerpts from sermons delivered in Jerusalem in 2002, as translated in "Palestinian Christian Leader in Praise of Marytrdom Operations," MEMRI Special Dispatch No. 459, <http://www.memri.org/bin/articles/cgi?Page=archives&Area=sd&ID=SP45903>. Hanna was eventually fired.

57. Excerpts from April 22, 2002, message on Palestine Television, as translated in "Arab Christian Clergymen," <http://www.memri.org/bin/opener.cgi?Page=archives&ID=IA9302>.

58. Excerpts from message on *Al-Manar* Television (Lebanon) April 24, 2002, ibid.

59. Excerpts from article by Khalil in *Al-Maydan* (Egypt), April 22, 2002, as cited in *Al-Quds Al Arabi* (London), April 24, 2002, ibid.

60. Only a fanatical fringe of Israelis are not willing to compromise to achieve peace. Sadly, the fanatical is sometimes misrepresented as typical Israeli sentiment, even in respected evangelical Christian sources, for instance, Gary Burge, "The Land: Who Owns the Holy Land?" *Books & Culture* 9, no. 4 (July–August 2003):40–41.

61. "Muslim Countries of the World," Muslim Educational Trust, May 2003, <http://members.tripod.com/arabicpaper/country.html>.

62. Avi Shlaim, *The Iron Wall: Israel and the Arab World* (London: Penguin Books, 2001), 484.

Chapter 15: Just Peace in the Land

1. Any reference to any individual who may bear this name is purely coincidental.

2. Shipler, 459–60, tells the same legendary tale, and I have drawn heavily from Shipler's embellished account.

3. *Zondervan Pictorial Bible Dictionary*, 812.

4. After World War I, the land was designated for a Jewish homeland by the League of Nations' British Mandate. (See chapter 13.)

5. Abba Eban, *An Autobiography* (New York: Random House, 1977), 392.

Chapter 16: Israel on a Last Days' Altar

1. Melissa Radler, "Kirkpatrick Blasts UN's Antisemitism," *Jerusalem Post* Internet, October 29, 2002, <http://www.jpost.com/servlet/Satellite?pagename=JPost/A/JPArticle/ ShowFull&cid=103>.

2. "Israel Action Alert," undated open letter (Los Angeles: Simon Wiesenthal Center, 2002).

3. Mike Evans, *Israel—America's Key to Survival* (Plainfield, N.J.: Logos International, 1981),101.

4. Simon Wiesenthal Center, "UN NGO Document Is a Call for Dismantling Israel," Wiesenthal Press Information, September 1, 2001, <http://www.wiesenthal.com/social/press/pr_item.cfm?ItemId=3626>. The American delegation walked out of the conference in protest.

5. Ibid.

6. UN Commission on Human Rights Resolution 2003/6 entitled "Question of the Violation of Human Rights in the Occupied Arab Territories, Including Palestinians"; see also Melissa Radler, "Rights and Wrongs," *International Jerusalem Post*, June 27, 2003, 15.

7. Andras Kovacs, Budapest Central European University, as quoted in Ruth E. Gruber, "Anti-Semitic Violence Across Europe," JTA Global News Service of the Jewish People, April 30, 2002, <http://www.jta.org/page_view_story.asp?intarticleid=12248&intcategoryid=2>.

8. These events took place in France, Russia, Italy, England, Belgium, Ukraine and Germany. The attitude behind government tolerance of anti-Semitism may be aptly reflected in French ambassador Daniel Bernard's explicit remark that the world's troubles are the fault of "that s _ _ _ _y little country, Israel." Reported by Jeff Jacoby, "The Canary in Europe's Mine," *Boston Globe*, September 28, 2002.

9. "Speaker: Antisemitism Alarming," JTA Global News Service of the Jewish People, May 13, 2003, <http://www.jta.org/brknews.asp?id=63787>.

10. Joseph Farah, "Harvard President Warns of Antisemitism," *WorldNet Daily*, September 20, 2002, <http://www.worldnetdaily.com/news/article.asp?ARTICLE_ID=29013>.

11. Rosie Dimanno, "Latest Attack on Jews Brings a Deafening Silence," *Toronto Star,* December 2, 2002, as quoted by Stand With Us <http://www.stand withus.com>.

12. Keith Intrater, *From Iraq to Armageddon: The Final Showdown Approaches* (Shippensburg, Pa.: Destiny Publishers, 2003), 192.

13. Some say the fourth Temple pertains to the new heavens and earth; others, to heavenly Jerusalem.

14. See also Thomas Ice and Randall Price, *Ready to Rebuild: The Imminent Plan to Rebuild the Last Days Temple* (Eugene, Ore.: Harvest House Publishers, 1992), 205–6.

15. The Scriptures do not associate the *Shekhinah* with the third Temple but with the fourth, in Ezekiel 43:4–5.

Chapter 17: The Sacrament of Sacrifice

1. Richard Wurmbrand, *Tortured for Christ* (Bartlesville, Okla.: Living Sacrifice Book Co., 1967); Idem, *Christ on the Jewish Road* (Bartlesville, Okla.: Living Sacrifice Book Co., 1970).

2. Nanos, 274.

3. As quoted in Evangelical Sisterhood of Mary, 207. Used by permission.

4. Don Gillerman, in speech to the UN Security Council, October 5, 2003, during Security Council meeting called to censure Israel for her attack on the Ein Tzahib Islamic jihad training base in Syria.

5. Corrie ten Boom, *The Hiding Place* (Grand Rapids: Chosen Books, 1996), 77.

6. Ibid., 95.

7. Leora Eren Frucht, "Chosen Homeland: The Death of Abigail Litle Has Brought the Baptist Community in Israel into the Public Eye," *International Jerusalem Post,* April 4, 2003, 16–17.

8. Barry Segal, *Jerusalem-On-The-Line,* Vision for Israel Ministries Open Email Letter, March 13, 2003. Used by permission.

9. Eitan Shishkoff, "A Seed That Falls," *Tikkun International* 12, no.3 (April 2003): 5, quoting Yuval Steinitz.

10. Bonhoeffer, 89.

11. Don Finto, *Your People Shall Be My People: How Israel, the Jews and the Christian Church Will Come Together in the Last Days* (Ventura, Calif.: Regal Books, 2001), 171–72.

Bibliography

Apisdorf, Shimon. *Judaism in a Nutshell: Israel*. Pikesville, Md.: Leviathan Press, 2003.

Arnold, Caroline, and Herma Silverstein. *Anti-Semitism: A Modern Perspective*. New York: Julian Messner, 1985.

Ateek, Naim Stifan, and Rosemary Radford Ruether. *Justice and Only Justice: A Palestinian Theology of Liberation*. Maryknoll, N.Y.: Orbis Books, 1990.

Awad, Alex. *Through the Eyes of The Victims: The Story of the Arab-Israeli Conflict*. Bethlehem, Israel: Bethlehem Bible College, 2001.

Baron, Salo W. *The Russian Jew Under Tsars and Soviets*. New York: Macmillan, 1976.

Bauer, Walter. *A Greek-English Lexicon of the New Testament and Other Early Christian Literature*. 2d ed. Chicago: University of Chicago Press, 1979.

Ben-Sasson, Hillel Haim, and Yehuda Slutsky. "Blood Libel." In *Encyclopedia Judaica*. Vol. 4. Jerusalem: Keter, 1974.

Berkowitz, Ariel, and D'vorah Berkowitz. *Torah Rediscovered: Challenging Centuries of Misinterpretation and Neglect*. Littleton, Colo.: First Fruits of Zion, 1996.

Bernstein, Herman. *The Truth About The Protocols of Zion: A Complete Exposure*. New York: Ktav Publishing House, 1935.

Bjoraker, Bill. *Hebrew Nuggets: Truth That Impacts You, Mined from the Riches of Our Hebrew Heritage*. Pasadena: Operation Ezekiel, 1997.

Bonhoeffer, Dietrich. *The Cost of Discipleship*. New York: Simon & Schuster, 1995.

Boskey, Avner. *A Perspective on Islam*. Nashville: Final Frontier Ministries, 2001.

Brown, Francis. *The New Brown-Driver-Briggs-Gesenius Hebrew and English Lexicon*. Boston: Houghton Mifflin, 1983.

Brown, Michael L. *Our Hands Are Stained with Blood*. Shippensburg, Pa.: Destiny Image, 1992.

———. *Answering Jewish Objections to Jesus*. Vols.1, 2, 3. Grand Rapids: Baker, 2000–2003.

Buttrick, George, gen. ed. *The Interpreter's Dictionary of the Bible*. Vol. 2. Nashville: Abingdon Press, 1981.

Caner, Ergun Mehmet, and Emir Fethi Caner. *Unveiling Islam*. Grand Rapids: Kregel, 2002.

Carroll, James. *Constantine's Sword: The Church and the Jews*. Boston: Houghton Mifflin, 2001.

Chapman, Colin. *Whose Promised Land? The Continuing Crisis Over Israel and Palestine*. Grand Rapids: Baker, 2002.

Cohen, Abraham. *Everyman's Talmud: The Major Teachings of the Rabbinic Sages*. New York: Schocken, 1949.

Cranfield, C. E. B. "Romans." In *The International Critical Commentary*. Vol. 2. Edited by J. A. Emerton and C. E. B. Cranfield. Edinburgh: T. & T. Clark, 1979.

Curtis, Michael, et al, ed. *The Palestinians: People, History, Politics*. New Brunswick, N.J.: Transaction Books, 1975.

Curtiss, John Shelton. *An Appraisal of the Protocols of Zion*. New York: Columbia University Press, 1942.

Dimont, Max I. *The Indestructible Jews*. New York: Signet, 1973.

Doron, Reuven. *One New Man*. Cedar Rapids, Iowa: Embrace, 1993.

Duvernoy, Claude. *The Prince and the Prophet*. Translated by Jack Joffe. Jerusalem: Christian Action for Israel, n.d.

Eban, Abba. *An Autobiography.* New York: Random House, 1977.

Elwell, Walter A., ed. *Baker Encyclopedia of the Bible.* Vols. 1, 2. Grand Rapids: Baker, 1989.

Epstein, Isadore, ed. "Sanhedrin 99b." In *The Babylonian Talmud.* London: Soncino Press, 1935.

Evangelical Sisterhood of Mary, ed. *Changing the Future by Confronting the Past: Talks and Testimonies—Jerusalem 2001 Convention.* Darmstadt, Germany: Evangelical Sisterhood of Mary, 2001.

Evans, Mike. *Israel—America's Key to Survival.* Plainfield, N.J.: Logos International, 1981.

Finto, Don. *Your People Shall Be My People: How Israel, the Jews and the Christian Church Will Come Together in the Last Days.* Ventura, Calif.: Regal Books, 2001.

Flannery, Fr. Edward. *The Anguish of the Jews: Twenty-Three Centuries of Antisemitism.* New York: Paulist Press, 1985.

Foxe, John. *The Acts and Monuments of John Foxe.* Vol. 4, 4th ed. London: Religious Tract Society, n.d.

————. *Foxe's Annals of Martyrs.* Burlington, Ontario: Inspirational Promotions, n.d.

Frankel, Ellen, and Betsy Platkin Teutsch. *The Encyclopedia of Jewish Symbols.* Northvale, N.J.: Jason Aronson, 1995.

Friedman, David. *They Loved the Torah: What Yeshua's First Followers Really Thought About the Law.* Baltimore: Lederer Books, 2001.

Fruchtenbaum, Arnold G. *Israelology: The Missing Link in Systematic Theology.* Tustin, Calif.: Ariel Ministries Press, 1993.

Goll, Jim W. *Exodus Cry.* Ventura, Calif.: Regal Books, 2001.

Gruber, Dan. *The Church and the Jews: The Biblical Relationship.* Hagerstown, Md.: Serenity Books, 1997.

Guthrie, D., ed. *The New Bible Commentary Revised.* Grand Rapids: Eerdmans, 1981.

Hagee, John. *Attack on America.* Nashville: Thomas Nelson, 2001.

Hay, Malcolm. *The Roots of Christian Antisemitism.* New York: Liberty Press, 1981.

Horowitz, David. *Why Israel Is the Victim in the Middle East.* Los Angeles: Center for the Study of Popular Culture, 2003.

Horowitz, Edward. *How the Hebrew Language Grew.* New York: Ktav Publishing House, 1960.

Howe, Irving, and Carl Gershman. *Israel, the Arabs and the Middle East.* New York: Bantam, 1972.

Hsia, R. Po-chia. *The Myth of Ritual Murder: Jews and Magic in Reformation Germany.* New Haven, Conn.: Yale University Press, 1988.

Hubbard, David A., and Glenn W. Barker, gen. ed. *Word Biblical Commentary.* Vol. 38B. Dallas: Word, 1988.

Ice, Thomas, and Randall Price. *Ready to Rebuild: The Imminent Plan to Rebuild the Last Days Temple.* Eugene, Ore.: Harvest House Publishers, 1992.

Intrater, Keith. *From Iraq to Armageddon: The Final Showdown Approaches.* Shippensburg, Pa.: Destiny Publishers, 2003.

Johnstone, Patrick, and Jason Mandryk. *Operation World: 21ˢᵗ Century Edition.* Pasadena: U.S. Center for World Missions; and Bulstrode, Gerrards Cross, England: WEC International Research Office, 2001.

Juster, Daniel C. *The Irrevocable Calling.* Gaithersburg, Md.: Tikkun Ministries, 1996.

Kaiser, Walter C. Jr. *Mission in the Old Testament: Israel as a Light to the Nations.* Grand Rapids: Baker, 2000.

———. "The Land of Israel and the Future Return." In *Israel: The Land and the People,* edited by H. Wayne House. Grand Rapids: Kregel, 1998.

Katz, Samuel. *Battleground: Fact and Fantasy in Palestine.* New York: SPI Books, 1986.

Kaufman, Myron. *The Coming Destruction of Israel.* New York: American Library, 1970.

Keil, C. F., and F. Delitzsch. "Genesis." In *The Pentatuch.* Translated by James Martin. Vol. 1 of *Commentary on the Old Testament.* Grand Rapids: Eerdmans, 1983.

Kevan, Ernest F. "The Principles of Interpretation." In *Revelation and the Bible,* edited by Carl F. H. Henry. Grand Rapids: Baker, 1958.

Kjaer-Hansen, Kai, and Bodil Skjott. *Facts and Myths About the Messianic Congregations in Israel.* Jerusalem: United Christian Council and Caspari Center for Biblical and Jewish Studies, 1999.

Ladd, George Eldon. *The Gospel of the Kingdom.* Grand Rapids: Eerdmans, 1990.

Laenen, J. H. *Jewish Mysticism: An Introduction.* Louisville: John Knox, 2001.

Lewis, David Allen. *The Last War.* Green Forest, Ariz.: New Leaf Press, 2001.

Lindsey, Hal. *The Road to Holocaust.* New York: Bantam, 1990.

―――. *The Everlasting Hatred: The Roots of Jihad.* Murietta, Calif.: Oracle House Publishing, 2002.

Loden, Lisa, Peter Walker and Michael Wood, eds. *The Bible and the Land: An Encounter.* Jerusalem: Musalaha, 2000.

Longenecker, Richard N. *Biblical Exegesis in the Apostolic Period.* Grand Rapids: Eerdmans, 1975.

Marshall, Paul, Roberta Green and Lela Gilbert. *Islam at the Crossroads: Understanding Its Beliefs, History and Conflicts.* Grand Rapids: Baker, 2002.

McQuaid, Elwood. *The Zion Connection.* Eugene, Ore.: Harvest House Publishers, 1996.

McTernan, John, and Bill Koenig. *Israel: The Blessing or the Curse.* Oklahoma City: Hearthstone Publishing, 2002.

Meir, Golda. *My Life.* London: Futura Publications, 1989.

Morey, Robert. *The Islamic Invasion.* Eugene, Ore.: Harvest House Publishers, 1992.

Murray, Andrew. *Humility.* Springdale, Pa.: Whittaker House, 1982.

Murray, Iain H. *The Puritan Hope: Revival and the Interpretation of Prophecy.* Edinburgh: Banner of Truth Trust, 1991.

Myers, J. M. *Grace and Torah.* Philadelphia: Fortress Press, 1975.

Nanos, Mark D. *The Mystery of Romans: The Jewish Context of Paul's Letter.* Minneapolis: Fortress Press, 1996.

Netanyahu, Benjamin. *A Durable Peace: Israel and its Place Among the Nations.* New York: Warner, 2000.

Nicholls, William. *Christian Antisemitism: A History of Hate.* Northvale, N.J.: Jason Aronson, 1995.

Otis, George Jr. *The Last of the Giants: Lifting the Veil on Islam and the End Times.* Tarrytown, N.Y.: Chosen Books, 1991.

Packer, J. I. *Knowing God.* Downers Grove, Ill.: InterVarsity Press, 1973.

Pentecost, J. Dwight. *Things to Come: A Study in Biblical Eschatology.* Findlay, Ohio: Dunham Publishing, 1958.

Peters, Joan. *From Time Immemorial: The Origins of the Arab-Jewish Conflict Over Palestine.* New York: Harper & Row, 1984.

Pinson, Koppel S., ed. *Essays on Antisemitism.* New York: Council on Jewish Relations, 1946.

Piper, John. *The Justification of God: An Exegetical and Theological Study of Romans 9:1–23.* Grand Rapids: Baker, 1993.

Potok, Chaim. *Wanderings: Chaim Potok's History of the Jews.* New York: Fawcett, 1990.

Prittie, Terence. *Israel: Miracle in the Desert.* Baltimore: Penguin, 1971.

Ross, Allen P. *Creation and Blessing: A Guide to the Study and Exposition of the Book of Genesis.* Grand Rapids: Baker, 1988.

Sachar, Howard M. *A History of Israel.* New York: Knopf, 1976.

Seekins, Frank I. *Hebrew Word Pictures.* Phoenix, Ariz.: Living Word Pictures, 1994.

Shipler, David K. *Arab and Jew: Wounded Spirits in a Promised Land.* New York: Time Books, 1986.

Shlaim, Avi. *The Iron Wall: Israel and the Arab World.* London: Penguin Books, 2001.

Shorrosh, Anis A. *Islam Revealed: A Christian Arab's View of Islam.* Nashville: Thomas Nelson, 1988.

Stern, David H. *Complete Jewish Bible.* Clarksville, Md., and Jerusalem, Israel: Jewish New Testament Publications, 1998.

Strong, James. *The Exhaustive Concordance of the Bible.* Nashville: Abingdon, 1977.

Tasker, R. V. G., ed. *The Tyndale New Testament Commentaries.* Grand Rapids: Eerdmans, 1963.

Ten Boom, Corrie. *The Hiding Place.* Grand Rapids: Chosen Books, 1996.

Tenney, Merrill C., ed. *The Zondervan Pictorial Encyclopedia of the Bible.* Vol. 1. Grand Rapids: Zondervan, 1976.

Teplinsky, Sandra. *Out of the Darkness: The Untold Story of Jewish Revival in the Former Soviet Union.* Jacksonville, Fla.: Hear O Israel Ministries Publishing, 1998.

Tozer, A. W. *The Knowledge of the Holy.* San Francisco: Harper & Row, 1961.

Unger, Merrill F. *Unger's Bible Dictionary.* Chicago: Moody Press, 1966.

Vine, W. E. *A Comprehensive Dictionary of the Original Greek Words with their Precise Meanings for English Readers.* Iowa Falls: Riverside Book and Bible House, n.d.

Waltke, Bruce K., and M. O'Connor. *An Introduction to Biblical Hebrew Syntax.* Winona Lake, Ind.: Eisenbrauns, 1990.

Walvoord, John F., *The Prophecy Knowledge Handbook.* Wheaton, Ill.: Victor Books, 1990.

Wilson, Marvin R. *Our Father Abraham: Jewish Roots of the Christian Faith.* Grand Rapids: Eerdmans, and Dayton, Ohio: Center for Judaic-Christian Studies, 1989.

Wurmbrand, Richard. *Tortured for Christ.* Bartlesville, Ok.: Living Sacrifice Book Co., 1967.

———. *Christ on the Jewish Road.* Bartlesville, Okla.: Living Sacrifice Book Co., 1970.

Zuck, Roy B. *Basic Bible Interpretation: A Practical Guide to Discovering Biblical Truth.* Wheaton, Ill.: Victor, 1991.

Index

Sandra Teplinsky, B.A. (University of Illinois), J.D. (Indiana University School of Law), is founder and director, together with her husband, Kerry, of Light of Zion, a Messianic Jewish ministry to Israel and the Church associated with Harvest International Ministries. A former litigation attorney, Teplinsky, now a licensed minister, speaks and ministers internationally on God's heart and prophetic plans for Israel, where she spends significant time.

Teplinsky's previous books include *Out of the Darkness: The Untold Story of Jewish Revival in the Former Soviet Union* and *The Blessing of Israel: What Christians Need to Know to Intercede and Interrelate with the Jewish Nation.*

You may contact the author through:

Light of Zion
P.O. Box 27575
Anaheim Hills, CA 92808
www.lightofzion.org